W9-AKD-372

APR 1 7 2006

PLANTING
FOR COLOR

THE Horticulture GARDENER'S GUIDES
PLANTING FOR COLOR

Susan Chivers

HORTICULTURE
BOOKS
www.hortmag.com

A HORTICULTURE BOOK

Horticulture Publications, Boston, Massachusetts

First published in the US in 2005 ISBN 1-55870-763-8

Horticulture is a subsidiary of F+W Publications Inc. Company
Distributed by F+W Publications Inc.
4700 East Galbraith Road, Cincinnati, OH 45236
1-800-289-0963

Printed in Singapore by KHL Printing Co Pte Ltd
for Horticulture Publications, Boston, Massachusetts

Visit our website at www.hortmag.com

Commissioning Editor Mic Cady
Art Editor Sue Cleave
Production Beverley Richardson

Series Editor Sue Gordon, OutHouse Publishing
Winchester, Hampshire SO22 5DS
Art Editor Robin Whitecross
Editor Polly Boyd
Design Assistant Caroline Wollen
Proofreader Audrey Horne
Indexer June Wilkins

Series consultant Andrew McIndoe

American edition by
Creative Plus Publishing Ltd.
53 Crown Street
Brentwood, Essex CM14 4BD

ORNAMENTAL PLANT OR PERNICIOUS WEED?

In certain circumstances ornamental garden plants
can be undesirable when introduced into natural habitats, either
because they compete with native flora or because they act as
hosts to fungal, bacterial, and insect pests. Plants that are
popular in one part of the world may be considered undesirable
in another. Horticulturists have learned to be wary of the effect
that cultivated plants may have on native habitats, and
as a rule, any plant likely to be a problem in a particular area if
it escapes from cultivation is restricted and therefore is not
offered for sale.

Contents

Introduction

I became a gardener because I had to. Faced with a neglected old cottage garden, I started gardening over 30 years ago with a distinct lack of enthusiasm and scant knowledge. To my amazement, my enforced labor proved to be the most satisfying of pastimes, and it wasn't long before I experienced a sort of Damascene conversion that opened my eyes to the wonderful world of plants.

With unbridled enthusiasm I set about filling my patch with small trees, shrubs, perennials, bulbs, fruit trees, and vegetables—anything that took my fancy. Luckily, this random, untutored approach did not result in too awful a picture. I ended up with an archetypal cottage garden, with its own higgledy-piggledy kind of charm; but no doubt it would have been a much more exciting and satisfying one had I known even a little about color theory and how to use plants to create specific color effects. In those days I was happy simply growing anything, and the terms "color harmonies," "contrasts," "shades," "tones," "saturation," and "intensity" had yet to enter my lexicon. It was only later, when I began to read the works of great gardening writers such as Gertrude Jekyll, Russell Page, Penelope Hobhouse, Rosemary Verey, and Christopher Lloyd and started visiting gardens of all kinds, that I began to appreciate that there is much more to making a good garden than simply building up a collection of plants.

Today, as a writer and lecturer on garden-related subjects, I am often asked about color, and it strikes me that there are many amateur gardeners who are somewhat intimidated by the thought of working with color. Some people are at a loss as to how to make their garden colorful throughout the year, while others simply find putting color schemes together difficult. Moreover, I find that many gardeners have definite color preferences, and they want me to suggest plants to fit into their particular schemes. Others, often urban gardeners, have problems finding colorful plants for shade, and there are some country gardeners who are perplexed about how they can blend their gardens into the landscape beyond. With the emphasis now on gardens used as outside rooms, there are also people keen to know how to use color to create specific moods.

In writing *Planting for Color* I have tried to address some of these questions, but principally my aim has been to illuminate this somewhat complex subject and encourage readers to cast aside their prejudices and be more willing to experiment with color. In keeping with the current interest in English-style planting schemes, this book describes plants that suit this style of planting, and the illustrations are of old European gardens.

Susan Chivers

6

INTRODUCTION

CHOOSING PLANTS FOR COLOR

Plants are seductive, and it is easy to buy them on impulse without considering whether they are suited to your soil. Similarly, you can be so intent on creating a color scheme that you overlook the plants' cultivation requirements. Flowering times have an impact, too. Some plants flower repeatedly, while others are quickly over. For this reason, include foliage plants to fill the gaps left by short-lived flowers.

Availability

Some of the species mentioned are new cultivars and others are traditional British varieties, which, if you can find them, will give authenticity to your design. The following sources should help you on your way to your traditional, English-style planting:
Plant Delights Nursery, Inc., 9241 Sauls Road, Raleigh, NC 27603, tel (919) 772-4794
Select Seeds – Antique Flowers, 180 Stickney Hill Road Union, CT 06076-4617, tel (800) 684-0395

USDA HARDINESS ZONES

Most species described in this book will thrive in temperate areas (around Zone 7), and the seasonal changes described apply to these areas. With the exception of annuals, zones are indicated next to each species name, and cultivars are suitable for the same zones unless otherwise stated. Remember that a plant's site can also affect its hardiness.

Zone	Avg. annual min. recorded temp.	Zone	Avg. annual min. recorded temp.
1	Below -50°F	7	0°F to 10°F
2	-50°F to -40°F	8	10°F to 20°F
3	-40°F to -30°F	9	20°F to 30°F
4	-30°F to -20°F	10	30°F to 40°F
5	-20°F to -10°F	11	Above 40°F
6	-10°F to 0°F		

To find your zone, see the USDA zone map on the back flap of this book.

LEFT: *Papaver somniferum* 'Black Paeony'

INTRODUCING COLOR IN THE GARDEN

To use color successfully in a garden, it is necessary not only to grasp something of color theory but also to have an awareness of the importance that color has played in gardens of the past and how its use differed from today. Gardeners also need to be aware of how changing light affects color, and how it can best be utilized to enhance a garden's size and shape, as well as its mood.

RIGHT: *Cirsium rivulare* 'Atropurpureum' and *Hesperis matronalis*.

Frescoes like this one in Pompeii, Italy, dating from from the 1st century A.D., give us an idea of the kind of formal and largely green gardens that were made in ancient Roman times.

Garden design through the ages

We take color in our gardens very much for granted, not always appreciating that only comparatively recently has it assumed such a high level of importance. Plant breeders today are constantly producing new cultivars in an amazing diversity of colors, which means that modern-day gardeners can devise planting schemes in a variety of styles and moods. This wide choice was not available to the majority of our gardening ancestors.

From the writings of Pliny the Younger (*c*.62–113 A.D.) we know that the ancient Romans were accomplished gardeners, yet they tended to regard plants as raw materials—like stone or marble—to be trained, trimmed, and clipped to fit into the formal designs that were characteristic of their gardens. Green was the principal color at this time.

In the medieval era the most resourceful gardeners were monks and nuns; but they grew plants for food and for medicinal purposes, rather than for their decorative qualities. Tapestries of the period reveal that flowers such as roses, lilies, violets, irises, hollyhocks, peonies, lavender, periwinkles, and columbines were grown at the time, although sometimes it seems they were valued more for their symbolism than for their beauty. Color certainly didn't feature in the first gardening book written in English—*The Feate of Gardening*, by Jon Gardener, written in 1440—in which the writer instructs his readers on how best to grow wild herbs and a few vegetables, plants that are hardly likely to make a garden a riot of color.

TUDOR AND ELIZABETHAN GARDENS

Flamboyant color was a feature of the gardens at Hampton Court and Nonsuch near London, created for Henry VIII. However, it was the brightly colored artifacts such as banqueting pavilions, painted seats, arbors, fences, and gilded heraldic beasts on long posts,

Some flowers, including roses, have been cultivated since antiquity; but for centuries they were grown mainly for their symbolic meaning, or for medicinal or culinary purposes, rather than for their aesthetic qualities. In the Middle Ages, for example, roses were cooked and served with honey.

This baroque fountain at Het Loo Palace in Holland shows how elaborate gardens had become by the 17th century, though color was often in artifacts rather than in plants. Tulips arrived in Europe from Turkey in the 1500s and began to be grown solely for their beauty, making gardens more colorful.

rather than the plants, that would have dazzled visitors. The gardens of the Tudor monarch were designed to reflect his brilliance, but there was no such splendor for the more humble of his subjects, whose gardens would have been used primarily for growing food.

All this was to change, however, when Elizabethan navigators and explorers returned home with plants and seeds from all over the known world. This influx of new plant material began to transform British gardens and, in the process, made them much more colorful. For the first time, individual plants became the focus of interest,

Green was the principal color in the large parterres of beds lined with boxwood (*Buxus sempervirens*) that were made, often in complex patterns, in grand gardens in France, Holland, and England in the 17th century.

and a new breed of plant connoisseurs, notably John Gerard and the John Tradescants, father and son, created gardens full of rarities. By the time James VI of Scotland became James I of England in 1603, a keen English gardener could acquire many colorful flowering plants, including tulips, bearded irises, dog's tooth violets, hyacinths, anemones, and bulbs such as narcissi.

17TH-CENTURY FORMALITY

During the 17th century, people in Europe with money and power were largely preoccupied with making grand gardens as a mark of their status; although good plantsmanship was not lost, the interest in growing unusual and interesting plants was kept alive by only a minority of gardeners. With the Restoration of King Charles II in England in 1660, French gardens became the vogue. The Frenchman André Mollet began transforming the gardens at the London palaces of Whitehall and St. James's for Charles II. At nearby Hampton Court, he began the canal, called the Long Water. Later, after the accession of William III and Mary II in 1688, Dutch gardens (which were strongly influenced by the French) came into favor.

Both French and Dutch styles were formal; and as in all formal gardens, the predominant color was green. Some color was provided by flowering shrubs and

Many 18th-century aristocrats in Britain created landscapes, complete with grand buildings and artifacts, like this Palladian bridge, in Prior Park, in Bath. Older gardens were frequently destroyed in the process.

RARE PLANTSMAN

The London apothecary John Parkinson was a connoisseur of plants. In 1629, he published *Paradisi in Sole, Paradisus Terrestris*—a rich source of knowledge about 17th-century garden design and the plants grown at the time. What makes it unique for its day is that Parkinson demonstrates a love of flowers for their own sake and argues that they are worthy of growing solely for their beauty.

Left: *Alcea rosea*, the original hollyhock, is mentioned by Parkinson.

choice flowers, but it was the greens of hedges, topiary, and trees that contributed most. We can see a late 17th-century, Dutch-inspired garden at the palace of Hampton Court, in England, today, as the King's Privy Garden has been restored to its original splendor.

18TH-CENTURY LANDSCAPES

The famous British landscapers of the mid-18th century—Charles Bridgeman, William Kent, and Lancelot (Capability) Brown—were commissioned to produce harmonious settings for the grand houses of their patrons. Each in his own way produced schemes where there was an interplay between landscape, water, buildings, and trees, and so once again green was the predominant color of their creations. (At Rousham, in

13

Oxfordshire, in England, perhaps William Kent's finest garden, there is a range of greens provided by evergreens and deciduous trees, but virtually no other colors.) However, it is a misconception that 18th-century English landscape gardens always lacked flowers and shrubs. It is true that they were often confined to walled gardens, away from public view, but by the 1750s the word "shrubbery" had become commonplace, and shrubberies began to appear even in grand gardens. In some they played a pivotal role, for example at Painshill Park, the Hon. Charles Hamilton's garden in Surrey.

Hamilton planted vast numbers of "new" plants from America to create colorful shrubberies for his many visitors to admire—it was a style much ahead of its time. Thomas Whateley, in his *Observations on Modern Gardening*, published in 1770, described Painshill as "a park happily united with the capital beauties of a garden," and it is now generally agreed that at Painshill, Hamilton successfully melded landscape with colorful shrubberies, setting in train the fashions of the 19th-century English garden.

Color certainly played a part in the gardens created by Humphry Repton, the last of the great 18th-century landscapers. Recognizing that tastes were moving away from the pure landscape of the mid-18th century, Repton remodeled his clients' parks and made them more "gardenesque." He achieved this by introducing flower gardens and shrubberies close to the houses and, by means of less structured planting farther away, blending the more distant parts of the ground seamlessly into the landscape.

INSTANT TRANSFORMATIONS

Humphry Repton (1752–1818), who described himself as a "landscape gardener," was a marketing genius. In his famous "Red Books," he invented a way of demonstrating his design ideas to prospective patrons. The books contained watercolor sketches of the existing grounds, which could be altered by the turning of flaps or the pulling of tabs to show how they would look after his suggestions had been carried out. Such was the success of his practice that during his career he designed 330 gardens throughout Britain, some of which survive (for example Endsleigh, in Devon).

19TH-CENTURY FLAMBOYANCE

England at the start of the 19th century was becoming increasingly affluent, as industrialization of the country grew apace. While the working class, for the most part, lived in appalling conditions, the upper and emerging middle classes had money to spend and were keen to improve their properties and gardens. The age of ostentation had arrived and, with it, a desire for color in the home and the garden. Rich patrons commissioned the building of grand terraces and parterres around their

country houses, from architects such as Sir Charles Barry and William Andrews Nesfield, and it became the fashion for the beds in parterres to be bedded out with annuals twice or three times a year. "Carpet bedding," as it was called, relied on the skill of head gardeners who, armed with improving technology (it was now possible to heat glasshouses reliably), could produce vast numbers of plants as and when they were needed to create the sensationally colorful displays.

The most colorful and popular plants used for bedding schemes were from South America and

Affluent 19th century British landowners often displayed their wealth by commissioning architects to make them grand gardens with elaborate terraces and parterres, like this one at Bowood House, Wiltshire, England.

included zinnias, calceolarias, petunias, verbenas, and *Salvia splendens*. To start with, the displays were mixtures of plants, but gradually it became the fashion to group similar plants together in large, single-color masses. The schemes were usually planned with contrasting colors, and to our eyes many would have seemed garish or daring in the extreme. Their coloring zenith was reached in the 1840s and 1850s, for by the end of the 1860s, bedding schemes were more restrained and the colors more muted. Foliage, rather than flowers, became the vogue, with succulents such as echeverias, sempervivums, and sedums used to create the patterns, some of which were as intricate as the designs on oriental carpets. The superintendent of the park at Crystal Palace, London, in England, George Thomson, used succulents to create a design featuring six species of butterfly.

A MORE NATURAL APPROACH

While large, prestigious gardens and parks in Britain were still full of vast bedding schemes in the 1860s, some gardeners were advocating more naturalistic planting. Gardening writer the Reverend Shirley Hibberd led the field, and he had very definite views about the use of color. He suggested that his readers should try growing plants with neutral colors and eschew those with primary ones; he dismissed repetitive plantings of vividly colored plants, such as scarlet pelargoniums with yellow calceolarias, as tasteless; and declared that bedding schemes were vastly overrated.

Hibberd's ideas led the way for William Robinson, the high prophet of naturalistic planting, who published his groundbreaking book *The Wild Garden* in 1870. Robinson loathed the artificiality of the bedding system and, with missionary zeal, set himself the task of changing the way the world gardened. Robinson's premise was that plants grown in a garden should be given the same conditions they would have enjoyed in the wild, and that native and exotic plants should be planted together in woods, on the edge of woodlands, and in meadows, as well as in the more conventional setting of a bed or a border. This ecological approach seems utterly sensible to us today, but at the time Robinson was writing it was considered radical. However Robinson, who tried out many of his ideas in his own garden at Gravetye Manor, West Sussex, in England, soon had an army of followers, who began to change and develop gardens following his principles. While Robinson was not primarily a colorist, his ideas

The trend toward more naturalistic gardens began in the late 1800s, especially after William Robinson's *The Wild Garden* appeared in 1870.

were adopted by those who were, and they in turn had a significant influence on the way that gardens developed during the 20th century.

THE 20TH-CENTURY COLORISTS

In the latter years of the 19th century the Arts & Crafts Movement was gaining ground in Britain, and Robinson's ideas were very much in accord with their beliefs. However, the gardens made by members of the movement harked back to medieval times, when clipped hedges, trellis-covered rose bowers, and beds full of simple flowers, such as hollyhocks and columbines, provided the perfect setting for a troubadour to woo his maiden. This was the style taken up by perhaps the greatest English colorist gardener, Gertrude Jekyll, who modified and expanded it to embrace her views on the use of color and planting.

Miss Jekyll trained as an artist when young, and this gave her great insights into how to use color. In the gardens she designed, she planted reds, yellows, and oranges together, and used blues and yellows as contrasts. In the long perennial borders for which she was renowned, she advocated planting hotter colors at the center and cooler colors at the ends, so that, as

After 1889 Edwin Lutyens and Gertrude Jekyll collaborated in designing more than 100 gardens, in which Lutyens, an architect, designed the hard landscaping and artifacts, like this seat at Hestercombe, in Somerset.

In 1907, Lawrence Johnston bought the land for the garden at Hidcote, Gloucestershire, in England, and in the 1920s and 1930s Vita Sackville-West and Harold Nicolson designed their gardens in Long Barn and Sissinghurst Castle, in Kent. When they began making their famous gardens, they followed the precepts for planting and for the use of color fostered by Robinson and Jekyll. Hidcote's Red Borders and the Sissinghurst White Garden have become world famous, and paved the way for the fashion for single-colored, themed borders and for colorist gardens.

Today, there are numerous examples of gardeners demonstrating the art of using color in the garden. Nori and Sandra Pope's garden at Hadspen, Somerset, in England, started in the 1980s, features monochrome plantings; Marylyn Abbott's historic garden at the National Trust's West Green House, Hampshire, in England, which she began restoring in the mid-1990s, is renowned for its flamboyant use of color; and Pam Lewis's garden at Sticky Wicket, Dorset, in England, is admired for its colorist naturalistic plantings.

someone walked along them, the colors rose in a crescendo and then tailed off to a muted ending. As a friend and disciple of Robinson, she was in accord with his ideas about plants and the wild garden.

Gertrude Jekyll was already well known in gardening circles when she met the architect Edwin Lutyens in 1889. They began working together right away, designing houses and gardens in a partnership that lasted 20 years and during which they completed over 100 commissions. Such was their brilliance that their collaborations came to be recognized as the epitome of good taste and set the standard for many years to come. Lutyens designed the houses and the layout of the gardens, including their structural elements, such as paths, arbors, pools, terraces, and steps, while Miss Jekyll designed the planting, which owed much to the romantic ideal of the traditional English-style cottage garden, with masses of plants spilling out of borders and draping arbors and walls. Today, their work can be seen in the restored gardens, such as those at Hestercombe, in Somerset, and at The Manor House, Upton Grey, in Hampshire, England.

Miss Jekyll was an accomplished gardener by the time she met Lutyens. Because she had trained as an artist in her youth, she had a particular interest in color theory. Her planting schemes, many of which were on a grand scale, reflected this.

17

Color theory

It goes without saying that color is a vital ingredient of all gardens, and learning how to use it to best advantage adds another string to a gardener's bow. Color not only makes gardens more interesting, it creates their mood. A skillful gardener can use color to manipulate space, for example, by making small gardens seem larger or large gardens seem more intimate.

If a light beam is passed through a prism, the beam is split into separate and distinct colors, the colors we see in a rainbow. These colors are red, orange, yellow, green, blue, and violet, and they are known as the "spectrum."

While we can see all the colors of the rainbow, in fact our eyes' retinas contain light-sensitive cells, called cones, which can distinguish only three colors: red, yellow, and blue. These are known as the primary colors of the spectrum. The other colors that we see in a rainbow—orange, green, and violet—we see because they are mixtures of the three primary colors. These are called secondary colors. Anyone who has mixed paints knows that mixing red with yellow produces orange, while yellow and blue produce green, and mixing red and blue makes violet. By altering the amounts of red and yellow when trying to produce an orange color, blue and yellow when making green, and red and blue when making violet, it is possible to produce an enormous number of different oranges, greens, and violets. Likewise, the spectrum is really composed of an infinite number of colors, although at a glance we can pick out only a few.

COLOR WHEEL

If the colors of the spectrum are painted side by side to produce a colored band, and the band is then bent to make a circle, the resulting structure is called a color wheel. Half the wheel is composed of hot or warm colors, such as red, orange, and yellow, and the other half consists of cold or cool colors, including blues, greens, violets, and indigos. The color wheel's main use for gardeners is to demonstrate the differences between harmonies and contrasts.

HARMONIES

If, when planting a border or bed, we use plants with colors that are near each other in the color wheel, a harmony is produced. However, not all harmonies have the same character. There are soothing, relaxing harmonies, and exciting, vibrant harmonies. A planting scheme incorporating blue- and yellow-flowering plants and evergreen foliage produces a calming harmony, for example, a parterre edged with *Buxus sempervirens* (boxwood) (Zones 6–9), bedded out with the cream- and green-flowered *Veronica spicata* ssp. *incana* (Zones 5–8) and the pale blue-flowered *Muscari armeniacum* 'Valerie Finnis' (Zones 3–8). On the other hand, a harmony produced by planting orange-flowered plants with yellow and red ones, such as the orange-flowered *Alstroemeria aurea* (Zones 8–10) grown in proximity to red crocosmias, such as *Crocosmia* 'Lucifer' (Zones 7–9), and the yellow grass *Carex elata* 'Aurea' (Zones 5–9), results in a vibrant, energetic effect. Christopher Lloyd, in his Great Dixter garden, in East Sussex, England, has magnificent plantings of hot, vibrant harmonies.

Top row from left: A relaxing harmony with *Buxus sempervirens* (boxwood), *Alchemilla mollis*, and *Veronica spicata* ssp. *incana*. **Bottom row from left:** An exciting harmony with *Alstroemeria aurea*, *Crocosmia* × *crocosmiiflora* 'Jackanapes', and *Carex elata* 'Aurea'.

COLOR INTENSITY

The intense contrasts produced by putting opposites in the color wheel together are best managed by ensuring that the saturation levels of the colors are approximately equal. For example, a muted violet will contrast most happily with a yellow if it is a dull yellow. The same applies to harmonies, as seen above: The silver and purple combination would not work so well if the purple were more intense. When using a single color, however, choose plants that display differing degrees of saturation, or intensity, as this adds interest. This technique is used by Mr. and Mrs. Pope in their garden at Hadspen, Somerset, in England, in their color-themed borders.

CONTRASTING AND COMPLEMENTARY COLORS

A planting scheme with flowers or leaf colors that are not close to each other on the color wheel is known as a "contrast." Contrasts always involve a hot color being matched by a cold color. Contrasting colors placed together do not soothe but shock and even disturb. For example, the pale purple flowers of *Campanula glomerata* 'Superba' (Zones 3–8) would make a sharp contrast to the yellow of *Aquilegia chrysantha* 'Yellow Queen' (Zones 3–8), because purple and yellow are not near each other on the color wheel. (See "Contrasting and Complementary Schemes," below.)

Colors that are opposites on the color wheel are known as "complementary" colors, because each makes up for everything that its opposite in the wheel lacks. Complementary colors are red and green, orange and blue, and yellow and violet. Planting combinations of these colors will always result in the most shocking of vibrant color schemes, as the most intense contrasts are between colors that are opposite in the wheel. (See "Contrasting and Complementary Schemes," below.)

CONTRASTING AND COMPLEMENTARY SCHEMES

The clear yellow *Hemerocallis lilioasphodelus* (1) (Z. 4–10) grown in front of *Ceanothus* 'Blue Mound' (2) (Z. 9–10) contrasts with and highlights the mauve-blue.
The contrast produced by growing bright blue *Agapanthus* 'Blue Giant' (3) (Z. 8–10) in a sea of orange flowers of *Heliopsis helianthoides* var. *scabra* (4) (Z. 4–8) is a complementary scheme designed to stimulate and surprise. In the picture that is created when the deep red climber *Tropaeolum speciosum* (Z. 7–9) scrambles up a dark, rich green yew hedge (5) (Z. 5–7), the color saturation levels are approximately equal.

SATURATION AND TONE

A saturated color is a color at its most intense and pure. So, the more saturated a color is, the stronger it is and the more it stands out from its surroundings. Obviously this has to be considered when devising planting schemes, especially those that incorporate saturated reds, oranges, and yellows. Saturated colors can be useful when a dash of rich, strong color is needed. Pots of bright red pelargoniums on a dark balcony never fail to attract attention, for example, and the orange berries of *Pyracantha* 'Orange Glow' (Zones 6–9) show up brilliantly against the dark green of its evergreen leaves. Many late-blooming daisy-flowered perennials, like heleniums and rudbeckias, have vivid yellow flowers, whose color will dominate a planting. The less saturated a color, the less intense it is, so the more it will blend and recede into its surroundings, particularly if they are shades of blue. *Salvia patens* (Zones 8–10) has saturated blue flowers that instantly capture the attention, whereas those of *Veronica gentianoides* (Zones 4–7) are less noticeable, as they are a pale, unsaturated blue.

In this well-composed grouping, the strong lime green color of the euphorbia's flowers is perfectly balanced by the rich orange of the leaves of the heuchera planted beside it.

These alliums have a lighter tone than that of the purple foliage behind, so they stand out. The dark-toned leaves of the smoke bush (*Cotinus*) are much less dominant, and they recede into the background.

Whereas saturation is a measure of a color's intensity, tone is a measure of its lightness or darkness. All colors have an intrinsic tone, which may be light or dark. Yellow has a light tone, and violet has a dark tone. The rod cells in the human eye can detect differences of tone, and they function better in dim light than the cones, the other light-sensitive cells in the eye. This makes it possible to pick out tonal differences in a garden even when their colors are lost in darkness. In a garden, distinct tonal differences can be exploited to produce dramatic effects; for example, the black-stemmed bamboo *Phyllostachys nigra* (Zones 7–10) can be grown in front of a pale-colored wall, or the silver-leaved *Cynara cardunculus* (Zones 6–9) in front of a yew hedge.

Speaking botanically

Many people ask why it is necessary to use Latin names for plants rather than common names, which are often better known. The reason is that Latin is an international language, so it allows us to communicate accurately with other gardeners, wherever they are in the world. Just a basic knowledge of botanical Latin can give us a lot of information about plants.

The oak tree, *Quercus robur* (left), provides us with an excellent example of why Latin botanical names are so useful. In North America and Britain this tree is known as the English oak, yet it has several alternative names (including the common oak and the pedunculate oak). To add to the confusion, it grows not just in Britain but throughout Europe, and no doubt it has colloquial names wherever it is found. However, if it is referred to by its Latin name, *Quercus robur*, confusion is avoided, because any gardener with knowledge of botanical names can identify the plant exactly.

GENERA AND SPECIES All botanical names have at least two words to describe them. The first always has a capital letter and is the name of the genus, or plant group, to which the plant  belongs. For example, all oak trees belong to the genus *Quercus* (Latin for "oak"). Within each genus, plants can vary enormously, but they all share some characteristics. In the genus *Quercus*, for instance, there are 600 kinds of oaks—they all produce acorns, but they differ widely in many other ways: some are evergreen, some are semi-evergreen, and others are deciduous. Each kind of oak is known as a species. To differentiate one from another, an adjective is placed after the word *Quercus* that defines all members of one particular species. So *Quercus robur* is one species, while *Quercus rubra* (above) is another.

The species component of a plant's name may refer to its origins or its native habitat; for example, *Quercus georgiana* is an oak that is a native of Georgia. Alternatively, it may give a clue to size and shape, as in the case of *Quercus rotundifolia*, which is an oak with round leaves (*rotundifolia* means "round leaves"). The species part of the name may also refer to a botanist or plant hunter; for example, *Quercus douglasii* is an oak that commemorates David Douglas, the Scottish plant hunter who discovered many plant treasures in northwestern United States. Alternatively, it may describe a color exhibited by the plant. For example, the Latin name of the water oak is *Quercus nigra* and that of the American red oak is *Quercus rubra. Nigra* is the Latin for "black," while *rubra* is an adjective meaning "red."

CULTIVARS AND HYBRIDS Plant breeders often select species that manifest slightly different or interesting qualities to propagate from cuttings. These

---

COLOR CHARTS FOR GARDENERS

Throughout the plant world there are species with names that give a clue to their color. We understand what this means as we have an expectation of what a color will look like. However, the standardization of color has happened only comparatively recently. John Parkinson, in his *Paradisi* of 1629 (see page 13), talks of an orange tree as having red fruits because the word "orange" was unheard of at the time. It wasn't until the early 1900s that the first color charts, such as the *Code des Couleurs*, were created. This was originally intended for mycologists, who studied fungi, but it was taken up by British gardeners and some horticulturalists in the United States. However, it is not used exclusively in North America—for example, the American Rose Society uses their own color chart.

COLOR DESCRIPTIONS USED IN BOTANICAL NAMES

Below is a chart listing some Latin color adjectives found in plant names. As with nouns, Latin adjectives have male, female, and neuter versions, and their gender usually matches that of the noun they describe. For example, *Quercus* is a female noun, so the adjectives accompanying it are also in the female form—for instance, *Quercus nigra* or *Quercus rubra*. (The male forms are *niger*, *ruber*, and the neuter are *nigrum* and *rubrum*.) Alternative gender endings of the adjectives are given after the male form.

Color in Latin	Translation	Example	Color in Latin	Translation	Example
argenteus, -a, -um	silvery	*Salvia argentea*	*griseus, -a, -um*	pearly gray	*Acer griseum*
armeniacus, -a, -um	apricot	*Muscari armeniacum*	*lacteus, -a, -um*	milky white	*Cotoneaster lacteus*
aurantiacus, -a, -um *aurantius, -a, -um*	orange	*Primula aurantiaca*	*lividus, -a, -um*	grayish brown/blue	*Helleborus lividus*
			luteus, -a, -um	yellow	*Asphodelus luteus*
aureus, -a, -um *auratus, -a, -um*	golden yellow	*Lilium auratum*	*niger, -nigra, -um* *nigrescens*	black	*Sambucus nigra*
azureus, -a, -um	sky blue	*Penstemon azureus*	*purpureus, -a, -um*	purple	*Euphorbia amygdaloides* 'Purpurea'
caeruleus, -a, -um	blue	*Polemonium caeruleum*			
candidus, -a, -um	pure white	*Lilium candidum*	*roseus, -a, -um*	rosy pink	*Hyssopus officinalis* 'Roseus'
canus, -a, -um or *incanus, -a, -um*	grayish white (caused by hairs)	*Philadelphus incanus*	*ruber, -rubra, -um* *rubescens,* *rubellus, -a, -um*	red	*Centranthus ruber*
coccineus, -a, -um	scarlet	*Schizostylis coccinea*			
dealbatus, -a, -um	whitened, e.g. by hairs	*Acacia dealbata*	*sanguineus, -a, -um*	blood red	*Geranium sanguineum*
flavus, -a, -um or *lutescens*	pale yellow	*Crocus flavus* ssp. *flavus*	*violaceus, -a, -um*	violet	*Passiflora × violacea*
			viridis, -is, -e	green	*Santolina viridis* (now called *Santolina rosmarinifolia* ssp. *rosmarinifolia*)
glaucus, -a, -um *glaucescens*	glaucous	*Rosa glauca*			

The fascinating subject of plant names and their meanings is fully explored in Horticulture's *Plant Names Explained*.

plants are known as cultivars (from culti-vated var-iety). Cultivars may have the standard two names with another name added or simply a generic name, for example *Quercus* 'Pondaim'. This part of a cultivar's name is always enclosed in single quotation marks. *Quercus rubra* 'Aurea' (left) has young leaves that are golden (*aurea* is the Latin word for "gold").

If two species cross-pollinate the result is a hybrid. A hybrid's name always contains an ×—for example, in *Quercus × sargentii*, which is a hybrid of *Quercus prinus* and *Quercus robur*.

NAME CHANGES

In the ancient world it was difficult to have precise names for colors, as they varied depending on the way the pigments were extracted and then handled. Also, the ancients' perceptions of colors often differed from ours.

Tyrian purple, known to the Greeks as *porphyra* and the Romans as *purpurea*, was reserved for imperial robes and aristocrats' togas, as it was a highly expensive dye. It was extracted from small glands found in a particular sea snail (*Murex brandaris*), with 8,000 snails being needed to produce one gram of dye. Today, using our modern color definitions, we would describe this sumptuous color as crimson, not purple.

THE ORIGIN OF *COCCINEUS* (SCARLET)

The color adjectives in plant names have come down to us from the ancient Greeks' and Romans' dyestuff and pigment industries. The ancients extracted a red dye from an insect that lives in certain oaks, including *Quercus suber* (cork oak). However, initially they mistook the female insects swollen with eggs for berries growing on the trees. In Latin, the word for "berry" is *coccus*, so *coccineus* became the adjective used to describe the scarlet dye extracted from the insects. In botanical names, this is the adjective used to describe something that is scarlet, and is applied to berries or flowers when appropriate. *Schizostylis coccinea* has scarlet flowers in late summer and early fall.

The impact of light

Light changes according to the time of day, the season, and the climate; in the process, it alters our perception of color. Knowledgeable and creative gardeners take the variable nature of light into account when planning their plantings and make use of this phenomenon to make their gardens more beautiful and atmospheric.

Planting red, yellow, or orange flowers, such as these poppies (*Papaver rupifragum*), where they are touched by low, golden sunlight in the evening or early morning emphasizes their colors.

One of the great pleasures of owning a garden is being able to stroll around it in the early morning or evening, when the rising or setting sun appears to bathe everything in a beatific light. This soft glow occurs because the sun is at its lowest point in the sky, so light passes through the atmosphere at a low angle. As this happens, it tends to pick up dust, much more than when the sun is high in the sky at midday. The dust particles have the effect of diffusing the light and emphasizing the warm end of the spectrum, making it appear red and giving it a familiar glow. When creating a color scheme, we can make use of this by planting reds, oranges, and yellows in places where they will pick up the morning and evening sun. There is no point in doing the same for

schemes featuring blue, violet, or white, as these colors look dark and lifeless when the sun is rising and setting.

After the sun has set, everything changes. The light ceases to have a reddish glow and becomes bluer. As the light fades, warm hues are lost and the only colors discernible are blue and white. Again, one can exploit this by selecting plants that feature these colors for terraces, patios, and other areas used for evening entertaining in summer. A simple idea would be to plant some pots with white annuals, such as petunias, and others with blue agapanthus.

A walk around the garden at midday reveals that at this point the light appears to be colorless. In fact,

A table in a shady seating area has been painted blue, and a planter is filled with blue-flowered grape hyacinths. This is effective because blue shows up well in shade or when the sun has set in the evening.

Some colors are more prevalent in one season than another. In spring many trees and shrubs—like this *Amelanchier lamarckii*—have white blossoms, so make the most of this in your spring planting schemes.

sunlight has a yellow tinge but this is not apparent because the blue of the sky cancels it out. The sky's ability to reflect blue light is most powerful in shade, which is why shadows appear bluer at midday. Again, we can use make use of what nature offers by planting blues, white, and purples in areas that receive no midday sun, because these colors make their most telling impression in blue light.

SEASONAL CHANGE

Many of us who live in northern, temperate climates enjoy the fact that each season has its own character. In Britain, for example, winter sunlight is something of a rarity, and the northern light seems gray and muted; if the sun does appear, it creates long shadows. This is the best time of year to appreciate some subtle nuances of color—for example, the varying browns of bark, the russet of beech leaves, and the pearly white of flowers such as snowdrops (*Galanthus*) (Zones 4–8) and *Helleborus niger* (Zones 4–8).

In spring and fall, the sun is more evident; it slants across the sky, and its light appears to be cool and soft.

In spring this has the effect of lessening the impact of some of the bright yellows we associate with the season. The misty light of a British autumn has a similar effect on that season's glowing leaf color. When planning our color schemes for spring and fall, again it is wise to follow nature's example and base them on seasonal colors. So plantings featuring blues, yellows, cream, and white are good for spring, as these are the colors we associate with the season, while yellows, oranges, and reds are right for fall.

In the same way, gardens in temperate climates in summer look best if they reflect the colors of indigenous plants, which tend to be more muted than those found in hotter and tropical climates. They should, therefore, have a predominance of pinks, mauves, blues, purples, and dark reds, as well as pale yellows and greens, while gardens designed to look subtropical should feature hot, exciting primary colors. It is also worth noting that in high summer, when the sun is at its highest and strongest, even in temperate climates, colors seem more washed out in the middle of the day, and the best time to see them is in early morning and evening.

WINTER STRUCTURE

If a garden has "good bones," in the form of evergreen and deciduous trees and shrubs and elements of hard landscaping, it will manifest all kinds of subtle but immensely satisfying color associations in winter. Examples of winter color include the whiteness of silver-birch bark against a yew hedge, silhouettes of deciduous trees and shrubs against a leaden or a clear blue sky, stone paving after a bout of rain, crystals of hoarfrost on brown earth, or herbaceous seed heads skirted with drifts of gleaming snow.

Color in the past and present

When we consider traditional use of color in the garden, we must look to British landscape gardener Gertrude Jekyll (1843–1932), who was arguably the most influential gardener of her generation. Although the subject of color was much discussed in gardening magazines from the 1820s onward, it was Miss Jekyll—with her prodigious knowledge of plants, their cultivation needs, and their flowering times, combined with her insights about colors—who became the supreme garden colorist. She continues to be an inspiration to gardeners today.

Miss Jekyll trained as an artist and learned color theory—invaluable knowledge when, in middle age and with failing eyesight, she began to design planting schemes. Today, many people imagine that Gertrude Jekyll began the trend for planting schemes of subtle pastel shades that have become so familiar and are often seen as epitomizing traditional English-style gardens. In fact, consciously tasteful, muted plantings owe much more to Miss Jekyll's disciples, notably Vita Sackville-West, than to Miss Jekyll herself. It is true that, for the most part, Jekyll created harmonies rather than contrasts, and preferred using subtle shades rather than pure spectral colors, but it is not the case that all her schemes were muted or featured restrained colors. Sometimes she chose hues that were decidedly bright—garish even—as she admired all colors and believed that all had their uses.

Generally, it was Miss Jekyll's practice to arrange plants in irregularly shaped drifts. This meant that the colors of individual plants were woven together

Hot harmonies using reds, oranges, and yellows featured in many of Gertrude Jekyll's planting plans.

to produce "kaleidoscopes," whose impact depended on the color juxtapositions of neighboring plants. Her skill lay in devising schemes where the flowers appeared at just the right moment to provide the subtle gradations of tone she was aiming for. Sometimes she created hot harmonies, with reds merging into oranges and then into yellows; in other situations she chose the cooler combinations of blues, violets, and grayish greens. She added depth and balance to her compositions by the careful use of foliage, as well as flowers, contrasting rounded and upright shapes and, when necessary, using bright colors as focal points.

Miss Jekyll studied the paintings of J.M.W. Turner, and it was his use of color she most admired. He believed that the substance of the visible world could be represented by the spectrum's three primary colors: red, blue, and yellow. In his impressionistic painting *The Fighting Temeraire* the picture's blood red sunset and its reflection dominate the canvas, while the ship, surrounded by blue, seems to recede into the distance. The sky is a blaze of color that gradually changes from rich red above the sun to golden yellow and then into a pale yellow; the pale yellow then progresses to the white of the moon, and this transmutes finally into the pale blue of the sky. This color sequence was often employed by Turner and, in turn, by Miss Jekyll. Indeed, this was the basis of the planting for the famous long herbaceous (perennial) border in her own garden at Munstead Wood, near Goldalming, Surrey, in England. Vibrant reds dominated the middle of the border, while on either side the colors gradually cooled from the hotter oranges and yellows to the whites and blues at either end.

BARRINGTON COURT

Examples of Gertrude Jekyll's use of color may be seen at Barrington Court, Somerset, in England, where she designed the planting for a group of gardens in the early 1900s. The National Trust has restored the gardens, basing the planting schemes on Miss Jekyll's designs.

In the United States, there is only one garden designed by Gertrude Jekyll, namely the small area surrounding the Glebe House Museum at Roxbury, in Connecticut. This garden has been skillfully restored using Miss Jekyll's original planting plans, but without the delphiniums, which do not fare well in the New England climate.

Cool, calm harmonious plantings of blues, mauves, and grays, like this one, were favored for the ends of the long, color-themed borders designed by Gertrude Jekyll.

As a painter Miss Jekyll was greatly influenced by Turner's use of color, and often her plantings reflected this. In the long borders for which she became famous, her practice was to grade the colors from cool to hot, with the hottest hues in the center and the cooler, recessive ones at both ends. To create these spectacular effects she had to know a great deal about the flowering times and the needs of the many plants she used.

FROM JEKYLL TO THE PRESENT DAY

The subject of color in the garden is discussed as much today as in the 19th century, and Gertrude Jekyll still continues to inspire many gardeners in this respect. Penelope Hobhouse, whose classic book *Color in Your Garden* was published (in the United States) in 1985, describes how reading Miss Jekyll's books and the theories of the French Impressionists inspired her to stop being what she calls "a good taste gardener," and transformed her into someone who was excited by the "infinite possibilities of weaving color pictures with plants." Moreover, Miss Jekyll opened her eyes to the fact that it was just as rewarding to create contrasts as harmonies, and that color can be used to evoke different moods and to manipulate perspectives.

While everyone would agree that Miss Jekyll's contribution to our understanding of color and how to use it has been enormous, there are significant differences in the way color is used in gardens today.

This is especially because, thanks to plant hunters and breeders, today's gardeners have a much greater range of plants to choose from, many of which feature tones that Miss Jekyll could only have dreamed of (see "Modern cultivars," below). Newer cultivars of trees, shrubs, herbaceous perennials, and bulbs now offer us the possibility of using color in exciting and very different ways from those used in the past.

SINGLE-COLOR BORDERS

Although harmonies—rather than clashing or vibrant contrasts—have traditionally held sway in English gardens, one-color borders have also been ingredients of many gardens. Indeed, several of these—for example the White Garden at Sissinghurst, Kent, in England—are renowned all over the gardening world. Single-color borders first became popular at the end of the 19th century, after the Reverend Shirley Hibberd (see page 16)

MODERN CULTIVARS

It is interesting to speculate about the look of plantings Gertrude Jekyll would have created had she been able to use some modern herbaceous cultivars. For example, picture a border with the grayish plum-colored Oriental poppy *Papaver orientale* **'Patty's Plum'** (1) (Z. 3–8), the dusky pink *Verbascum* **'Jackie in Pink'** (2) (Z. 6–8), the burnt orange daisy *Helenium* **'Waldtraut'** (3) (Z. 3–8), the muted red *Astrantia* **'Hadspen Blood'** (4) (Z. 5–8), the bluish gray leaves and purple flowers of the annual *Cerinthe major* **'Purpurascens'** (5), and the almost black-leaved cow parsley, *Anthriscus sylvestris* **'Ravenswing'** (6) (Z. 7–10).

The Red Border at Hadspen Garden, Somerset, in England, is a fine example of a monochrome border. Monochrome borders create their own mood and rhythm and allow an onlooker to enjoy the plants' textures and shapes without being too distracted by their color.

had written about creating schemes using plants exhibiting varying tones of a single color. Contrary to popular belief, Gertrude Jekyll did not care for monochrome borders and advised her readers to include small amounts of other colors in them to provide "punctuation marks."

Today, there are still many gardeners who prefer to plant in monochromes, taking the view that single-color schemes create mood, provide rhythm, and highlight the textures, shapes, and nuances of plants. Nori and Sandra Pope, creators of the monochromatic colorist garden at Hadspen, near Castle Cary, Somerset, in England, prefer one-color schemes because, as they say in their book *Color by Design*, it allows them to "control the colour shift, the saturation of colour and the tonal change from dark to light." Moreover, they feel that if colors are separated, the full impact of each can be appreciated. Like the majority of today's gardeners, who want their gardens to look enticing for as long as possible, the Popes design their plantings to look good for about seven months of the year. This is in stark contrast to Gertrude

Jekyll, who could plan schemes that would look their best at a certain time of year and then be closed off when another scheme came into its own.

Some gardeners prefer to create plantings of mixed colors, rather than monochromes. The one shown here was designed by plantswoman Carol Klein and has yellows, purples, and silvers in close proximity.

Large naturalistic plantings of perennials and grasses, like this one designed by Piet Oudolf at the RHS Garden at Wisley, in England, have been made in recent years for public spaces in the United States, Britain, and continental Europe. Gardeners are increasingly adapting this idea for their own gardens.

NATURALISTIC PLANTINGS

A major factor that has contributed to the changing use of color has been the burgeoning interest in gardens that look "natural." This has manifested itself in the widespread creation of wildflower meadows and in large perennial plantings featuring plants whose natural habitats are the prairies. For this reason, grasses have become increasingly popular, and their neutral shades—browns, straws, and parchments—have come to play an increasing role in modern gardens. Added to this, there are now many small urban gardens whose owners want simple, stylish, low-maintenance, minimalist schemes, where hard landscaping takes precedence over plants. In these situations, a restricted palette featuring the greens of evergreens, blacks, whites, and neutrals is often the theme of choice. When a color is included, it is often provided by plantings in containers or by a few choice plants, selected as much for their foliage as their flowers. The concept is one of "furnishing" the space.

EXOTIC PLANTINGS

The availability of inexpensive air travel and the popularity of garden-makeover programs on television have also affected the way many people garden and use color today. In particular, there is increasing interest in

As the interest in creating jungle-style gardens has grown, so has a desire to grow more unusual plants, such as the tree fern *Dicksonia antarctica*.

creating exotic gardens or, at least, in growing some subtropical plants in among more traditional plantings. These days it is not unusual to find gardens given over to yuccas, cordylines, tree ferns, elephant ears, and various palm species, not to mention bananas, as owners attempt to capture the exoticism of a favorite vacation spot or to emulate designs featured on television. The strong architectural forms of many subtropical plants, allied to the desire to create a "jungle" effect, call for bold use of color, with the result that there are now many gardens featuring vibrant, exciting harmonies and contrasts quite unlike those commonly associated with traditional English-style gardens.

Moreover, there are now more garden writers and commentators urging readers to be more imaginative and brave with their colors, especially when trying out contrasts. Christopher Lloyd, one of England's most respected gardeners and garden writers, urges readers of his book *Color for Adventurous Gardeners* not to be "too precious" or to "play it too safe." In his garden at Great Dixter, in Kent, Lloyd practices what he preaches: dazzling, flamboyant plantings consist of daring color combinations worthy of Henri Matisse and Les Fauves. (They were painters in France in the early 1900s who, bored with the conventional use of colors of their predecessors, chose to paint with "barbaric" colors to create vivid harmonies and clashing contrasts.) In late summer, Lloyd's Exotic Garden vibrates with reds, oranges, greens, purples, whites, and yellows, a spectacle that has all the senses tingling—just the sensation Mr. Lloyd wants his visitors to experience, for he considers gardens should be exciting as well as calming places. He also believes that everyone should try putting even the most clashing colors together because, as he says, "violent contrasts will sometimes work against all the odds, depending on the light and the time of day, on the time of year and on our own mood."

In general, however, there seems to be a consensus among today's colorist gardeners and designers that the way we use color in the garden is entirely up to us, to our own personal tastes, and that there is no right or wrong when it comes to using color. Of course we can learn from the past, but it does not always pay to be bound by convention.

British gardener and garden writer Christopher Lloyd has an exotic garden at Great Dixter, East Sussex, in England, full of stark contrasts (left) and hot harmonies (right). He believes we should all be braver when choosing color schemes for our gardens.

Scale and distance

Color has a vital role to play in establishing a garden's atmosphere and can also alter the viewer's perception of scale and distance. Careful use of color in a small garden can create a feeling of spaciousness and light, while in a larger garden it can act as a link, melding the garden into the surrounding landscape and providing cohesion within.

It is possible to create illusions of space and depth by positioning pale and dark colors together in a planting scheme. In this border at White Windows, in Longparish, Hampshire, in England, an illusion of depth has been created by placing plants with yellow foliage and flowers, including *Euonymus fortunei* 'Emerald 'n' Gold', *Potentilla fruticosa* 'Elizabeth', and *Achillea* 'Moonshine', in front of the dark-leaved *Physocarpus opulifolius* 'Diabolo'.

The important thing to remember when using color to deceive the eye with regard to space is that pale and warm, bright colors will appear closer, while cool colors, such as dark green and blues, will appear farther away. This is important when planning the hard landscaping of a garden, as well as its plantings. A small walled garden, for instance, will be made to appear smaller if it is surrounded by brightly colored walls but will feel larger if the walls are dark and merge into the undergrowth. Also, a planting of white or pale pastel shades in front of a dark hedge at the far end of a long garden will appear closer and make the garden seem shorter. If rich blue flowers were planted in front of the hedge, instead, the garden would not appear foreshortened.

COLOR IN SMALL GARDENS

Every small garden, whether it is a front garden on view to the world or a private back garden, has to be attractive throughout the year. For this reason, foliage plants are the most important constituents and form the backdrop against which more colorful flowers can be introduced. In temperate zones, these background plants should be subtle—dark greens, reds, browns, blacks, and silvery grays—as they will not clash with the brighter flower colors and, being dark, will make a garden seem larger. Small trees, evergreen and deciduous shrubs with dark leaves (for example black-leaved *Sambucus nigra* f. *porphyrophylla* 'Gerda' [Zones 5–7]), and ferns and leafy perennials are all suitable foliage plants for a small garden, and it is a good idea to include some that will provide interest in more than one season; for example, the small tree *Amelanchier* × *grandiflora* 'Ballerina' (Zones 4–7) has pretty, fluffy white blossom in spring, followed by pinkish green fresh young leaves that turn a dramatic crimson in the fall.

The choice of more ephemeral color for a small garden will depend on the mood one wishes to create. If the aim is to have a tranquil space for relaxing, then calming colors—blues, pinks with touches of violet, silver, and white—will obviously work best. On the other hand, gardens designed for activity could include vibrant, lively colors such as bright oranges, reds, and yellows. Whatever the color scheme, the rule of thumb is to place the strongest colors nearest the house and the

A garden seems larger if the strongest colors are placed nearest the house and muted ones are on the garden's perimeters. Here, purple alliums form a belt of strong color in the foreground, while the subtle colors beyond increase the sense of distance to the garden's boundaries.

most muted colors nearest the boundaries, as this will help to make the space seem larger. When reds, oranges, and yellows are being used, the brightest should be planted close to the house and darker tones, such as ocher and brown, farther away. Deeper blues, pinks, and mauves should also be in the foreground, with grayer, more discreet tones graduating toward the perimeter of the garden. Reds may be used at the boundaries, provided they are sufficiently dark and on the blue side of the spectrum rather than the orange. Mixing crimson with violets, purples, and mauves in boundary plantings works well too.

LIGHTENING SMALL GARDENS

Small gardens tend to have dark areas that can be lightened using light-reflecting plants. Those with variegated or light-reflecting leaves, such as epimediums, asarums, hellebores, and silver-leaved plants are best, while plants sporting white or yellow flowers are

RESTRICTING COLOR

It is always wise to restrict the number of colors used in a small garden, perhaps to three or four. However, avoid limiting a small garden to one color only: it demands great skill to avoid producing something very dull indeed. One-color gardens work best when they are constituents of larger gardens, where, as Sir Roy Strong says in his book *Creating Small Gardens*, "there is room for indulgences."

Compositions featuring silver and golden leaves, yellow-flowered plants, and light-reflecting foliage are guaranteed to bring light and cheer to any part of the garden. This group includes *Thalictrum flavum* 'Illuminator', *Milium effusum* 'Aureum', *Euphorbia schillingii*, and golden forms of feverfew and origanum.

invaluable in these situations, too. Shrubs with silver or variegated foliage and those with shiny, light-reflecting leaves, such as skimmias and *Viburnum davidii*, should be placed in the foreground, as they will make the space seem smaller if planted on the boundaries. When a small garden doesn't have a view, the perimeter walls or fences assume greater importance, so care needs to be taken to select climbers and wall shrubs that will not close in the space even more. Dark-leaved shrubs and plants with small and unobtrusive, pale yellow, cream, apricot, blue, or turquoise flowers fool the eye into believing the space is larger than it is.

PLANTING FOR A DARK CORNER

A small dark corner can be enlivened by underplanting a *Fatsia japonica* 'Variegata' (1) (Z. 8–9) with snowdrops interspersed with *Corydalis lutea* (Z. 5–7) or *Epimedium* × *versicolor* 'Sulphureum' (2) (Z. 3–8) for spring interest. White-flowering tobacco plants such as *Nicotiana sylvestris* (3) (Z. 8–10) would give height in summer, while at ground level *Cyclamen hederifolium* (4) (Z. 7–9) would provide attractively mottled leaves and pink flowers in fall.

In larger gardens, where extensive plantings do not look out of place, there is the opportunity to experiment with interesting and unusual color combinations.However, colors should always be repeated throughout the planting to provide a sense of unity. In a predominantly red border at White Windows, in Longparish, Hampshire, in England, the planting is pulled together by the repetition of bronze and silver foliage.

COLOR IN LARGE GARDENS

By their very nature, large gardens tend to be found in rural settings and often have a view of the landscape beyond. Boundaries of such gardens are vitally important. The best solution is to keep them muted in a variety of greens. Mixed plantings of shrubs, such as willows, species roses with subtly-colored flowers, and elders will not jar and will act as a link between garden and landscape. For more dense living boundaries, through which, perhaps, a view can be glimpsed, the choice could be a hedge of indigenous species. These will vary, depending on the situation of the garden—it is a good idea to look at established hedges in the area and replicate them. Across the United States, a hedge

may include plants such as highbush cranberry, hawthorn, holly, yew, honeysuckle, privet, and dog roses. Hedges help to place a garden in its context; they also provide a haven for wildlife.

Large gardens offer the opportunity to create a number of smaller gardens within them, each with its own mood; they also enable the gardener to make large plantings, with great swaths of color that would be overwhelming in a small space. Colors should always be repeated throughout a large planting, as this will lead the eye around it, giving it character and a sense of unity, and there should always be a focal point to draw the eye. Large plantings of gentle, harmonious colors will be given a touch of excitement if deliberate contrasts are added here and there.

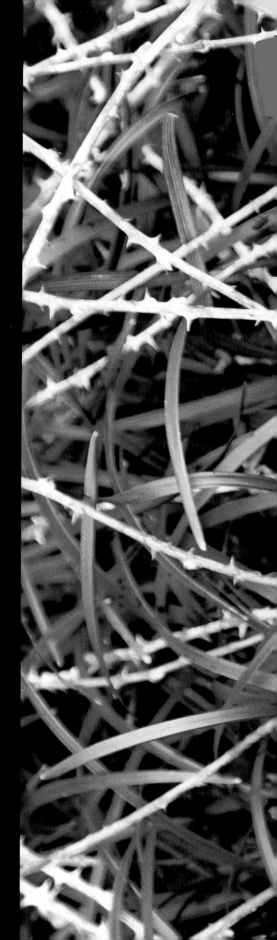

COLORS

There are plants with flowers in every color of the rainbow, so gardeners have the richest of palettes to play with. In order to make the most of this diversity, it is a good idea to get to know something of each color's individual character and potential. One also needs to understand how colors behave when placed alongside each other—information that is of the utmost importance when constructing planting schemes for a garden.

RIGHT: *Rubus cockburnianus* 'Goldenvale' underplanted with *Ophiopogon planiscapus* 'Nigrescens'.

Black

Coco Chanel, the high priestess of Parisian chic, always wore black and white, for she thought they were the most elegant of colors. Plants with black flowers have the same aura of glamour and sophistication; and perhaps because they do not occur in nature, plant breeders have been trying to produce them for centuries.

The novel *The Black Tulip* by Alexandre Dumas, written in 1850, may be a fictionalized account of the Dutch craze for tulips (known as tulipomania) in the early 17th century, but it gives us an insight into the passion that black has always ignited in some horticulturists—a passion that is still as intense today. Luckily for those caught up in the black mystique, there are now more plants sporting black flowers than ever. In addition, there are perennials and shrubs displaying striking black leaves and stems.

It should not be forgotten that true black does not exist in nature. Flowers, leaves, and stems that we think of as black always contain an element of red or purple. So, the popular "black" tulip *Tulipa* 'Queen of Night' (Zones 4–8) is, in fact, a deep purple, and the leaves of the lesser celandine *Ranunculus ficaria* 'Brazen Hussy' (Zones 4–7) are a very dark bronze.

Black plants certainly give a planting scheme drama. Since the strength of their color tends to draw the eye away from the paler items, they should be repeated at regular intervals throughout the scheme.

When black plants are planted with whites, they accentuate each other in the way that complementary colors do.

The drama of the composition is heightened by the shadows created by the dark tones, as in a chiaroscuro drawing. So, a combination of the black-flowered hollyhocks *Alcea rosea* 'Nigra' (Zones 8–10) and *Alcea rosea* 'Black Beauty' (Zones 8–10) with white-flowered perennials—for example, *Eupatorium rugosum* (Zones 5–8) or

BLACK FLOWERS

Today's gardeners are fortunate to have black to plant in a variety of situations. *Iris chrysographes* 'Black Knight' (Z. 2–9) is a beardless iris with dark violet to almost black flowers; it will grow happily in sun or shade but prefers a dampish soil. *Veratrum nigrum* (Z. 6–8) is an imposing perennial that will bring a touch of class to a shady corner but needs a cool, deep, humus-rich soil. It has pleated leaves and plumes of very dark, reddish brown flowers, which may appear black in some situations, on stems up to 4 ft. (1.2m) tall.

Shown left is a *Helleborus* × *hybridus* (Z. 5–8), one of a variable group whose flowers may be white, yellow, green, pink, or purple. The purple blooms are sometimes so dark they appear black, as here.

Lysimachia clethroides (Zones 4–8)—will make the flower colors of each seem considerably more intense. The dark leaves of **Actaea simplex** Atropurpurea Group **'James Compton'** (Zones 3–8) will appear in silhouette, especially if combined with large white flowers—for example, those of the statuesque *Galtonia candicans* (Zones 7–9).

Minimalist gardens can look very elegant when given a black and white color scheme. The black-stemmed bamboo *Phyllostachys nigra* (Zones 7–10), grown in large white or silvery pots, would be eye-catching in a small urban courtyard. On a smaller scale, stone pots planted with the black, grasslike **Ophiopogon planiscapus 'Nigrescens'** (Zones 6–9) and white snapdragons or marguerites would be chic in summer; add white crocuses or snowdrops for winter decoration.

Occasionally, black and white are found in a single plant. The Oriental poppy **Papaver orientale 'Black and White'** (Zones 3–8) has flowers with papery white petals with a black blotch at their bases, and the English native cow parsley **Anthriscus sylvestris 'Ravenswing'** (Zones 7–10) has dark purple, almost black leaves and white or pink flower heads. *Sambucus nigra*, the common elder (Zones 5–7), has a number of attractive cultivars that are

now available, such as **Sambucus nigra f. porphyrophylla 'Gerda'** (formerly *Sambucus nigra* 'Black Beauty'), which has fernlike purple-black leaves and rich pink flowers, and **Sambucus nigra f. porphyrophylla 'Eva'** (formerly *Sambucus nigra* 'Black Lace'), with black-purple leaves and pale pink flowers. These shrubs will grow in sun or shade, although they prefer sun.

Silver or gray foliage (see pages 56–57) also enhances black-flowered plants. The tiny **Viola 'Bowles' Black'** (Zones 5–8), interspersed with the finely silver-leaved *Artemisia schmidtiana* 'Nana' (Zones 3–7), would make an eye-catching edging for a stone path, while the silvery foliage of *Cynara cardunculus* (cardoon, see page 57) (Zones 6–9) would make a dramatic backdrop for the striking black flowers of **Iris 'Study in Black'** (Zones 2–9).

Ophiopogon planiscapus 'Nigrescens' with cyclamens and snowdrops.

Above, left to right: *Tulipa* 'Queen of Night', *Sambucus nigra* f. *porphyrophylla* 'Eva', *Cornus alba* 'Kesselringii', *Pittosporum tenuifolium* 'Tom Thumb', *Alcea rosea* 'Nigra', *Iris* 'Study in Black'.

OTHER BLACK PLANTS

Aeonium 'Zwartkop' (Z. 9–11) Succulent with shiny black, purple-tinged leaves.

Aquilegia vulgaris var. *stellata* 'Black Barlow' (Z. 4–8) Perennial with double black flowers in late spring.

Cornus alba 'Kesselringii' (Z. 2–8) Deciduous shrub with blackish purple winter shoots.

Geranium phaeum var. *phaeum* 'Samobor' (Z. 7–8) Perennial with near black flowers and brown-marked leaves.

Hermodactylus tuberosus (Z. 7–9) Perennial with black, irislike flowers in spring.

Lysimachia ciliata 'Purpurea' (Z. 5–8) Perennial with purple, near black leaves.

Pittosporum tenuifolium 'Tom Thumb' (Z. 9–10) Compact, evergreen shrub with dark purple or bronze foliage.

Rhodochiton atrosanguineus (Z. 10) Climber with deep purple and black flowers from summer to fall.

Trifolium repens 'Purpurascens Quadrifolium' (Z. 4–8) Four-leaved clover with purple or maroon, green-edged leaves.

Blue

Gardeners are beguiled by blue perhaps more than by any other color. Who has not been moved by a sea of woodland phlox (*phlox divaricata*) in a beech wood in the South in spring, or marveled at billowing *Mertensia virginica* in the woods of Pennsylvania in May? We all want to include blue in our gardens, for it is one of the most soothing colors and combines beautifully with a wide variety of other plants.

Plants with true blue flowers are rare in nature and, despite the best efforts of plant breeders, in cultivation, too. Many of the plants described as having blue flowers or leaves are actually tinged with other colors. For example, the cottage-garden favourite *Centaurea montana* (see page 140) has flowers with reddish blue petals, and the leaves of *Hosta* 'Halcyon' (Zones 4–8), known for their blueness, are more green than blue.

The prize for the truest of blue flowers probably goes to **delphiniums** and **salvias**. Towering delphiniums in a border are, for many, a defining image of an English garden in summer, and the fact that they have names such as *Delphinium* 'Blue Nile' (Zones 4–7) and *Delphinium* 'Blue Jay' (Zones 4–7) leaves no doubt about the color. However, delphiniums are found in a range of tones that illustrates just how

varied blues can be. *Delphinium tatsienense* (Zones 7–8) is cornflower blue; *Delphinium grandiflorum* 'Blue Butterfly' (Zones 4–7) is a much deeper color, while the flowers of *Delphinium* 'Cliveden Beauty' (Zones 3–8), a Belladonna Group hybrid, are sky blue. Among salvias, *Salvia patens* (Zones 8–10) has the clearest, purest blue flowers, followed closely by *Salvia uliginosa* (Zones 6–9). These South American natives flower in late summer and fall, at a time when blue in the garden is a rare sight.

All-blue plantings create an aura of calm; but there are fewer blues found in perennials than any other color, so it may be necessary to add some annuals, such as **forget-me-nots** (*Myosotis*) and **love-in-a-mist** (*Nigella*). The beauty of these simple cottage-garden plants is that they will self-seed and so reappear

year after year. On light, well-drained soil one could also sow the flax *Linum grandiflorum* and the larkspur *Consolida ajacis* (formerly *Consolida ambigua*), removing stems that produce white or pink flowers instead of blue.

While all-blue plantings are cool and restful to the eye, they can be enhanced and lightened by the introduction of greens and whites. In early spring, the mottled dark green and cream leaves of *Arum italicum* ssp. *italicum* 'Marmoratum' (see page 124) provide a perfect foil for blue-flowered bulbs and perennials. A striking effect can also be achieved by planting the white *Tulipa* 'White Triumphator' (see page 54) with pale blue *Brunnera macrophylla* 'Hadspen Cream' (Zones 4–8).

The sharpest of all contrasts are achieved by planting blue with orange, because the two are complementary

colors. Planting a bugleweed, such as *Ajuga reptans* (Zones 4–7), and allowing the orange tulip *Tulipa* 'Prinses Irene' (see page 46) to grow through it produces this kind of sizzling contrast in a spring planting. Late in summer, one could achieve a similar effect by planting orange cannas, such as *Canna indica* (see page 148), with the tall, intensely blue *Salvia uliginosa* (Zones 6–9).

Planting blue with yellow produces a less intense contrast than in the case of orange and blue. We have all seen blue and yellow combinations in spring gardens, for at this time of year there are many yellow- and blue-flowering bulbs: *Scilla siberica* (Zones 5–8) or *Chionodoxa forbesii* (also known as *luciliae*) (Zones 5–8) planted among drifts of daffodils, for instance; or the bright yellow-flowered *Epimedium × perralchicum* (Zones 5–9) combined with the intense blue of the evergreen perennial *Omphalodes cappadocica* (see page 127). These combinations accentuate both colors, with the yellows appearing more prominent and the blues seeming to recede.

Above, left to right: *Iris sibirica* 'Ego', *Delphinium grandiflorum* 'Blue Butterfly', *Anemone blanda*, *Hosta* 'Fragrant Blue', *Agapanthus* Headbourne hybrids, *Nigella damascena* 'Miss Jekyll'.

BLUES FOR THE GARDEN

Pale blue flowers
Allium caeruleum (Z. 3–7)
Amsonia tabernaemontana (Z. 3–9)
Camassia cusickii (Z. 5–9)
Campanula cochlearifolia (Z. 6–8)

Medium blue flowers
Agapanthus Headbourne hybrids
  (Z. 7–10)
Ceratostigma willmottianum
  (see page 165)
Echium pininana (Z. 8–10)
Iris sibirica 'Ego' (Z. 4–8)
Meconopsis × sheldonii (Z. 7–8)

Deep blue flowers
Aconitum carmichaelii 'Arendsii' (Z. 4–8)
Anchusa azurea 'Loddon Royalist'
  (see pages 134, 135)
Baptisia australis (see pages 140, 141)
Gentiana verna (Z. 4–7)
Pulmonaria 'Blue Ensign
  (see pages 62, 115, 116)

Glaucous blue leaves
Echeveria elegans (Z. 10–11)
Eryngium × oliverianum (Z. 5–8)
Festuca glauca 'Blaufuchs' (Z. 4–8)
Helictotrichon sempervirens (Z. 5–9)
Hosta sieboldiana var. *elegans*
  (see page 127)

BLUES IN SHADE AND SUN

Blues show up best and look their most stylish in shade. If you do not have the space to grow drifts of bluebells or mertensias, try planting blue-flowered bulbs such as *Anemone blanda* (Z. 5–8), or low-growing perennials such as *Omphalodes cappadocica* (1) (Z. 6–8) under a specimen tree—perhaps a white-stemmed birch, such as *Betula utilis* var. *jacquemontii* cultivar (2) (Z. 4–7), for similar effects on a small scale.

Blues in sunshine appear pinkish, so in a sunny site they look best teamed with pinks and mauves to produce subtle harmonies. Pale blue veronicas, such as *Veronica gentianoides* (3) (Z. 4–7), pink geraniums, and *Allium hollandicum* (4) (Z. 5–9), at the front of a border combine to create a simple but harmonious planting.

Green

To be a gardener in a temperate climate is to be immersed in a world of greens—the rich dark green of yew, the yellowish green of young euphorbias, the soft green of young beech leaves, the glistening blackish green of laurel, the brownish green of unfurling ferns, and the intense bright green of springy new turf. Green soothes and calms and acts as a foil for every other color in the garden. It also provides a vital, seamless link between garden and landscape.

Dark greens in the garden recede into the distance, while yellowish greens advance into the foreground. However, since the leaves of most perennials are medium green, they neither stand out from nor disappear into a planting; instead, as they interweave among the colors, they tend to bring an element of unity to the whole.

Medium greens are neither on the warm side of the color wheel with the reds, oranges, and yellows, nor on the cool side with the blues and violets. This explains why they perform so well as buffers, soothing contrasting colors that, if placed side by side, would clash. The brightest reds, magentas, and oranges may all be planted together, provided there is plenty of green mixed among them; for example, the bright red Oriental poppy *Papaver orientale* 'Allegro' (Zones 3–8) may be planted

GREEN FLOWERS

We associate green with leaves and shoots, but there are also plants that produce green flowers; these have cast a spell over gardeners from John Parkinson (see page 13) onward. They may not be rare, but their color makes them seem so. The quirky, many-petaled rose *Rosa × odorata* 'Viridiflora' (1) (Z. 6–10) is far from being the showiest, but it has an avid following of growers. The early flowers of *Viburnum opulus* 'Roseum' (2) (Z. 3–8) are a soft lime green before the flower heads develop into creamy white snowballs. Later in the year, the prize for sheer class goes to the pale green racemes of the bulb *Eucomis bicolor* (3) (Z. 8–10) and to *Allium* 'Mount Everest' (4) (Z. 4–9), whose creamy white, green-eyed flowers quickly change to attractive green seed heads. (For more green flowers, see box, opposite.)

close to the magenta *Geranium psilostemon* (Zones 5–7) and the brick red *Geum coccineum* (Zones 5–8) because their medium green foliage enables the colors to work together.

Gardens with a predominantly green theme can be very striking, and the color has assumed a new importance in the perennial plantings of landscapers such as Piet Oudolf, Wolfgang Oehme, and James van Sweden, who make much use of grasses, arranging them in subtle gradations of green. On a smaller scale, a green herbaceous planting consisting of interesting variations of texture and color could include green-flowered hellebores—for example, *Helleborus orientalis* 'Hillier Hybrid Green'

(Zones 5–8)—and heucheras such as *Heuchera* 'Key Lime Pie' (Zones 4–8). These are good interspersed with hostas—for example, the large, bluish green leaves of *Hosta sieboldiana* var. *elegans* (see page 127)—and grasses, for example, the green and creamy edged leaves of *Calamagrostis × acutiflora* 'Overdam' (see page 171) and *Stipa tenuissima* (Zones 7–9), with erect, bright green leaves and feathery panicles in summer (see also page 171).

Green-themed gardens need to exploit plants' textures, shapes, and tones. They should include pale and dark greens, as well as those veering toward blue and with a hint of yellow. A simple but satisfying green garden can be made by planting walls of yew (*Taxus baccata*) (Zones 6–7) and laying out a pattern of beds lined with boxwood (*Buxus sempervirens* 'Suffruticosa') (Zones 6–9) inside the yew walls, with standard green hollies like *Ilex aquifolium* 'J.C. van Tol' (Zones 6–9) as centerpieces for the beds. Adding *Tulipa* 'Spring Green' (Zones 4–8) and white forget-me-nots will provide spring interest; and the annuals *Zinnia* 'Envy' or the tobacco plant *Nicotiana* 'Lime Green' may be planted in the beds for summer color. Large pots of the foliage plant *Melianthus major* (Zones 8–9) will add glaucous green.

Above, left to right: *Helleborus × hybridus*, *Heuchera* 'Key Lime Pie', *Cornus controversa* 'Variegata', *Stipa tenuissima*, *Nicotiana* 'Lime Green', *Matteuccia struthiopteris*.

OTHER GREEN PLANTS

Green flowers
Alchemilla mollis (see page 154)
Astrantia major (Z. 5–8)
Euphorbia palustris (Z. 5–8)
Euphorbia schillingii (see page 127)
Galtonia viridiflora (Z. 7–9)
Garrya elliptica (Z. 8–9)
Helleborus argutifolius (Z. 6–8)
Kniphofia 'Green Jade' (Z. 6–9)
Paris polyphylla (Z. 6–9)
Tulipa 'Spring Green' (Z. 4–8)

Shiny green foliage plants
Asarum europaeum (see page 178)
Fatsia japonica (see page 78)
Ilex latifolia (Z. 7–9) and other hollies
Prunus lusitanica (see page 82)

Dramatic green foliage plants
Acanthus spinosus (Z. 5–8)
Darmera peltata (Z. 7–8)
Gunnera manicata (Z. 7–10)
Rodgersia podophylla (see pages 65, 101)

Green ferns
Athyrium filix-femina (Z. 2–9)
Matteuccia struthiopteris (see also page 73)
Polypodium interjectum 'Cornubiense' (Z. 5–9)
Polystichum setiferum (Z. 7–8)

Yellow

After green, yellow is the color most easily manufactured by plants, which explains why in spring and summer there are so many yellow flowers beside roads, on hillsides, in hedgerows, and in gardens. We all feel happier for seeing primroses on a mossy bank shyly lifting their heads to the sun. However, while there are some gardeners who love yellow for its brightness and cheerfulness, there are others who shun it, fearing its overpowering brilliance.

In temperate gardens, pure yellow looks best in spring and fall; this is because the sun, which is relatively low in the sky, produces a soft light that dilutes its intensity. In contrast, the summer sun, being higher in the sky, casts dark shadows that intensify the impact of yellow and may make it seem too harsh. This is not the case in Mediterranean gardens, where the sun is so strong that all colors are leached and no yellow seems too intense.

Because yellow is such an intense primary color, it can dominate more subtle colors and make strident contrasts with stronger ones if not used carefully. The skill lies in choosing the best shade for a particular planting, remembering that yellow harmonizes with oranges and reds and its complementary color is blue. The contrast between intense blues and yellows can appear too sharp, so when combining blue and yellow, try adding paler and darker shades of both colors.

YELLOW PLANTS

Today we have a wealth of yellow-flowering bulbs, perennials, and shrubs to choose from. There are also plants with yellow stems, as well as trees whose leaves turn yellow in fall and those with variegated foliage. Many plants have leaves that are yellow as soon as they appear, such as the false acacia *Robinia pseudoacacia* 'Frisia' (Zones 3–8), the bright yellow Mexican orange blossom *Choisya ternata* 'Sundance' (Zones 8–10), and *Dicentra spectabilis* 'Gold Heart' (Zones 4–7).

Primrose yellow is the easiest shade to accommodate in a garden, as it harmonizes with fresh young leaves and makes pleasing contrasts with lots of blue-flowering bulbs and perennials, such as *Brunnera macrophylla* (see page 62). The dangling flower clusters of the upright shrub *Corylopsis sinensis* (Zones 6–8) are lemon yellow, which makes it a good shrub for acid or neutral soil in mid-spring. Another beautiful yellow flower is found on the primrose yellow Caucasian peony, *Paeonia mlokosewitschii* (Zones 5–8), whose single, bowl-shaped flowers, the texture of tissue paper, appear in late spring. In summer, another Caucasian plant, *Cephalaria gigantea* (giant scabious) (Zones 3–7) has primrose-colored flowers. Carried aloft on stems 8 ft. (2.5 m) tall, they add luster to the back of any border. The prize for the prettiest primrose yellow, daisylike perennial must go to the chamomile *Anthemis tinctoria* 'E.C. Buxton' (Zones 2–8).

Some of the earliest flowers to appear in the year are those of the winter aconite *Eranthis hyemalis* (Zones 3–8). Naturalized in grass under deciduous trees, its cheery, buttercup-like flowers, with ruffs of shiny leaves, are especially welcome where they bloom in winter. (See Good Companions, pages 115 and 178.) Winter is also the time for the sweetly scented flowers of witch hazel to make an appearance. Among the most desirable of these is the sulfur-flowered *Hamamelis* × *intermedia* 'Pallida' (see page 177), a beautiful specimen shrub for a winter garden.

Sunflowers and daisies, such as **rudbeckias** and **heleniums**, provide rich yellows for late-summer borders. While they make an impact on their own, interspersing them with paler yellow flowers enriches plantings, providing interesting gradations of tone and helping to emphasize individual flower shapes and textures. For more dramatic, exotic borders, intermingle the yellow flowers with reds and oranges.

Above, left to right: *Kniphofia* 'Little Maid', *Corylopsis sinensis*, *Robinia pseudoacacia* 'Frisia', *Paeonia mlokosewitschii*, *Clematis cirrhosa* var. *balearica*, *Magnolia* × *brooklynensis* 'Yellow Bird'.

YELLOW-FLOWERED PLANTS

Spring
Corydalis lutea (Z. 5–7)
Doronicum × *excelsum* 'Harpur Crewe' (see page 126)
Fritillaria imperialis 'Maxima Lutea' (Z. 4–8)
Kerria japonica 'Golden Guinea' (Z. 4–9)
Lysichiton americanus (Z. 6–7)
Magnolia × *brooklynensis* 'Yellow Bird' (Z. 4–8)
Uvularia grandiflora (see page 126)

Summer and fall
Allium moly (Z. 4–10)
Clematis 'Bill MacKenzie' (Z. 6–9)
Helenium 'Butterpat' (Z. 3–8)
Inula magnifica (Z. 4–8)
Kniphofia 'Little Maid' (Z. 6–9)
Meconopsis cambrica (Z. 6–8)
Phlomis russeliana (Z. 5–8)
Rosa 'Graham Thomas' (Z. 5–10)
Rudbeckia fulgida var. *sullivantii* 'Goldsturm' (Z. 4–8)
Sternbergia lutea (Z. 3–9)

Winter
Clematis cirrhosa var. *balearica* (Z. 7–9)
Crocus × *luteus* 'Golden Yellow' (Z. 3–8)

BRIGHTENING DARK AREAS

Plants with yellow flowers and/or leaves are invaluable for lightening dark corners, shady walls or the shade cast by trees beside ponds. The captivating, pale yellow-flowered *Erythronium* 'Pagoda' (1) (Z. 4–8) fares well under trees and makes a lovely companion for the mottled leaves of the variegated arum, *Arum italicum* ssp. *italicum* 'Marmoratum' (see page 124).

Beside pools, *Caltha palustris* (marsh marigold) (Z. 3–7) planted with *Carex elata* 'Aurea' (2) (Z. 5–9) and the water iris *Iris pseudacorus* (yellow flag) (Z. 5–8) will produce a shimmering spectacle.

Yellow-variegated ivies, such as *Hedera colchica* 'Sulphur Heart' (3) (Z. 6–9) and *Hedera helix* 'Goldchild' (Z. 4–9), will give a glow to walls that are partially shady. However, their variegations are more pronounced if they are grown in full sun.

Orange

Orange is not a color for the fainthearted. It demands attention like a lively, spoiled child. "Look at me," it seems to say, and so has a reputation for not sitting easily with other colors. For this reason, perhaps, it is the color that arouses most passion among gardeners. There are those who think it a "must" for its glowing warmth and intensity, while others wouldn't consider using it because of its relentless attention-grabbing quality.

Orange is found across the plant world, from the flowers of tiny bulbs to the bark, stems, and autumn leaves of trees. Numerous annuals and perennials sport orange flowers, and some shrubs make orange berries that are magnets for birds in fall. Moreover, the glowing vivacity of orange may be enjoyed in every season.

In spring there are the eye-catching bracts of *Euphorbia griffithii* 'Dixter' (Zones 5–7) and the majesty of the crown imperial *Fritillaria imperialis* 'Rubra Maxima' (Zones 4–8) (see also page 66). There are also plenty of early-flowering **tulips** (see box, right). Nothing will banish the winter blues better than orange tulips planted in blue pots. Summer brings the cheery deep orange of *Geum* 'Borisii' (Zones 3–7) at the front of a border and, later in the season, the elegant *Canna* 'Wyoming' (Zones 8–11) and the burnt orange

Helenium 'Moerheim Beauty' (Zones 3–8). In fall the rich orange-red leaves of *Sorbus sargentiana* emerge (see page 163), as well as the striking, papery orange lanterns of *Physalis alkekengi* (Chinese lantern, see page 163), while in winter the impressive orange stems of the lime *Tilia cordata* 'Winter Orange' (Zones 3–7) and the burnt orange-copper bark of *Acer griseum* (Zones 4–7) are a spectacular sight.

PARTNERS FOR ORANGE

The pure, saturated color of orange calls for boldness when combining it with other plants. Mixing orange with those colors nearest to it on the color wheel, namely orange-red and golden yellow, yields vibrant, energized harmonies, like the flames of fire from which a devil might leap—a planting of yellow, orange, and red tulips, for example,

EARLY-FLOWERING TULIPS

Tulipa 'Daydream' (opposite top) (Z. 4–8) Yellow-orange flowers.

Tulipa 'Ballerina' (Z. 4–8) Lily-flowered tulip in orange, red, and yellow.

Tulipa 'Generaal de Wet' (Z. 4–8) Early tulip with fragrant orange blooms.

Tulipa linifolia Batalinii Group 'Bronze Charm' (Z. 4–8) Orange/bronze flowers.

Tulipa 'Orange Emperor' (Z. 4–8) Tangerine, bowl-shaped flowers.

Tulipa 'Orange Favorite' (Z. 4–8) Parrot tulip; green blotches on orange tepals.

Tulipa 'Orange Nassau' (Z. 4–8) Double, orange-red petals flushed with rich red.

Tulipa 'Prinses Irene' (right) (Z. 4–8) Pale orange flowers flushed with purple tones.

gives a lively, harmonious display with orange at its center. However, a planting of orange and blue, as in the case of marigolds growing through annual blue lobelia, creates a "shock" effect, because both colors are complementary and therefore intensified.

For those who prefer colors to have less shock value, the impact of pure orange may be lessened by placing it in proximity to bronze or ivory, which are darker or paler, unsaturated versions of itself. Bronze-colored flowers are hard to find, but there are plenty of plants that have bronze-colored leaves—for example, the bronze-leaved fennel and heucheras such as *Heuchera* 'Ebony and Ivory' (Zones 4–8), which has dark bronze leaves and ivory flowers. Bronze phormiums and cordylines also make effective foils for orange flowers.

Reddish browns and earthy colors also associate very well with orange. Many grasses have yellow, brown, and beige stems and flowering spikes, and dramatic results can be achieved by adding architectural grasses, such as the stately *Stipa gigantea* (see pages 67 and Good Companions, page 151) and the elegant *Calamagrostis* × *acutiflora* 'Karl Foerster' (see page 75), with its attractive, pink-bronze inflorescences, to plantings featuring orange. (See also pages 170–71.)

Pale orange and apricot, and other unsaturated forms of orange, make

Above, left to right: *Fritillaria imperialis* 'Rubra Maxima', *Physalis alkekengi*, *Alstroemeria aurea* with *Kniphofia* 'Royal Standard', *Acer griseum*, *Achillea* 'Terracotta', *Tulipa* 'Daydream'.

happy partnerships with cream, pale yellow, and yellowish pink. The flowers of ***Rosa* 'Gloire de Dijon'** (Zones 6–11) demonstrate how well these colors work together, as they are pinkish apricot in bud, deeper apricot when they open, and they then fade to cream as they age. As its flowers appear over a long period, all these colors are sometimes present together in close proximity, and yet the overall impression is one of a pleasing harmony.

LATE-SUMMER COMBINATION

A vibrant planting for late summer of oranges, reds, and browns could be made with the soft orange-flowered *Crocosmia* × *crocosmiiflora* 'Solfatare' (Z. 7–10), which has bronze-tipped leaves, and *Kniphofia uvaria* 'Nobilis' (Z. 6–9), with its erect, rich orange and yellow pokers. *Dahlia* 'Bishop of Llandaff' (1) (Z. 9–11) would add scarlet flowers and dark purple foliage. *Helenium* 'Moerheim Beauty' (Z. 3–8), with dark copper-red flower heads with brown centers, and *Helenium* 'Waldtraut' (2) (Z. 3–8), with golden brown flower heads with brown centers, would also be attractive elements in this planting.

ORANGE-FLOWERED PLANTS

Achillea 'Terracotta' (Z. 3–8)
Achillea 'Walther Funcke' (see page 153)
Alstroemeria aurea (Z. 8–10)
Canna 'Striata' (Z. 8–11)
Colutea × *media* (Z. 5–7)
Crocus flavus ssp. *flavus* (Z. 4–8)
Dahlia 'Ellen Huston' (Z. 8–10)
Hedychium coccineum 'Tara' (Z. 8–11)
Helianthemum 'Henfield Brilliant' (Z. 5–8)
Hemerocallis 'Indian Paintbrush' (Z. 4–10)
Kniphofia 'Royal Standard' (Z. 6–9)
Lilium 'Fire King' (Z. 4–8)
Meconopsis cambrica (Z. 6–8)
Potentilla 'William Rollison' (Z. 3–9)

Red

Red is the most volatile of colors. Our language is peppered with "red" metaphors to express our most violent emotions: We speak of "a red rag to a bull," "red-hot passion," and "seeing red." Red never fails to ignite a response in us, and we can't take our eyes off it. So much so that in a garden red needs skillful handling. However, more than any other color, it has a power that can enliven, enrich, and add a sense of drama.

Although we talk of red as a single entity, there are, in fact, two distinct kinds of red: the warm reds that veer toward orange, such as scarlet and vermilion; and the cool reds that veer towards violet, such as crimson, cerise, and magenta. Mixing the two types in a planting makes a stimulating composition, although it can create a discordant effect—for example, when pinks are combined with scarlet and vermilion.

RED PLANTINGS

Red and green are complementary colors, which means that seeing intense reds and green together, as in a red border, produces a sensation of tension and excitement. On the other hand, combining pure red with darker reds and bronze or coppery foliage makes a less showy effect—one with deeper and richer resonances. Some red-flowered plants, such as *Dahlia* 'Bishop of Llandaff' (see page 47) and *Dianthus barbatus* 'Nigrescens Group' (Zones 3–8), have dark foliage, so they are doubly welcome in such plantings.

Pure red is best seen at close range, because, on the whole, it absorbs, rather than reflects, light. To make a border of bold reds that continues to radiate color over a long period requires an assortment of both hardy and tender

RED FLOWERS FOR SPRING

Red flowers are something of a rarity in spring. However, there are several flowering quinces—among the first shrubs to flower—that sport red flowers. *Chaenomeles* × *superba* 'Crimson and Gold' (left) (Z. 4–8) has dark red flowers with yellow anthers, and *Chaenomeles* × *superba* 'Nicoline' (Z. 4–8) bears scarlet flowers. In addition, tulip breeders are producing ever-increasing varieties of red tulips, but perhaps there is none to beat the elegance of the species *Tulipa sprengeri* (Z. 5–8).

perennials and annuals. For example, *Papaver orientale* 'Türkenlouis' (Zones 3–8) and *Papaver orientale* (Goliath Group) 'Beauty of Livermere' (Zones 3–8) are scarlet Oriental poppies that can be relied upon to provide vivid early summer color, and *Potentilla* 'Gibson's Scarlet' (Zones 5–8) flowers over a long period from early to late summer. *Lychnis chalcedonica* (Zones 2–8) has clusters

of star-shaped flowers that appear in midsummer, and *Kniphofia* 'Prince Igor' (Zones 6–9) has dramatic orange-red pokers from early to mid-autumn. Other red plants, which flower from midsummer to autumn, include dahlias such as *Dahlia* 'Zorro' (Zones 8–10) and *Dahlia* 'Scarlet Comet' (Zones 8–10), cannas, including *Canna* 'Rosemond Coles' (Zones 8–11) and *Canna* 'Endeavour' (Zones 8–11), and tender salvias such as *Salvia fulgens* (Zones 9–10) and *Salvia* × *jamensis* (Zones 9–10). The shrub *Salix alba* ssp. *vitellina* 'Britzensis' (Zones 2–9) has bright orange-red winter shoots.

RED WITH OTHER PLANTS

In a mixed color planting, large patches of saturated or intense red will draw the eye like a magnet and so upset the balance and rhythm of the scene. In these circumstances it is a good idea to dot the red throughout the planting. *Geum* 'Mrs. J. Bradshaw' (Zones 4–7) and certain potentillas, for example *Potentilla atrosanguinea* (Zones 5–8), *Potentilla* 'Gibson's Scarlet' (Zones 5–8) or *Potentilla fruticosa* 'Red Ace' (Zones 2–7), are ideal for this purpose.

Combining scarlet and vermilions with oranges and yellows gives bright, invigorating effects. Mixing bluish reds with deeper colors, such as rich dark blues, violets, purples, and indigos or gold, copper, bronze, and browns, produces very rich results. In these dark, sultry plantings, where colors should meld into the whole, avoid pastels, white, yellow, or orange, all of which stand out too much. Such a planting might include the crimson roses *Rosa* 'William Lobb' (Zones 4–9) and *Rosa*

Above, left to right: *Tulipa* 'World's Favorite', *Potentilla* 'Gibson's Scarlet', *Salix alba* ssp. *vitellina* 'Britzensis', *Acer palmatum* 'Fireglow', *Papaver orientale* (Goliath Group) 'Beauty of Livermere', *Penstemon* 'Port Wine'.

'Charles de Mills' (Zones 4–8), *Berberis thunbergii* 'Atropurpurea Nana' (Zones 4–8), with red-purple leaves, the dark red *Astrantia* 'Hadspen Blood' (Zones 5–8), *Aconitum carmichaelii* 'Arendsii' (Zones 4–8), with its deep indigo flowers, and the stately dark blue *Delphinium* 'Blue Nile' (Zones 4–7).

PLANTS WITH RED FLOWERS

Warm reds

Canna 'Assaut' (Z. 8–11)
Crocosmia 'Lucifer' (see page 148)
Lobelia 'Cherry Ripe' (Z. 3–9)
Papaver orientale 'Ladybird' (Z. 3–8)
Rosa 'Frensham' (Z. 4–9)
Salvia fulgens (Z. 9–10)
Watsonia 'Stanford Scarlet' (Z. 9–10)

Cool reds

Achillea millefolium 'Cerise Queen' (Z. 4–8)
Anemone blanda 'Radar' (Z. 5–8)
Angelica gigas (see page 70)
Centranthus ruber var. *coccineus* (Z. 4–8)
Clematis 'Abundance' (Z. 5–7)
Geranium psilostemon (Z. 5–7)
Penstemon 'Port Wine' (Z. 6–9)
Weigela 'Bristol Ruby' (Z. 5–9)

RED FOLIAGE

Bright red leaves are not common, although *Acer palmatum* 'Fireglow' (Z. 6–8) (see above) and *Acer palmatum* 'Bloodgood' (see page 161) have dark red foliage, and some pieris, photinias, and *Leucothoe* 'Scarletta' (right) (Z. 4–7) have new growth that emerges scarlet. However, there are numerous shrubs and trees whose fall color comes within the red palette. Among the most brilliant are the crimson foliage of *Euonymus alatus* (Z. 3–8), and *Acer rubrum* cultivars (see page 160).

Pink

We tend to think of pink as being either fluffy, frivolous, and fun, like cotton candy, or gentle and comforting—a baby color. However, pinks are much more varied than that. While the palest pinks suggest innocence and purity, one could not say the same for the brittleness of magenta or the sugariness of shocking pink—these are strident, assertive tones, very far removed from the softness of baby pink.

It is natural to assume that pink is a simple color, as it is produced by mixing red with white, but in fact the composition of pinks is very complex. Moreover, there are two distinct groups of pinks: those derived from reds on the yellow side of the color wheel, and those derived from reds on the blue side (see pages 18–19). Warm, peachy pinks are the product of mixing scarlet, vermilion, and orange-reds with white. Cool pinks are produced by mixing white with bluish reds such as crimson, carmine, and cerise. The cool, bluish pinks outnumber the warm pinks. We find both kinds in the foxglove clan, where *Digitalis purpurea* (Zones 4–8) has deep bluish pink flowers, while those of *Digitalis × mertonensis* (Zones 5–8) are a warm buff.

Warm pinks, if they have a high yellow content, will appear more apricot and pale orange than pink. Their inherent yellowness makes them the only pinks that will harmonize well with pale yellow. The climbing rose *Rosa* 'Albertine' (Zones 5–9) has warm pink blooms with hints of apricot, while *Verbascum* 'Helen Johnson' (Zones 6–8) has coppery pink flowers that appear yellowish brown in certain light.

PINK ROSES

Many shrub and species roses have flowers in beautiful pink shades. The soft, cool pinks are found in the simple flowers of *Rosa canina* (dog rose) (Z. 3–8) and the many-petaled Gallica *Rosa* 'Duchesse de Montebello' (Z. 4–8). The spreading *Rosa* 'Raubritter' (1) (Z. 5–9) has double flowers in a warmer pink. *Rosa × centifolia* 'Cristata' (Z. 4–9) has deep, silvery pink flowers, and those of *Rosa* 'Ballerina' (2) (Z. 4–9) are pale pink with white centers, while the Californian species *Rosa nutkana* 'Plena' (Z. 3–9) has deep bluish pink flowers with a hint of lilac. A good magenta-flowered rose is *Rosa* 'Charles de Mills' (Z. 4–8), which has flowers with magenta-purple petals.

Experts on using color advise keeping the two kinds of pink apart, because they clash when seen together. Interestingly, some pink flowers seem to change from being a cool pink to a warm one, depending on their planting partners or the light shining on them. This is particularly true at sunset, when the sun has a yellow glow. When making pink harmonies, it's best to plant the cool pinks with blues, violets, and whites, and the warm pinks with apricots and yellowish greens.

PINKS FOR ALL SEASONS

There are innumerable plants with pink flowers, some of which are suitable for shade as well as sun. For example, several hellebores have flowers in pale to deep pink and, as a breed, are shade-loving woodland plants (see page 180).

Pinks are also found in every season: The pretty winter flowers of *Cyclamen coum* (see also pages 168–69) appear in a range of pinks, and winter-flowering deciduous and evergreen **viburnums** sport pink flowers, too. Spring produces **tulips** in pink, from the palest shades to the showiest magenta. Summer brings a vast array of pinks, from the flowers of the smallest alpines to the largest perennials. In fall, some late-flowering perennials, such as the Japanese anemones *Anemone* × *hybrida* and

Anemone hupehensis var. *japonica* (see pages 163 and 167), and **origanums** go on producing their pink flowers right up until frosts appear.

ALL-PINK PLANTINGS

With such a wealth of pink material available, it is tempting to create all-pink plantings. Since plantings of a single pink shade look too bland, it is preferable to vary shades and tones and to add interest by selecting plants exhibiting differing textures, forms, and shapes. Another approach with small plantings is to select one plant whose flowers come in several pinks and grow them all together. **Diascias** or **verbenas** could be grown together in this way.

In early summer, one could create a pink planting by mixing the magenta-flowered *Gladiolus byzantinus* (Zones 6–10) and *Geranium psilostemon* (Zones 5–7) and interspersing them with the Oriental poppy *Papaver orientale* **'Cedric Morris'** (Zones 3–8), which has pale pink tissue-paper flowers. *Allium cernuum* (Zones 4–8), with its pale pink to deep rose globes, and *Geranium* **(Cinereum Group) 'Ballerina'** (Zones 5–7) could spill from the front of the bed, while the knapweed *Centaurea montana* **'Carnea'** (Zones 4–8) provides pretty, pale pink star-shaped flowers over a long period.

Above, left to right: *Diascia rigescens, Digitalis* × *mertonensis, Geranium* (Cinereum Group) 'Ballerina', *Cyclamen coum, Viburnum* × *bodnantense* 'Charles Lamont', *Rhododendron* Loderi Group.

PINK-FLOWERED PLANTS

Spring
Erythronium dens-canis (Z. 4–8)
Magnolia × *soulangeana* 'Lennei' (Z. 4–9)
Rhododendron Loderi Group (Z. 8–10)
  (see pages 132–133)
Tulipa 'China Pink' (Z. 4–8)

Summer
Astrantia maxima (Z. 5–7)
Diascia rigescens (Z. 7–9)
Geranium 'Ann Folkard' (Z. 5–7)
Lychnis coronaria (Z. 4–8)
Weigela florida 'Variegata' (Z. 5–9)

Fall
Anemone hupehensis 'Hadspen
  Abundance' (Z. 6–9)
Colchicum autumnale (see page 167)
Cyclamen hederifolium (see page 169)
Eupatorium purpureum (Z. 5–8)
Origanum laevigatum 'Herrenhausen'
  (see page 74)
Phlox paniculata 'Mother of Pearl' (Z. 4–8)

Winter
Cyclamen coum (see pages 168–69)
Erica carnea 'King George' (Z. 5–7)
Viburnum × *bodnantense* 'Charles
  Lamont' (Z. 6–8)
Viburnum farreri (see page 176)
Viburnum tinus 'Eve Price' (Z. 8–9)

Violet

True violet and purple are the most sumptuously rich colors a gardener will ever have to work with. The deeper shades suggest the majesty of royalty and opulence, and tend to inspire awe rather than joy. There's also something mysterious about violet—it lies at the very rim of the rainbow, next to ultraviolet rays, which can't be seen by the human eye, and so it appears to melt into the void.

As a cool color, violet has a recessive quality, which means that in a garden it may get lost in a sea of greenery or be eclipsed by stronger colors. Astute gardeners overcome this by isolating it from other colors and planting it in large masses.

Violet loses its identity as soon as it is mixed with another color. Combined with red, it becomes purple; and blue makes it into a rich blue, rather than violet. When black is added, it becomes dark and somber, the kind of color that has overtones of melancholy. No doubt this is the reason why it is frequently associated with death and mourning. However, gardeners can capitalize on its soulful air to create plantings that give a garden a meditative mood.

On the other hand, lilac and lavender (the unsaturated tones of violet) and mauve (the unsaturated tone of purple) can create an entirely different mood.

When partnering pinks and blues, these understated colors make soothing, subtle harmonies that are particularly easy to create in high summer, when there are so many plants in flower. The only drawback of these paler colors is that they may be overlooked, because

the tendency of violet to recede into the background is even more pronounced in the lighter shades. For this reason, it is sometimes a good idea to plant unsaturated violets and purples with other closely related colors that will not overshadow them. And remember that

DARK, MOODY COMBINATIONS

There are several tulips that have almost black flowers, including *Tulipa* 'Queen of Night' (see page 38) and *Tulipa* 'Black Hero' (Z. 4–8). Planting lots of these mixed with mauve wallflowers would provide a quietly reflective setting for a seat in a small garden. On a larger scale, the seat and its planting could be the focal point for an iris walk, with dark violet, tall bearded irises in parallel beds running alongside the path. A compact lavender, for example *Lavandula angustifolia* 'Hidcote' (left) (Z. 5–8), could be used to edge the path and would add its own soporific scent in high summer. *Iris* 'Blackout' (Z. 3–8) has very dark violet flowers, which could mix with the almost black *Iris* 'Dusky Challenger' (Z. 3–8), which has ruffled falls and a delicious scent.

Above, left to right: *Syringa vulgaris* 'Katherine Havemeyer', *Clematis* 'Jackmanii Superba', *Allium* 'Globemaster', *Salvia lavandulifolia*, *Penstemon* 'Alice Hindley', *Phlox paniculata*.

SOFT HARMONIES

There are many geraniums with violet flowers that can be included in harmonies with pinks and blues. The flowers of *Geranium pratense* 'Plenum Violaceum' (see pages 63, 141) growing with *Geranium* (Cinereum Group) 'Ballerina' (see page 50) and *Viola cornuta* (Z. 5–7), would make a charming edging for a sunny path. A lovely harmonious planting for summer could include *Geranium pratense* 'Mrs. Kendall Clark' (Z. 4–7) among pink roses, with the flowers of *Thalictrum aquilegiifolium* (right) (Z. 5–8) and *Delphinium* 'Lord Butler' (Z. 4–8), which has medium blue, semidouble flowers with hints of purple at their centers.

large masses of color are needed to create impact. Lavender, the essential ingredient of every romantic garden, certainly looks best when it is planted in large groups, or as a hedge.

RICH, INTENSE EFFECTS

Dark violet, purple, and shades of magenta planted together will produce a rich, opulent, intense effect totally removed from the soft effects of the pastel harmonies—violet and purple will calm down fiery reds and give the planting depth. Planting several **clematis** in these shades against a wall, or to ramble over a shrub so that their flowers intermingle, will produce this kind of effect. The magenta *Indigofera heterantha* (Zones 6–10) makes a

perfect framework for dark violet and purple late-flowering clematis to clamber through.

Violet and yellow are complementary colors, so when they are planted together a sharp contrast is set up, with the intensity of both heightened. One has only to imagine wild buttercups and violets growing together in a hedgerow to see that this is the case. In these kinds of plantings, the yellows will tend to dominate and the violet will recede into the background—to create a balance, it is necessary to have much more of the violet than of the yellow. Around a pool in early summer, such a contrast could be produced by generous plantings of *Iris sibirica* 'Caesar's Brother' (Zones 4–8) and globeflowers such as *Trollius × cultorum* 'Lemon Queen' (Zones 5–7).

VIOLET-COLORED PLANTS

Dark and medium violets
Allium 'Globemaster' (Z. 4–10)
Allium hollandicum 'Purple Sensation' (Z. 5–9)
Callicarpa bodinieri var. *giraldii* 'Profusion' (see page 165)
Clematis 'Jackmanii Superba' (Z. 4–8)
Gaultheria mucronata 'Mulberry Wine' (Z. 6–7)
Iris sibirica 'Ruffled Velvet' (Z. 4–8)
Lavandula angustifolia 'Hidcote' (Z. 5–8)
Penstemon 'Purple Bedder' (Z. 7–9)
Phlox paniculata (see page 75)
Rhododendron 'Purple Splendor' (Z. 5–8)
Viola riviniana Purpurea Group (Z. 5–8)

Paler, softer violets
Abutilon vitifolium (Z. 9–11)
Allium cristophii (Z. 4–10)
Aster amellus 'King George' (Z. 5–8)
Baptisia australis (see page 140–41)
Iris japonica 'Variegata' (Z. 5–8)
Penstemon 'Alice Hindley' (Z. 7–10) (see also pages 79, 147)
Polemonium 'Lambrook Mauve' (Z. 4–7)
Salvia lavandulifolia (Z. 5–9)
Syringa vulgaris 'Katherine Havemeyer' (Z. 3–7)

53

White

White suggests purity, simplicity, lightness, order, and romance. We marvel at pristine new snow transforming the landscape and the white tips of emerging snowdrops on a cold winter's morning. Gardens devoted to white have long fascinated gardeners for their elegance, so much so that they have become something of a cliché. However, white plants continue to cast their spell, because as well as looking beautiful in monochrome plantings, they combine well with other colors.

To satisfy this yen for white, today's gardeners have at their disposal large numbers of trees, shrubs, perennials, bulbs, grasses, and alpines that exhibit the color. Of course, lots of plants have white flowers, but there are also many that have white stems or seedpods or white-variegated leaves. Some trees, such as the **jacquemontii birches**, have striking white bark (see also pages 41, 175). There are also whites for every season, with **snowdrops** (*Galanthus*) in winter, numerous bulbs and woodland plants, such as **anemones**, in spring, and white berries in fall, for example, those of *Sorbus cashmiriana* (see page 166) or the snowberry *Symphoricarpos albus* (see page 166).

We tend to use the term "white" loosely, covering colors that are, in fact, creamy or have an inherent pinkness or blueness. Nothing could be more white than the flowers of *Lilium candidum*

(the Madonna lily) (Zones 6–8), but the tulips *Tulipa* 'Purissima' (see page 125) and *Tulipa* 'White Parrot' (Zones 4–8) are perhaps more ivory than pure white, and *Geranium clarkei* 'Kashmir White' (Zones 5–7) has flowers whose petals are crisscrossed with fine purple veins, so they appear pinkish gray.

The natural brilliance of white means that it stands out in any setting, and so plants with large white flowers in a

mixed color planting will dominate the picture. This may be the effect wanted in predominantly green gardens, but when using white with other colors it is preferable to select plants with smaller flowers, as their impact will be less, and the rhythm and balance of the planting won't be lost. *Gypsophila paniculata* 'Bristol Fairy' (Zones 4–8) and *Crambe cordifolia* (see page 138) perform the task perfectly in early

WHITE PLANTING FOR SHADY AREAS

In partial shade, a white planting for spring could include *Epimedium* × *youngianum* 'Niveum' (Z. 5–8), *Pulmonaria* 'Sissinghurst White' (Z. 4–8), and *Anemone nemorosa* (Z. 4–8) for the foreground, with *Polygonatum* × *hybridum* (Z. 4–8) behind. For early summer, try *Dicentra spectabilis* 'Alba' (Z. 4–7), *Astrantia major alba* (left) (Z. 5–8), and *Campanula alliariifolia* (Z. 3–8) with white foxgloves, such as *Digitalis purpurea* f. *albiflora* (Z. 4–8). Later in summer, *Monarda* 'Schneewittchen' (Z. 5–9), *Aster divaricatus* (Z. 3–8), and *Schizostylis coccinea* f. *alba* (Z. 6–8) can take over.

summer; and, although not as light and airy, **gauras** such as *Gaura lindheimeri* (Zones 6–9), with their thin spikes of bell-shaped flowers, can perform a similar function in late summer if scattered throughout a planting. *Astrantia major* (Zones 5–8) also provides "broken" white flowers, with a lightness that makes them ideal for mixing with other plants. As a bonus, if they are cut back after the blooms die they will flower until early fall.

The ethereal quality of white, and the fact that it reflects light, may be exploited in those areas of the garden that are somewhat dark and shady: Plants with white flowers will always lift the mood of a dark space. Their luminosity also means that they look marvelous in moonlight. Again, one can make the most of this propensity by planting white annuals such as **cosmos**, **tobacco plants** (*Nicotiana*), and **snapdragons** (*Antirrhinum*) beside a path, in a front garden, or around a seat—anywhere in the garden where visitors are likely to walk or sit. On balmy summer evenings there is nothing more enchanting than the feeling that you have strayed into a moonlight garden.

Above, left to right: *Betula utilis* var. *jacquemontii, Tulipa* 'White Triumphator', *Crambe cordifolia, Chamerion angustifolium* 'Album', *Salvia sclarea* var. *turkestanica* white-bracted, *Zantedeschia aethiopica.*

PLANTS FEATURING WHITE

Trees and shrubs

Carpenteria californica (Z. 8–11)

Davidia involucrata (see page 137)

Escallonia 'Iveyi' (see pages 61, 157)

Eucryphia glutinosa (Z. 8–10)

Exochorda × *macrantha* 'The Bride' (see page 123)

Magnolia stellata (see page 114)

Philadelphus 'Virginal' (see page 138)

Rosa 'Margaret Merril' (Z. 6–10)

Sorbus cashmiriana (see page 166)

Viburnum opulus 'Compactum' (Z. 3–8)

Perennials

Anthemis punctata ssp. *cupaniana* (Z. 3–9)

Artemisia lactiflora (Z. 5–8)

Salvia sclarea var. *turkestanica* (Z. 5–9) (see also page 158)

Zantedeschia aethiopica (Z. 9–11)

Bulbs

Galanthus elwesii (Z. 5–8)

Leucojum aestivum 'Gravetye Giant' (Z. 4–8)

Trillium grandiflorum (see page 96)

Tulipa 'White Triumphator' (Z. 4–8)

WHITE DOGWOODS

White is well represented in the genus *Cornus* (dogwoods), which includes a wide range of plants from low-growing, ground-creeping shrubs to small trees. The popular small tree, *Cornus florida* reaches 30 x 35 ft. (9 x 10.7 m). It has medium green leaves, which turn red and purple in fall and showy, white or pink bracts surrounding tiny yellow flowers in spring. On a smaller scale, *Cornus canadensis*, the creeping dogwood, seldom grows taller than 6 in. (15 cm) and has tiny green flowers surrounded by showy white bracts up to ¾ in. (2 cm) long. Another beautiful small tree, *Cornus controversa* 'Variegata' (see page 42) has tiers of shiny dark green leaves with white margins and flat heads of white flowers in early summer; it grows up to 25 x 25 ft. (8 x 8m). *Cornus* 'Eddie's White Wonder' (above) has showy greenish purple flower heads surrounded by four to six white bracts, which appear in late spring. When mature, this cornus reaches 20 x 15 ft. (6 x 5 m).

Gray and silver

We all know that nothing sets off the colors of a shirt and tie as well as an understated, elegant dark gray suit, and the same is true in a garden setting. Gray has the capacity to make pastel shades seem more intense and to neutralize brash, strident ones. Although gray is inconspicuous and recessive in nature, it plays a major "diplomatic" role, helping other more assertive colors to work together.

In most situations, gray seldom catches our eye, while silver (which is gray with a sheen) tends to sparkle. However, in the garden the two colors are interchangeable and will add luster to any planting. Many plants have gray or silver leaves, including some trees, such as *Olea europaea* (olive) (Zones 8–9) and *Hippophae rhamnoides* (sea buckthorn) (Zones 3–7), as well as many shrubs, succulents, and perennials. Most come from hot, dry places, so in gardens in dampish northern latitudes it is important to try to replicate as closely as possible the conditions these plants would have enjoyed in the wild, namely positions in sun in well-drained soil.

The foliage appears gray or silver because the leaves are covered with masses of tiny white hairs that grow on their surfaces; this is nature's way of preventing them from being scorched in hot sun. The texture of the leaves is variable. Some gray or silver foliage plants have thick, felted leaves—for instance, *Salvia argentea* (Zones 5–8), *Verbascum olympicum* (Zones 6–8) and *Stachys byzantina* (Zones 4–8)—while others have feathery, intricate leaves, for example the **santolinas** or **artemisias** (see box, left). Some have thick succulent leaves, namely the **echeverias** and **sempervivums**.

SILVER-LEAVED ARTEMISIAS

The 300 species of artemisias vary enormously, but most have gray or silver leaves with intricately cut and indented margins. The foliage of *Artemisia ludoviciana* 'Valerie Finnis' (1) (Z. 4–8) is silvery gray with deeply cut margins, while *Artemisia ludoviciana* 'Silver Queen' (2) (see also page 79) has lance-shaped, silvery white leaves. They are ideal for weaving into mixed perennial plantings, as is *Artemisia* 'Powis Castle' (3) (Z. 6–10), with its soft clouds of feathery silver leaves. The compact *Artemisia stelleriana* 'Boughton Silver' (4) (Z. 3–7) has silky leaves and looks best at the front of a bed or as an edging for a path.

SILVER OR GRAY WITH OTHER COLORS

Silver- or gray-leaved shrubs, perennials, and annuals are ideal candidates for including in plantings where the emphasis is on harmonious pastel shades, such as pinks, blues, and creams. *Artemisia* 'Powis Castle' (see box, opposite) is the perfect companion for pale pink roses, such as *Rosa* 'Mary Rose' (Zones 6–10), and blue veronicas, such as *Veronica gentianoides* (see box, page 41). The silver-leaved *Veronica spicata* ssp. *incana* (see page 135) and the low-growing *Anthemis punctata* ssp. *cupaniana* (Zones 3–9)

make a pleasing and harmonious underplanting for pale yellow roses. The latter's white daisy flowers have yellow centers that mirror the color of the roses, and its finely cut silvery foliage never looks shabby.

Grays and silvers can also make a valuable contribution in all-white planting schemes, acting as softeners for the whites, which can appear almost too bright when set against dark green foliage. Using a single gray-leaved plant, such as *Artemisia ludoviciana* 'Valerie Finnis' (see box, opposite), repeated at intervals throughout a planting, will not only soften the planting but also enrich and lighten it.

Above, left to right: *Agave americana, Stachys byzantina, Elaeagnus* 'Quicksilver', *Cynara cardunculus, Eryngium giganteum, Hebe pinguifolia* 'Pagei'.

Grays and silvers may also help to calm down highly charged colors, such as magenta, and to lighten plantings that include dark red and plum shades. The Oriental poppy *Papaver orientale* 'Patty's Plum' (Zones 3–8), with its faded plum-colored blooms, looks beautiful against a backdrop of gray- or silver-leaved plants such as *Helichrysum italicum* (with its yellow flowers removed) (Zones 8–10) or *Stachys byzantina* 'Silver Carpet' (Zones 4–8).

ARCHITECTURAL SILVER OR GRAY PLANTS

One of the boons of the grays and silvers is that among their number there are some statuesque or architectural plants, which add a great sense of theater to plantings. The Scotch thistle *Onopordum nervosum* (right) (Z. 6–8) has spiny-toothed, silver-gray leaves, to 20 in. (50 cm) long, and thistlelike, purplish flower heads and spiny bracts in summer. *Cynara cardunculus* (cardoon) (Z. 6–9) has spiny, silvery gray, deeply cut leaves, up to 20 in. (50 cm) long. Among the sea hollies there are also some striking silvers, for example *Eryngium giganteum* (Miss Willmott's Ghost) (Z. 4–7), which has "thimblelike" flowers surrounded by prickly silver bracts, 2½ in. (6 cm) long.

GRAY/SILVER-LEAVED PLANTS

Agave americana (Z. 8–11)
Artemisia schmidtiana 'Nana' (Z. 3–7)
Astelia chathamica (Z. 8–10)
Athyrium niponicum var. *pictum* (Z. 4–9)
Echeveria secunda var. *glauca* (Z. 10–11)
Elaeagnus 'Quicksilver' (Z. 3–9)
Hebe pinguifolia 'Pagei' (Z. 8–10)
Helictotrichon sempervirens (Z. 5–9)
Hippophae rhamnoides (Z. 3–7)
Pyrus salicifolia 'Pendula' (Z. 4–7)
Salvia argentea (Z. 5–8)
Teucrium fruticans (Z. 9–10)
Thymus × *citriodorus* 'Silver Queen' (Z. 5–8)

MOODS

People have long used paint to decorate their dwellings to produce specific moods. Similarly, the plants a gardener chooses, and the way they are arranged together, affect the mood of a garden. By making definite but limited color choices, it is possible to create a range of moods, and mastering the art of exploiting color to provide an aura of calm, subtlety, excitement, drama, or sophistication enriches every gardener's experience.

58

RIGHT: *Viburnum plicatum* f. *tomentosum* 'Mariesii' and *Meconopsis* × *sheldonii*.

Calming

Monks of old realized that an enclosed garden with a cloister around it was the perfect place for calm reflection. Not many of us can afford to make a garden with its own cloister, but it is very easy to create a sense of enclosure, perhaps in a corner of the garden, and to construct plantings that generate a mood of calm. Not surprisingly, these plantings should be filled with harmonious rather than contrasting colors.

The word harmony suggests quietness and calm but, as we have seen, there are hot, vibrant harmonies as well as soothing, tranquil ones. Naturally, a calm planting requires the most restful harmonies—those composed largely of blues and other cool colors with blue in their makeup.

Blue harmonies show up best in shade, where the light with its bluish tinge enriches the blues. Any planting will, of course, contain a lot of green, but green is almost as soothing as blue and makes the perfect backdrop. When building blue harmonies, the most soothing plantings are made by adding other harmonious colors, such as violet, lavender, lilac, bluish pink, broken white, pale primrose, and silver—all guaranteed to enrich plantings without destroying their mood.

While orange, sulfur yellow, and scarlet must be avoided, the darker, bluish reds, such as crimson and deep purples, added to blue plantings give a sumptuous feel without necessarily destroying their calming effect. In fact, dark, sultry plantings may be just what is needed if a calming garden is not to be too bland.

A FEELING OF ENCLOSURE

When creating a garden or a corner of a garden with a calming effect, it is a good idea to surround the area in some way with a hedge or fence, as enclosed spaces convey a feeling of sanctuary from the outside world and barriers may help muffle unwelcome noise. A trellis creates a similar effect, particularly if painted a color that complements the garden scheme, as here. *Taxus baccata* (common yew) (Z. 6–7) makes the most enduring and handsome of hedges and provides a rich dark green background to plantings, while *Ligustrum ovalifolium* (privet) (Z. 5–9) and *Prunus lusitanica* (Portugal laurel) (Z. 7–9) have lighter green leaves that are shiny and therefore reflect light.

CREATING AN ATMOSPHERE

When trying to create a calm mood it is worth remembering that a fountain or the sound of running water will add to the contemplative air. You may find wind chimes or the clattering of bamboo boxes calming, too. On the other hand, you may prefer to be calmed by silence or the gentle rustling of leaves or grasses in the breeze. A garden's atmosphere can also be affected by the color of its furniture, containers, doors, gates, and walls, so take them into consideration when planning the scheme.

PLANTS TO CREATE SHADE

To provide some shade in a calm, blue planting scheme in a small area, a tree such as *Prunus padus* 'Watereri' (bird cherry) (Z. 6–9) would be ideal. This small- to medium-size deciduous tree is very attractive in spring, when it bears dangling, white, almond-scented flower clusters, up to 8 in. (20 cm) long.

If a large enclosed area is required, use evergreen shrubs to provide weight and year-round interest when the blue plantings are not in flower. There are a number of evergreen shrubs that have attractive leaves and flowers in winter, for example *Escallonia* 'Iveyi'(1) (see also page 157), *Viburnum* × *burkwoodii* 'Anne Russell' (2) (see also page 117) and *Sarcococca hookeriana* var. *digyna* (3) (Z. 6–8). All bear fragrant white flowers when little else is in bloom. *Phillyrea latifolia* (4) (Z. 7–8) is an underused evergreen with glossy, dark green leaves; it makes a handsome addition to a shrub planting and may also be grown as a hedge. In colder areas it should be grown against a wall.

A HARMONIOUS PLANTING FOR SHADE

Various evergreen and deciduous shrubs will work well in a harmonious planting in a shady area, providing some structure, a good backdrop for herbaceous plants, and various shades of green at times of year when there are no flowers present. **Philadelphus** tolerate partial shade, and their scented white, early-summer flowers add a touch of the exotic to any scheme. *Philadelphus* 'Belle Etoile' (Zones 5–7), growing to 4 ft. (1.2 m) high, has highly fragrant white flowers with pale purple markings in the center, while the compact, bushy *Philadelphus* 'Manteau d'Hermine' (Zones 5–7), at no more than 30 in. (75 cm) high, suits the front

of a border. **Hydrangeas** could also be used to bulk out such a planting and provide flowers over a long period from summer to fall, when the philadelphus cease flowering. On acidic soil *Hydrangea serrata* 'Bluebird' (Zones 5–7) has deep, rich blue fertile flowers (more mauve on alkaline soil) with paler blue sterile flowers around them. There are several low-growing shade-lovers that provide good color before the main flowering period. For the front of a border, *Corydalis flexuosa* 'Purple Leaf' (Zones 5–8) has delicate, ferny purple leaves and pretty medium blue, hooded flowers, and *Brunnera macrophylla* (Zones 4–8) has forget-me-not flowers in powder blue. *Pulmonaria* 'Blue Ensign' (see also page 115 and Good Companions, page 116) has clear, deep

blue flowers with dark green leaves without markings or spots.

Other plants that would add to the scene in early spring, and grow in partial shade, include *Polygonatum* × *hybridum* (Solomon's seal) (see page 125), with its graceful sprays of bell-like flowers on stems up to 5 ft. (1.5 m) tall, and **camassias**. These are splendid blue-, purple- and white-flowered bulbous perennials, whose star- or cup-shaped flowers emerge in erect spires from spring to summer. They provide striking vertical accents above the mounds of foliage toward the front of a border. *Camassia cusickii* 'Zwanenburg' (Zones 5–9) has deep blue flowers.

As spring gives way to summer, the shade-loving **meadow rues** (thalictrums) come into their own. *Thalictrum*

Top row, left to right: *Philadelphus* 'Belle Etoile', *Philadelphus* 'Manteau d'Hermine', *Hydrangea serrata* 'Bluebird', *Nepeta* 'Six Hills Giant', *Aconitum* 'Spark's Variety', *Geranium pratense* 'Plenum Violaceum'.

Bottom row, left to right: *Pulmonaria* 'Blue Ensign', *Brunnera macrophylla*, *Corydalis flexuosa* 'Purple Leaf', *Thalictrum rochebruneanum, Iris sibirica* 'Annemarie Troeger'.

rochebruneanum (Zones 5–7) has tiny clusters of blue and rich mauve flowers on branching stems, which add a feeling of airiness to any planting.

Siberian irises thrive in partial shade; the flowers—borne on long, thin stems up to 4 ft. (1.2 m) tall—are the height of elegance in early summer. The species, *Iris sibirica* (Zones 4–8), has royal blue flowers. Some interesting cultivars could be added, such as *Iris sibirica* 'Annemarie Troeger', which has soft mauve-blue flowers with a cream throat, and *Iris sibirica* 'Sparkling Rosé', with lilac-rose flowers.

The catmints (nepetas) are just as content growing in partial shade as in sun; *Nepeta* × *faassenii* (Zones 3–9), which reaches 18 in. (45 cm) high, could be planted along the front of the border to provide a bluish "haze" that would soften the border's edge from early summer to early fall. *Nepeta* 'Six Hills Giant' (Zones 4–7) is taller, to 3 ft. (90 cm), with lavender blue flower spikes.

Later in the summer, a number of monkshoods (aconitums) produce panicles of flowers in blue and purple. *Aconitum* 'Spark's Variety' (Zones 4–8) has deep violet flowers on stems up to 5 ft. (1.5 m) tall from mid to late summer. Some salvias are also happy in shade and, if planted in pots, could be popped into the planting to add punch in late summer or early fall. Perhaps the best for this would be *Salvia patens* (Zones 8–10), with its rich blue flowers.

Geraniums weave among other plants, and many have flowers in cool colors that would fit well into a harmonious blue planting. *Geranium pratense* 'Plenum Violaceum' (see Good Companions, page 141) is a beautiful double cranesbill with violet-blue flowers, which keep appearing from early to midsummer.

BLUES FOR SUN

When planting blues in sunny spots, remember that the sun will make them appear less blue and more violet. However, there are lots of plants with blue flowers that you could use to make a calming planting. Delphiniums, such as *Delphinium* 'Bluebird' (Z. 4–7), could be the centerpiece for summer; later, provided the soil is well drained and not too rich, *Perovskia* 'Blue Spire' (Z. 5–8) provides clouds of violet-blue flowers for weeks.

Exciting, vibrant

Playing safe doesn't always pay. Treading carefully may give you a secure life, but the chances are it will be a dull one. The same is true in a garden. Playing safe with color and always opting for restful hues will more than likely produce an uninteresting garden. How much more stimulating to throw caution to the wind now and then and experiment with bold, loud color to produce a mood that stimulates rather than soothes.

When trying to create a mood of excitement, there is nothing to beat the brightest reds, oranges, and yellows that together make hot, vibrant harmonies, unmatched for generating a spirit of *joie de vivre*. Moreover, when placed together, the individual colors seem more intense. These harmonies could not be further removed from the calm, harmonious plantings of the blues. Because they are brimming with energy, these hot colors will overpower more muted and cooler plantings so, where space permits, it is often best to create a separate area surrounded by a trellis, a fence, or a wall. The owners of smaller gardens will have to decide whether they want to go for broke and "electrify" the whole garden or confine vibrant color mixes to containers.

SPRING BORDERS

Mid- to late summer is the time when vibrant and exotic colors are most numerous, but it is also possible to make exciting schemes from mid-spring on. (Continued on page 66.)

DAHLIAS

After years of being thought tacky, dahlias (Z. 9–11) have become fashionable again and rightly so, for they have wonderfully jazzy flowers in an amazing range of colors. They are native to Central America, which explains why they are often lifted and brought into a frost-free environment for winter. The shapes of the flowers are almost as diverse as their colors, varying from daisylike single-flowered dahlias to "ball", "pompon", "waterlily", "orchid", "peony", "decorative", and "cactus" dahlias. Among the best for an exciting, hot planting are *Dahlia* 'Glow Orange' (1), with small, bright orange, ball-shaped blooms, *Dahlia* 'Moonfire' (2) , a single-flowered variety with cream blooms with red centers and dark-colored leaves, and the spiky, "semi-cactus" *Dahlia* 'Nargold' (3), with pinkish orange, double flowers with slightly pointed petals (see also page 153).

ADDING FOLIAGE

When creating hot plantings it is vital to achieve a balance between color and foliage, bearing in mind that a mixture of highly charged colors needs an almost equal mass of foliage. Some of the leaves should be big and dramatic, and there should be a range of shapes and textures. The foliage in hot, exciting schemes is just as important as the flowers—these plantings call for bold statements.

Phormiums, with their large, spiked leaves, work well in these situations; also rheums, such as *Rheum palmatum* 'Atrosanguineum' (1) (Z. 5–7), with its giant rhubarb leaves. These are red when fresh, gradually becoming dark green on top; *Melianthus major* (Z. 8–9) makes an elegant addition, with its beautiful gray-green, toothed, pinnate leaves, as well as tall, wafting grasses such as *Stipa gigantea* (see page 67 and Good Companions, page 151). Ligularias and rodgersias, such as *Rodgersia podophylla* (2) (see also page 101), have magnificent leaves, as do bananas (*Musa*), guaranteed to give a lush tropical feeling to a planting. For their calming properties, dark red or crimson leaves are an asset, such as those of *Canna* 'Tropicanna' (3) (see also page 67), but they must be used sparingly as too many make a planting seem somber. The inclusion of lime green or yellow foliage will counteract this and help to lighten a scheme. Golden grasses such as *Milium effusum* 'Aureum' (Z. 6–9), bamboos including *Pleioblastus viridistriatus* (Z. 7–8), and golden-leaved shrubs such as *Choisya ternata* 'Sundance' (Z. 8–10) and *Cornus alba* 'Aurea' (Z. 2–8) are all useful "lighteners."

In a planting of strong contrasting colors like this mixture of yarrows, *Centaurea montana*, and poppies, it is important to have large amounts of green foliage to act as a buffer.

From mid-spring on, bulbs such as hyacinths, narcissi (see pages 120–21), tulips (see pages 130–31), and large fritillaries (see page 129), notably the orange crown imperial *Fritillaria imperialis* 'Rubra Maxima' (Zones 4–8), start flowering in earnest. Many tulips (Zones 4–8) are also brightly colored, and a high-octane planting could include the scarlet flowers of *Tulipa* 'Red Impression', the orangey gold of *Tulipa* 'Generaal de Wet', the soft pink of *Tulipa* 'Apricot Beauty', the golden yellow of *Tulipa* 'Golden Apeldoorn', and the scarlet-flowered *Tulipa praestans* 'Fusilier'. These would grow through a bed of emerging foliage, such as that of aquilegias or euphorbias, perhaps *Euphorbia palustris* (Zones 5–8) or *Euphorbia polychroma* (see

page 126), or the emerging bright yellow foliage of *Valeriana phu* 'Aurea' (Zones 4–8). Planting the tulips to emerge through the young leaves of bronze fennel or the rich crimson leaves of *Euphorbia dulcis* 'Chameleon' (Zones 5–7) will make the scheme even richer.

SUMMER COMBINATIONS

While spring offers the excitements of bulbs and emerging lush foliage, and early summer yields masses of perennials and statuesque plants such as oriental poppies *(Papaver orientale)*, tall bearded irises, delphiniums, and lupines, as well as roses (see page 145), it is late summer that takes the prize for providing gardeners with the most

dazzling palette of colors to play with. This is the time when half-hardy and tropical flowers come into their own, flowering for all they are worth. Kniphofias (see page 152), cannas, heleniums, rudbeckias, dahlias, (see page 65) and crocosmias, as well as sunflowers *(Helianthus)*, zinnias, gazanias, and numerous other annuals, are at their peak now, and when combined they make the sparks fly.

At the back of a summer border you could plant pollarded *Paulownia tomentosa* (Zones 5–9) for the impact of its vast leaves. *Berberis thunbergii* f. *atropurpurea* (Zones 4–8) and *Cotinus coggygria* Rubrifolius Group (Zones 4–8) would add calming red foliage. Mid-border architectural shapes could consist of *Phormium cookianum* ssp. *hookeri*

Top row, left to right: *Euphorbia polychroma*, *Ligularia* 'The Rocket', *Cotinus coggygria* Rubrifolius Group, *Stipa gigantea*, *Canna* 'Tropicanna', *Sambucus racemosa* 'Sutherland Gold'.

Bottom row, left to right: *Fritillaria imperialis* 'Rubra Maxima', *Tulipa* 'Red Impression', *Ligularia dentata* 'Britt-Marie Crawford', *Helenium* 'The Bishop', *Heuchera* 'Plum Pudding'.

'Cream Delight' (Zones 8–10), with cream-striped leaves, and *Ligularia dentata* 'Britt-Marie Crawford' (Zones 3–8), with its red-brown, kidney-shaped leaves and deep orange flowers. For a different but equally attractive leaf form, *Ligularia* 'The Rocket' (Zones 3–8) could provide dramatic, toothed dark green leaves and spires of yellow flowers. The "lifting" of the planting would rely on the yellow, finely cut foliage of *Sambucus racemosa* 'Sutherland Gold' (Zones 3–7) and the bamboo *Pleioblastus viridistriatus* (Zones 7–8). At the front of the border, the purple-leaved *Heuchera* 'Plum Pudding' (Zones 4–8) and *Milium effusum* 'Aureum' (Bowles' golden grass) (Zones 6–9) could be interspersed with some suitable flowering perennials.

Every planting needs its stars, and here they would be *Canna* 'Wyoming' (Zones 8–11), which has frilly trumpets of flowers in bright orange or vermilion red and purple foliage with darker veins, and *Canna* 'Rosemond Coles' (Zones 8–11), with its shimmering red flowers on 5 ft. (1.5 m) stems. The cannas will provide strong vertical accents. Many highly colored daisies would also bring great charm and would help to fill out the middle and front of the border. *Helenium* 'The Bishop' (Zones 3–8) has rich yellow flower heads, while those of *Helenium* 'Chipperfield Orange' (Zones 3–8) are rich orange. *Rudbeckia fulgida* var. *sullivantii* 'Goldsturm' (Zones 4–8) has golden flower heads 3–5 in. (7–12 cm) in diameter, while those of *Rudbeckia laciniata* 'Goldquelle'

(Zones 4–9) are moplike with numerous petals in lemon yellow. **Crocosmias**, with their yellow, orange, or red funnel-shaped flowers on arching spikes, would contrast with the daisies. *Crocosmia masoniorum* (Zones 6–9) has orange-red flowers, while those of *Crocosmia* 'Lucifer' (see page 148) are bright red. *Crocosmia* × *crocosmiiflora* 'Citronella' (Zones 7–10) has lemon yellow flowers. A few **dahlias** would add glamour, and any gaps could be filled by annuals such as *Bidens aurea* 'Hannay's Lemon Drop', with its sunny yellow flowers, and *Tithonia rotundifolia* 'Torch', which is a tall Mexican sunflower with orange-red flowers. For an exotic touch, pots of yellow and orange **lilies** could be added to the planting when needed.

67

Dramatic

Plantings of rich, sultry colors capture our attention and draw us into their depths in the same way as an oil painting of an interior by a Dutch master. Dark blues, dark reds, indigo, violet, red-browns, copper, bronze, and burnt gold—all are intense colors individually, yet together they seem to coalesce into a mélange in which no one color stands out but nevertheless has the power to hold us enthralled.

For dramatic plantings, avoid pastels and lighter colors, such as white and yellow, which draw the eye too much. Consider including some flowering shrubs—by selecting carefully, it is possible to have attractive leaves, flowers, and brilliant autumn color, thus prolonging the interest of the scheme beyond the flowering period of the herbaceous plants. All plantings need a mixture of shapes and textures, but in dramatic designs, where the aim is to create an overall impression of rich interwoven color, they are particularly important.

Alliums are dramatic plants in their own right and always provide strong vertical accents.

68

SHRUBS AND ROSES FOR DRAMATIC SCHEMES

The darker-flowered weigelas (Z. 5–9) are good shrubs for dramatic schemes. They are happy in sun or partial shade, and some produce leaves in unusual dark shades to complement their funnel-shaped flowers: *Weigela* 'Eva Rathke' (see page 71) has rich green leaves and crimson flowers, *Weigela florida* 'Foliis Purpureis' (Z. 5–9) has bronze tinged leaves and dark pink flowers, and *Weigela* 'Briant Rubidor' has yellow leaves and dark red flowers (see page 70). The smoke bushes (*Cotinus*) are perfect in these situations, too. *Cotinus* 'Flame' (Z. 4–8) has light green leaves and purple-pink fluffy flower heads, and *Cotinus* 'Grace' (1) (Z. 5–8) (see also page 162) is a large shrub with purple leaves that turn brilliant shades of red in fall.

Dark blue brings another dimension to rich plantings, as it does to Renaissance paintings, so it pays to include blue-flowered shrubs. *Ceanothus*, the Californian lilacs, are easy to grow—some bloom in late spring and early summer, others later in summer and into early fall. *Ceanothus* 'Concha' (2) (Z. 9–10) (see also page 136) has dark foliage and sapphire blue flowers in spring. *Ceanothus thyrsiflorus* 'Skylark' (Z. 8–9) grows up to about 6 ft. (2 m), with glossy, medium green leaves and dark, rich blue flowers. It flowers in late spring to early summer. *Ceanothus* 'Autumnal Blue' (Z. 9–10) bears deep sky blue flowers from late summer to fall.

Among the shrub roses there are ideal candidates for dark, moody plantings. The short flowering time of some cultivars is more than compensated for by the intensity and richness of color and scent. The scented Gallica rose *Rosa* 'Tuscany Superb' (Z. 4–9) blooms only once, but its velvet-textured, flattish, double flowers in deep crimson-maroon with a central boss of gold stamens make it a must. The Moss rose *Rosa* 'William Lobb' (Z. 4–9) is another worthy candidate. Its mosslike, prickly, arching stems bear abundant highly fragrant, double, rich purple or deep lavender flowers; the stems may be trained over bent canes to encourage lateral branches to bear more flowers. Another Moss rose, *Rosa* 'Nuits de Young' (Z. 4–9), has upright stems covered with brownish "moss" and scented saucerlike flowers in a dark maroon. So dark are the blooms that this rose's common name is "Old Black Rose"; it has a reputation for being prone to disease. On the other hand *Rosa* 'Roseraie de l'Haÿ' (3) (Z. 2–7) is a robust Rugosa rose that grows up to 7 ft. (2.2 m) and has healthy, light green, leathery leaves and strongly scented rich dark crimson flowers over a long period from summer to fall (see also Good Companions, page 135, and page 145). Another long-flowering rose is *Rosa* 'Reine des Violettes' (Z. 4–9), with double violet-purple, scented flowers from summer to fall.

DAYLILIES

Today there are daylilies (*Hemerocallis*) in a kaleidoscope of colors and, while each flower lasts only a day or two, the plants continue to bloom for at least a month. There are many kinds to try for rich plantings. *Hemerocallis* 'American Revolution' (Z. 3–9) has dark crimson flowers, which appear almost black, in midsummer, and *Hemerocallis* 'Bela Lugosi' (Z. 4–10) has black-purple flowers with green throats from mid- to late summer. The flowers of *Hemerocallis* 'Dominic' (Z. 4–10) are a rich dark red and appear in late summer, as do those of *Hemerocallis* 'Starling' (Z. 3–9), which are dark chocolate. *Hemerocallis fulva* 'Flore Pleno' (right) (Z. 2–8) has double, tangerine flowers with dark orange veining, and those of *Hemerocallis* 'Missenden' (Z. 4–9) are burnt marmalade with tangerine veins and centers.

ORIENTAL POPPIES

Oriental poppies (Z. 3–8), some of the *grandes dames* of the traditional herbaceous border in early summer, are blowsy and "over the top," and they leave gaps when they finish flowering. However, they give such breathtaking performances that it is worth finding a place for them. Choice cultivars include the crimson *Papaver orientale* Goliath Group 'Beauty of Livermere' (see page 49), the dusky mauve *Papaver orientale* 'Patty's Plum' (1), and the salmon pink semidouble *Papaver orientale* 'Garden Glory' (2). The best way to fill the gaps left in the border after the flowers are over is to plant out some annuals, perhaps zinnias or cosmos, or tender perennials such as salvias. *Salvia patens* (Z. 8–10) has beautiful, saturated blue, hooded flowers.

HERBACEOUS PLANTS FOR A DRAMATIC PLANTING

You can heighten the drama by including some plants with impressive foliage, for example *Angelica gigas* (Zones 4–8) or *Angelica archangelica* (see page 100), *Acanthus spinosus* (Zones 5–8), *Acanthus mollis* (Zones 8–9), and *Veratrum nigrum* (Zones 6–8). However, such dominating shapes need to be offset by more unassuming, clump-forming subjects such as **astrantias** and **geraniums**. Astrantias are good-value plants with decorative pincushion flowers and attractive lobed leaves. The dark red *Astrantia major* 'Claret' (Zones 5–8) or *Astrantia* 'Hadspen Blood' (see page 156) would

Top row, left to right: *Angelica gigas, Delphinium elatum* hybrid, *Weigela* 'Briant Rubidor', *Digitalis ferruginea, Weigela* 'Eva Rathke', *Eremurus stenophyllus.*

Bottom row, left to right: *Papaver somniferum* Peony Flowered Mixed, *Hemerocallis* 'Anzac', *Astrantia major* 'Claret', *Anthriscus sylvestris* 'Ravenswing', *Crocosmia masoniorum* 'Rowallane Yellow'.

fit perfectly in this context, as would *Geranium himalayense* 'Gravetye' (Zones 4–7), whose violet-blue flowers have reddish centers. For more ferny leaves, try *Thalictrum aquilegiifolium* 'Thundercloud' (Zones 5–8) or the dark-leaved cow parsley *Anthriscus sylvestris* 'Ravenswing' (Zones 7–10).

Tall, towering spires are always impressive and can bring real drama to a planting. **Delphiniums** have the showiest blooms and *Delphinium* 'Faust' (Zones 4–8), with semidouble, rich cornflower blue flowers with hints of purple and indigo, and *Delphinium* 'Blue Nile' (Zones 4–7), with midnight blue blooms with white eyes, are reliable performers. The **foxtail lilies** *(Eremurus)* have star quality also but, like some prima donnas, have a reputation for

being "tricky." *Eremurus* × *isabellinus* 'Cleopatra' (Zones 5–8) is worthy of her name, with exotic reddish orange flowers carried in 20-in. (50 cm) spears on stems that can grow to 5 ft. (1.5 m). *Eremurus stenophyllus* (Zones 5–9) is less showy but has dark, rich yellow flowers in 12-in. (30 cm)-long spikes that would suit a dark planting. *Digitalis ferruginea* (Zones 4–8), with thin spires of coppery flowers (see also page 96), and *Digitalis davisiana* (Zones 9–10), with orange-veined, pale yellow flowers, are classy foxgloves to consider.

When including "towering" plants it is wise to balance them with some glitzy perennials, for example **tall bearded irises**, **daylilies** (*Hemerocallis;* see box, page 69), **oriental poppies** (*Papaver orientale*; see box, opposite), **peonies**

(*Paeonia*), and **crocosmias**, perhaps *Crocosmia masoniorum* **'Rowallane Yellow'** (Zones 6–9) or dark orange and yellow *Crocosmia* × *crocosmiiflora* 'Jackanapes' (see page 151). Some stalwart perennials, such as **aquilegias** and **penstemons**, are worth including as minor players. Bulbs such as **alliums** would provide late spring interest, while grasses would provide a spectacle well into fall; some **pennisetums**, for example, have pinkish or purple plumes.

Plantings of deep sultry colors are at their best in summer and early fall, but one can prolong the drama by not cutting the plants down as winter approaches. Skeletons of grasses and perennials gilded with frost on a cold winter's day can be just as spellbinding as a planting in high summer.

Subtle

The word "subtle" comes from the Latin *subtilis*, meaning fine and delicate. We talk of a subtle meaning, subtle approach, and subtle lighting, and in each case we mean refined and understated. Interestingly, this is the mood of many contemporary gardens, which are often designed to be as naturalistic and restrained as possible. If a naturalistic planting is not for you, there are a number of other ways to produce a subtle mood within a garden.

Restricting plants to a few choice specimens and then arranging them with great precision will produce a subtle, low-key effect. The Japanese have perfected this technique (see box, opposite), although in Japanese gardens the subtleties extend beyond the plants to embrace all the gardens' elements and symbolism. Any small, enclosed space could receive this kind of treatment, with perhaps a single, beautifully shaped tree being the centerpiece. *Cornus controversa* 'Variegata' (see page 42) is an elegant tree with tiered branches like

The pendulous flowers of *Acer negundo* var. *violaceum* are a subtle shade of mauve.

a wedding cake and leaves with creamy white margins. Drifts of *Cyclamen coum* **ssp.** *caucasicum* 'Album' (Zones 6–8) beneath it will provide small white flowers in winter and early spring (see pages 168–69), and intermingling the evergreen *Asarum europaeum* (see Good Companions, page 178), with its shiny, round or kidney-shaped, dark green leaves, ensures attractive year-round ground cover.

Green gardens or plantings can create a subtle mood, but to be sufficiently interesting they must contain plants whose leaves show marked differences of form, texture, and color. In shade, a collection of ferns including *Dicksonia antarctica* (Zones 9–11), which has fronds up to 10 ft. (3m) long, would be both spectacular and subtle at the same time. (See box, below.)

Another way of creating a subtle mood is to dedicate certain areas of the garden to flowers that are understated and muted in color. This strategy is

JAPANESE GARDENS

Japanese gardens are perfect miniature landscapes, featuring mostly trees, shrubs, climbers, grasses, ferns, and mosses. Evergreens provide a framework and bring interesting texture and strong forms, while deciduous trees and shrubs are selected for their flowers as well as their leaf forms. Interestingly, if snow settles on branches of evergreens in winter it is regarded in Japan as being another of the gardens' flowers. Many gardens use the surrounding landscape as part of their composition; it may provide a view, or an element such as a large tree can provide shade. There has always been a tradition of using collected native species within Japanese gardens—a practice that has latterly been taken up by many gardeners in North America and Australia.

FERNS FOR FORM AND TEXTURE

Some hardy ferns are wonderfully architectural—for example, *Matteuccia struthiopteris* (ostrich or shuttlecock fern) (1) (Z. 2–7) (see also page 43), whose upright "shuttlecocks" of deciduous pale green, sterile fronds, borne in spring, are at least 4 ft. (1.2 m) long. Its fertile fronds appear in late summer; they are dark brown and only 12 in. (30 cm) long. *Asplenium scolopendrium* Crispum Group (Hart's tongue fern) (2) (Z. 5–9) has 1–2 ft. (20–60 cm) leathery, light green fronds with wavy margins. *Osmunda regalis* (royal fern) (3) (Z. 2–8) is a statuesque fern with sterile, bright green deciduous fronds, up to 3 ft. (1 m) long, in spring. In summer, these are joined by semifertile brown fronds, up to 6 ft. (2 m) long, with wavy tassels. *Dryopteris affinis* (golden male fern) (Z. 4–8) is almost evergreen and produces "shuttlecocks" of lance-shaped, pale green fronds, divided into small segments, or pinnae. The fronds darken as summer wears on but often stay green throughout winter. Shorter but still elegant, *Blechnum penna-marina* (Z. 10–11) is an evergreen with dark green leathery fronds up to 8 in. (20 cm) long, which are linear or divided into tiny lobes.

particularly suited to shady areas. On a larger scale, these kinds of plants will produce a perennially satisfying picture in a woodland garden. Woods look best if they are cultivated to appear as natural and uncluttered as possible.

Plantings of single colors in pastel shades, in which there are fine gradations of tone and shade, will create a subtle mood, too. The most delicate effects are produced using pale blue, bluish pinks, violets, grays and silvers, and beiges and browns, or harmonies of these colors. However, it is a mistake to believe that bright colors should always be banished from subtle-mood plantings. Nothing is more understated than a wildflower meadow, despite the fact that some of its flowers are highly colored.

A subtle mood can be created using pastel-colored flowers in various tones and shades, as seen in this drift of candelabra primulas.

Above top row, left to right: *Miscanthus sinensis* 'Morning Light', *Liatris spicata, Calamagrostis × acutiflora* 'Karl Foerster', *Dierama pulcherrimum, Phlox paniculata*.

Bottom row, left to right: *Monarda* 'Croftway Pink', *Veronicastrum sibiricum, Origanum laevigatum* 'Herrenhausen', *Sanguisorba officinalis, Echinacea purpurea*.

A PLANTING OF PINK-FLOWERED PERENNIALS AND GRASSES

Grasses always bring elegance and lightness to a planting. *Calamagrostis × acutiflora* 'Karl Foerster' (Zones 5–9) is a good grass, with pinky bronze inflorescences, 2–6 ft. (0.6–1.8 m) tall, which gradually fade to beige and light brown in fall. *Miscanthus sinensis* 'Morning Light' (Zones 5–9) (see also page 170) is another delicately beautiful grass, reaching 4 ft. (1.2 m). It bears fine curved leaves with white margins and midribs that appear silvery. Its flower heads are produced in fall and are gray tinted with maroon.

Like grasses, umbellifers—plants such as cow parsley, with umbrella-shaped inflorescences—can be relied on to help create subtle effects. An elegant umbellifer to add to a midsummer pink planting is *Anthriscus sylvestris* 'Ravenswing' (see page 71), which has white flowers and bronze ferny foliage.

Perennials to provide large areas of color in this late-summer planting could include *Echinacea purpurea* (Zones 4–8), with its pink daisies (see also page 156), and the phloxes *Phlox paniculata* 'Eva Cullum' (Zones 4–8), a free-flowering form with rich, bright pink flowers and deeper pink centers, and *Phlox paniculata* 'Norah Leigh' (Zones 4–8), with variegated leaves and pale pinkish lilac flowers. All reach about 3 ft. (1 m). Monardas, too, are useful, though susceptible to mildew: *Monarda* 'Croftway Pink' (Zones 3–7)

has medium pink flower heads on stems up to 3 ft. (1m). *Sanguisorba officinalis* (Zones 4–8) has fluffy "bottlebrushes" carried 4 ft. (1.2 m) high; they are maroon so appear as darker "dots" through the planting. Held on stems up to 5 ft. (1.5 m) tall, the bells of *Dierama pulcherrimum* (Zones 4–8) also provide subtle specks of colors, ranging from pink to dark purple, over the lower plants.

For strong vertical accents, add *Liatris spicata* (Zones 2–8), with long, tapering flower spikes in purplish pink or white, and *Veronicastrum sibiricum* (Zones 4–8), with spikes of lavender blue flowers above whorls of leaves. *Origanum laevigatum* 'Herrenhausen' (Zones 5–8), with its clusters of bluish pink flowers, is good for weaving in and out of plants at the front of the bed.

Sophisticated

Sophistication is the antithesis of naturalness, so perhaps some of the most sophisticated gardens ever created were 18th-century British landscapes made by aristocrats inspired by the classical landscape paintings that they had seen on their Grand Tours in Italy. They filled their gardens with temples and statuary, whose relevance was apparent only to those who had a classical education or had been on the Grand Tour. But sophistication comes in many guises.

A great modern garden to which the epithet might apply was created by the late David Hicks, in Buckinghamshire, England. There are classical influences here—the design consists of strong, formal lines, and both the color palette and the range of plants are restricted. Green predominates and, while there are the browns, grays, and black of bark and hardscaping, bright colors make only guest appearances. So perhaps the lesson for creating sophisticated moods is that less is more, and green handled carefully can be the epitome of chic.

Sophisticated plantings can be unpretentious, like this hollyhock with *Vitis vinifera* 'Purpurea'.

PLANTS FOR A SOPHISTICATED LOOK

The "little black dress" has long been the simplest way for a woman to ensure that she looks sophisticated, and the equivalent in a garden is perhaps the clipped evergreen hedge. *Taxus baccata* (English yew) (Zones 6–7) has been the traditional formal hedge of English gardens for centuries, no doubt because, being an indigenous species, it has always been close at hand. Making hedges of shrubs with variegated foliage brings lightness to a garden. **Hollies** (*Ilex*), with their shiny leaves, also make good hedges (see box, right).

Pleaching—the ancient art of creating hedges on stilts by training branches of standard trees (usually hornbeam or lime) along horizontal wires or bamboo canes—brings a definite air of sophistication.

Topiary is another way of introducing some distinction to a garden. **Yew** (*Taxus*) and **boxwood** (*Buxus*) topiaries are ubiquitous because they make such perfect subjects, but there are other plants that respond well to clipping. In milder areas, **Phillyrea angustifolia** (Zones 7–8), a Mediterranean and southwest Asian species with handsome lance-shaped, glossy, rich dark green leaves and insignificant greenish white flowers, is a good choice. *Prunus lusitanica* (Portugal laurel; see also page 82) (Zones 7–9) also adapts well to being clipped and is less susceptible to cold weather than *Laurus nobilis* (bay laurel or sweet bay) (Zones 8–9), which it closely resembles. Evergreen shrubs with eye-catching glossy leaves and flamboyant flowers, for example **camellias** (see box, page 78), are also sophisticates for either pots or in the soil. Adding a knot of low hedges, perhaps of **boxwood**, a lavender like *Lavandula* × *intermedia* 'Grosso' (Zones 5–9), or a gray-leaved

HOLLIES FOR HEDGES

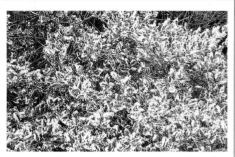

Some evergreen hollies, especially cultivars of *Ilex aquifolium* (Z. 6–9) and *Ilex* × *altaclerensis* (Z. 6–9), make handsome hedges. Variegated forms are choice subjects, such as *Ilex aquifolium* 'Handsworth New Silver' (see page 174), a female holly with distinctive dark purple stems and narrow, mid-green leaves finely edged with cream; the similarly variegated but broader-leaved (and male) *Ilex aquifolium* 'Silver Queen'; and *Ilex aquifolium* 'Ferox Argentea' (above; see also page 173), a male holly with wide creamy white margins. Planting male and female hollies together ensures that berries will form.

The neatly clipped box hedges at Bourton House and the pleached hornbeam at Hidcote bring an air of sophistication to these Gloucestershire gardens.

BAMBOOS

The more compact bamboos are useful for including in smaller-scale plantings as well as in containers. They should be trimmed and the older canes thinned from time to time. *Shibataea kumasasa* (Z. 6–10) is a well-behaved evergreen bamboo that is suitable for growing in a pot; it grows up to 24 in. (60 cm) and has rich dark green, lance-shaped leaves. *Pleioblastus auricomus* (Z. 8–9) has hollow purple and green canes and its leaves are bright yellow striped with green; it grows up to about 4 ft. (1.2 m) and has a tendency to spread. *Pleioblastus variegatus* (see page 79) is another small bamboo, about 40 in. (1 m) tall, with attractive cream-striped leaves. *Pleioblastus pygmaeus* 'Distichus' (Z. 7–8) has hollow medium green canes with purple tips and produces linear, medium green leaves; it reaches about 30 in. (75 cm) and is excellent as ground cover under other shrubs. *Sasaella masamuneana* 'Albostriata' (Z. 6–8) reaches about 5 ft. (1.5 m) and is sometimes invasive but may be confined to a pot. It has slender green or brown canes and narrowly elliptic, apple green leaves with white stripes; the stripes become more yellow as the leaves age.

CAMELLIAS

The camellias that have the widest range of flower color, size, and form are the cultivars of *Camellia japonica* (Z. 7–10). Most need some protection from midday sun and perform best if grown in free-draining acid soil with lots of leaf mould or well-rotted horse or cow manure. They prefer to be fairly dry when dormant but well watered in the growing season.

Camellia japonica 'Inspiration' (top left) bears miniature, soft pink flowers in what is known as a formal double configuration (flowers that have lots of rows of regular, overlapping petals with no stamens present). For those who like striped flowers, *Camellia japonica* 'Lavinia Maggi' (lower left) has medium-sized, formal double white flowers striped with pink and red. *Camellia japonica* 'Adolphe Audusson' makes a compact bush, producing large, semi-double red blooms in early spring.

plant like *Santolina chamaecyparissus* **'Lambrook Silver'** (Zones 6–9) or *Teucrium fruticans* (Zones 9–10), adds another layer of sophistication.

Minimalist gardens, with their strong emphasis on the cohesiveness and quality of all their elements, can be the height of sophistication. Plants that are interesting throughout the year and possess strong shapes are important in these settings. **Cordylines** and **yuccas**, and in warmer spots **aloes**, all have spearlike leaves so have instant impact. *Fatsia japonica* (Zones 8–9) (see page 83) is another classy but good-tempered evergreen shrub with large shiny leaves. Its great advantage is that it is quite happy growing in deep shade, and so it makes an ideal specimen for a dark courtyard garden. In recent years

Top row, left to right: *Fatsia japonica,
Camellia japonica* 'Adolphe Audusson',
Pleioblastus variegatus, Penstemon 'Alice
Hindley', *Clematis montana* var. *rubens*
'Tetrarose'.

Bottom row, left to right: *Lavandula
× intermedia* 'Grosso', *Scabiosa
caucasica* Perfecta Series 'Perfecta Alba',
Ophiopogon planiscapus 'Nigrescens',
Tulipa 'Black Hero', *Artemisia ludoviciana*
'Silver Queen'.

bamboos have become increasingly popular, and the smaller ones make good pot plants in modern minimalist compositions. (See box, page 77.)

A FORMAL PLANTING FOR SUN IN BLACK, WHITE, AND SILVER

Simple, clean-cut water features, such as rectangular pools with a paved surround, immediately say "sophisticated" and would be the perfect setting for this type of planting scheme. The garden, or area of the garden, could be enclosed by trellis painted in a neutral color, such as a soft gray.

Beds around a pool, or a paved area, could be edged with low hedges of *Buxus sempervirens* 'Suffruticosa'

(Zones 6–9), which might also zigzag through the beds to form a simple "knot garden." The spaces could be filled with white **grape hyacinths** (*Muscari*), black-leaved Mondo grass *Ophiopogon planiscapus* 'Nigrescens' (see also pages 36–37 and 39), and, in spring, *Tulipa* 'Black Hero' (Zones 4–8) and *Tulipa* 'Snow Parrot' (Zones 4–8). White annuals such as **snapdragons** (*Antirrhinum*) could follow. Standard roses always add formality; a good choice would be the white-flowered, scented English rose *Rosa* 'Winchester Cathedral' (Zones 5–10). These could be underplanted with the green- and silver-leaved *Heuchera* 'Mint Frost' (Zones 4–8), the gray-leaved *Artemisia ludoviciana* 'Silver Queen' (see page 56), *Viola* 'Bowles' Black' (Zones 5–8),

and the white-flowered *Penstemon* 'White Bedder' (Zones 6–9). The white-flowered scabious, *Scabiosa caucasica* Perfecta Series 'Perfecta Alba' (Zones 4–9), and the black-flowered *Scabiosa atropurpurea* 'Ace of Spades' (ann.) are good alternatives.

An attractive arbor could host the dark-leaved *Clematis montana* var. *rubens* 'Tetrarose' (Zones 6–9), with its sugar pink flowers in late spring, and the scented *Solanum laxum* 'Album' (Zones 9–10). Large pots of *Yucca filamentosa* 'Variegata' (Zones 5–8) and the black-flowered *Aquilegia vulgaris* var. *stellata* Barlow Series 'Black Barlow' (Zones 4–8) or, for a subtle touch of lilac blue, *Penstemon* 'Alice Hindley' (Zones 7–10) would complete the picture.

79

SITUATIONS

In our minds we associate certain colors with specific situations. For example, washed-out, sun-bleached pale blues and yellows seem to be appropriate in gardens beside the sea, as do an array of greens in woodland. When planning a garden's colors, the wise gardener bears in mind the situation and takes into consideration the colors of the hard landscaping and any containers. These are all factors that play a part in creating a satisfying overall picture.

RIGHT: Candelabra primulas.

Town gardens

Many town gardens are pocket-handkerchief size, but it's amazing what can be achieved using a bit of imagination, a few pots and plants, and perhaps some paint. Part of the fun of walking around a town is seeing the way people personalize their outdoor spaces, including making the most of the areas around front doors and windows.

By training climbers (here, *Rosa* 'Albertine') on the front wall of a town house, it is possible to create a verdant look even when there is no front garden.

It is always good to highlight the entrance to a house. One way is to pick out the color of the door in the planting. A purple front door can be complemented by plants sporting pink, mauve, magenta, and purple flowers or foliage. Another idea is to train climbers around the door—a dark green **ivy**, such as *Hedera helix* 'Parsley Crested' (Zones 4–9), on a diamond trellis looks good on a brick wall, as does *Jasminum nudiflorum*, the winter-flowering jasmine (Zones 6–10), trained into an arch on a stone façade. Pots containing matching plants placed to either side of the door will transform an entrance. Try something dramatic, like **cordylines**, or topiary (see page 84). Trimmed **hollies** (*Ilex*), such as the variegated *Ilex aquifolium* 'Silver Queen' (Zones 6–9), always look smart;

corkscrew **hazels** in large pots or, on a north-facing aspect, trimmed *Garrya elliptica* (Zones 8–9) work just as well.

Cordyline australis 'Torbay Dazzler'

URBAN JUNGLE OR MINIMALIST STYLE?

Many back gardens in towns don't have a view. Nearby tall buildings or trees may create permanent shade. One way to treat this kind of garden is to create a green "jungle," using large-scale plants and climbers. With a few big specimen plants and some tall evergreen shrubs, you can create a private domain, rich in atmosphere, where you can experiment with exotic plants and vivid but ephemeral "tropical" color.

Background foliage could be provided by evergreen shrubs such as *Viburnum tinus* (Zones 8–9), *Prunus lusitanica* 'Variegata' (Zones 7–9), *Elaeagnus* × *ebbingei* 'Gilt Edge' (Zones 7–11), and Japanese laurels—the most elegant are *Aucuba japonica* 'Nana Rotundifolia'

Viburnum tinus

Prunus lusitanica 'Variegata'

Musa lasiocarpa

A jungle effect has been created in this garden by planting evergreen shrubs, including *Fatsia japonica*, in close proximity to the seating area.

Lapageria rosea

(Zones 7–10), with rounded lance-shaped leaves, and *Aucuba japonica* 'Crotonifolia' (Zones 7–10), with gold-streaked foliage. Principal players should be more exotic plants such as **large-leaved hostas, ferns, tree ferns, phormiums, bamboos,** and **bananas.** The most suitable banana for general cultivation, if space allows, is *Musa* 'Dwarf Cavendish' (Zones 8–10), which has medium green, paddlelike leaves up to 5 ft. (1.5 m) long; it grows up to 10 ft. (3 m) high, with a similar spread. *Musa lasiocarpa* (Zones 7–10), regarded as the hardiest banana, has shorter leaves, up to 3 ft. (1 m) long, reaches only 5 ft. (1.5m), and is suitable for growing in a pot.

The Chilean climber *Lapageria rosea* (Zones 10–11), with its waxy, bell-shaped, pinkish red flowers, will add a subtropical feel to an arbor, and large pots of ginger lilies would provide vivid spots of color in late summer. *Hedychium densiflorum* 'Assam Orange' (Zones 8–10) has rich dark orange, erect, bottlebrush-like flower spikes and long, shiny leaves. It is hardier than many people think.

The antithesis of the urban "jungle" is the minimalist garden. Simple, stream-lined gardens make the perfect accompaniment to building schemes where steel, concrete, and glass are used in the construction and interiors are characterized by bleached wood, stainless steel, and neutral colors. Plantings of white, cream, sand, and gray (bamboos and grasses have stems and flowers in the appropriate neutral shades) work well in these settings alongside bold architectural plants such as **agaves, yuccas, phormiums,** and **cordylines** (see box, page 84).

This sophisticated garden uses a restricted color palette of green and white. The stark geometric lines of the hard landscaping have been softened with pale-flowered plants.

TINY TOWN GARDENS

In those town gardens where space is severely limited, it is often worth keeping permanent plantings of foliage plants to a minimum while making maximum use of the garden's perimeter walls or fences to support wall shrubs and climbers.

Another option is to espalier trees around the perimeter, using plants such as **beech**, **hornbeam,** or **pyracantha**. This will give a formal, almost French feel to a garden, and that could be

In small urban gardens it is important to make maximum use of the vertical elements, namely the walls or fences and any dividers. Here a painted trellis adds a splash of color to a dark urban garden; its color is repeated in the planting.

ARCHITECTURAL PLANTS FOR POTS

When selecting succulents and other architectural plants for pots, choose slow growers. These include the succulent *Agave americana* (see page 56), with its spiky, grayish green leaves (in the ground these reach 6 ft. [2 m] eventually), and the dwarf fan palm *Chamaerops humilis* (above) (Z. 8–10), with its bluish green leaves dissected into many linear leaflets (it grows up to about 10 ft. [3 m] in the ground).

Yuccas also grow slowly and make good potted specimens. The variegated *Yucca filamentosa* 'Bright Edge' (Z. 5–8) is eye-catching, with long, pointed, dark green leaves, edged with bright yellow.

Feed architectural potted plants with blood meal, fish fertilizer, or bonemeal. Water the pots regularly. Check root balls periodically to ensure they are not frozen in winter or dried out and overheated in summer.

POTTED TOPIARY

The most obvious choice for potted topiary is *Buxus sempervirens* (common boxwood) (Z. 6–9). It can be trained into a wide variety of shapes including balls, pyramids, and spirals. Some flowering plants also respond well to trimming and will grow happily in containers.

Syringa meyeri 'Palibin' (Z. 3–8) is a slow-growing lilac with pale mauvish pink flowers in late spring; it makes an elegant specimen when trained into a standard with a "lollipop" head. Winter-flowering *Viburnum tinus* (see page 82) has dark green, shiny leaves and flattened clusters of white flowers in late winter and spring, and also makes a good lollipop shape. Another option is *Ligustrum delavayanum* (left) (Z. 7–9), which is semi-evergreen in milder cllimates.

The expert advice on trimming plants in pots and containers is "little and often."

reinforced by placing square Versailles-style containers or other decorative pots of topiary around the garden.

SHADY TOWN GARDENS

Many urban gardens are permanently shady. Damp shade results when overhanging trees allow little or no sun to warm the soil, and drips from the trees dampen the ground. Luckily, many plants thrive in these conditions.

For a planting scheme in damp shade, a lovely centerpiece would be a *Cercidiphyllum magnificum* (Zones 4–8), a medium-sized, Japanese tree with large, rounded leaves that turn brilliant shades in fall. Alternatively, for smaller spaces, use a witch hazel such as *Hamamelis × intermedia* 'Jelena' (see page 179), which has large, burnt orange, spiderlike flowers in winter and leaves that turn bright red in fall, or a dogwood such as *Cornus kousa* var. *chinensis* 'China Girl' (Zones 5–8). This has tiny, spherical green flower heads surrounded by white bracts in early summer, and the leaves become dark reddish purple in fall.

Attractive evergreen shrubs to use as background foliage in a scheme for damp shade include **camellias**, **hollies**, **laurels**, and **privets**, such as *Ligustrum quihoui* (Zones 6–9), with its fragrant white flowers in late summer. Hellebores

A small enclosed town garden with few plants can be dull in winter, but planting some evergreens can overcome this. Here clipped box hedges surround a sundial and variegated ivy covers the wall, providing color and structure all through the year. Growing shrubs in containers allows the owner to introduce variety, bringing them to the fore when they are in flower.

provide flowers in winter and early spring and could be interspersed with low, carpeting plants such as the shiny-leaved, vigorous *Asarum europaeum* (see page 178), *Soleirolia soleirolii* (baby's tears) (Zones 8–10), *Anemone nemorosa* (see page 96), with its understated white flowers, and the creeping dogwood, *Cornus canadensis* (Zones 2–7). The silvery perennial *Astelia chathamica* (Zones 8–10), with its arching, sword-shaped foliage, would provide vertical accents in the foreground planting.

PLANTS FOR DRY SHADE

Dry shade is caused by overhanging plants that prevent rain from reaching the ground. Certain trees, including robinias, gleditsias, and *Amelanchier lamarckii* (Z. 4–8), will grow in these conditions, as will shrubs such as the flowering currant *Ribes sanguineum* (1) (Z. 6–7), *Hippophae rhamnoides* (Z. 3–7), berberis, euonymus, and the evergreen *Lonicera pileata* (Z. 6–7). Perennials that spread happily include lamium, brunnera, vinca, bergenia, and *Liriope muscari* 'Variegata' (2) (Z. 6–9).

Country gardens

When considering the English-style country garden, people often conjure up the vision of a traditional cottage garden with winding paths and old-fashioned flowers, or perhaps a country-house garden with spectacular perennial borders and sweeping lawns reminiscent of grand Edwardian estates. However, while there are still a lot of gardens that fit these descriptions, country gardens today tend to be as diverse and idiosyncratic as the people who make them.

Many gardens today, especially rural ones, are looking more "natural" than they did a generation ago. The reason for this is that there is great interest in naturalistic planting—that is, planting schemes that use grasses, biennials, and perennials, including umbellifers (whose thousands of tiny flowers are carried in flat-topped clusters or umbels, like those of Queen Anne's Lace). In addition to this, many gardeners have responded to calls from gardening and environmental experts to make their gardens more eco-friendly and attractive to wildlife by growing native plants alongside garden cultivars. These trends have inevitably had repercussions on the colors found in these gardens.

NATURALISTIC PLANTING

Plantings containing grasses and wildflowers (see pages 88–89), or those close in appearance to their native ancestors, generally have more restrained colors than schemes made up of garden cultivars. This is because the flowers of grasses are muted in color, and wildflowers tend, on the whole, to have smaller flower heads and less brilliant colors than cultivars. Also, in naturalistic plantings, plants are generally intermingled rather than planted in large masses, so the colors are more diffuse.

For many people the classic English-style country garden has roses and a mixture of cottage-style perennials billowing over a path like the one shown here. The effect is informal, intimate, and enticing; and, although the colors are mixed, the garden has a distinctly harmonious feel.

Close planting of a mixture of perennials with grasses has become popular in recent years. An informal effect like the one shown here works well in country gardens.

NATURALISTIC DESIGN

Wildflowers are the inspiration for the planting schemes designed by many contemporary designers. In Britain, Dan Pearson uses wildflowers in his designs, which are renowned for blending seamlessly into the landscape. His philosophy is that gardeners should work *with* nature rather than trying to dominate it. Similarly, nature is what inspires Piet Oudolf, one of Europe's most famous contemporary garden designers, acclaimed for his naturalistic plantings of grasses and tall perennials. For Oudolf, successful plant combinations rely primarily on shapes, particularly those of flowers and seed heads. Leaf shape and texture are of secondary importance, and color is only the third consideration.

Some advocates of the naturalistic gardening style argue that gardeners should restrict themselves to growing only native species. There are situations in a country garden where planting nothing but native species can be a good idea—for example, at a garden's boundaries, when the garden merges into the surrounding countryside, or in an area devoted to wild plants. Elsewhere, however, intermingling native plants with introduced species and cultivars generally makes for a more interesting and perhaps more personal garden. **Primroses** (*Primula*), **violets** (*Viola*), and **forget-me-nots** (*Myosotis*) are ubiquitous in country gardens and are often found among spring bulbs or **snowdrops** (*Galanthus*, see page 177). And many gardeners allow the European **foxglove** (*Digitalis purpurea*), (Zones 4–8) to seed itself in their borders.

Planting some introduced species and cultivars in wilder parts of the garden can work well, too. In outer areas of his garden, English garden designer Tom Stuart-Smith has British native plants such as **cranesbills** (*Geranium*), **teasels** (*Dipsacus*), **scabious** (*Scabiosa*), and **wild carrot** (*Daucus*). But he mixes them with introduced plants that have a delicate, wild look, such as *Persicaria amplexicaulis* (Zones 4–7), with its

Umbellifers are a key ingredient in any naturalistic planting scheme.

spiky purple, red, or white flowers, *Veronicastrum virginicum* 'Album', (Zones 4–8), with its spikes of veronica-like, white flowers, and the grass *Hakonechloa macra* (Zones 6–9), which has smooth, arching, medium green leaves and pale green flower spikes from late summer to early fall. He advocates a gradient of naturalness in a garden, from highly cultivated areas close to the house to the semi-wild in its outer reaches. This is a gardening practice very well suited to country gardens.

Planting bulbs such as narcissi in grass gives a country garden the feeling that it is rooted in the surrounding landscape.

Enormous herbaceous borders were often features of large country house gardens in the past. Today, many borders are mixed—that is, they include shrubs, trees, grasses, and bulbs, as well as herbaceous perennials. In this border at White Windows, in Longparish, Hampshire, in England, shrubs are planted among perennials, in a color scheme featuring flowers in blue, cream, and yellow.

COUNTRY GARDEN BORDERS

In the past, many English country gardens had very large perennial borders, the grandest of which included thousands of plants and required an army of gardeners to tend them. We can still see these kinds of border in some public gardens—for example, Bellevue Botanical Garden, in Bellevue, Washington; Frederick Law Olmsted's

Dark blue sweetpeas and the flat heads of a yarrow provide contrasts of shape and color.

walled garden at Biltmore Estate in Asheville, North Carolina; and the Longwood Gardens in Kennett Square, Pennsylvania. The trend toward naturalistic gardening affects perennial borders created in country gardens today, and newer borders often sport selections of umbellifers and grasses, as well as traditional perennials. At Kingston Maurward, Dorset, in England, the grass *Calamagrostis* × *acutiflora* **'Karl Foerster'** (see page 75) is repeated along the entire length of its impressive double perennial borders, and pampas grass, *Cortaderia* (Zones 6–9) is used as dramatic vertical accents.

Planting randomly, using plants with a variety of flower color, can look wonderful in a country garden, but it is wise to include large amounts of green, in the form of foliage plants, as this will soften the impact of lots of bright colors and meld them together. **Aquilegias, thalictrums, heucheras, hostas, geraniums, epimediums,** and spotted-leaved **pulmonarias** all have attractive

leaves. For the front of a border, *Stachys byzantina* **'Big Ears'** (see page 138) is a handsome silver-leaved, low-growing plant with furry leaves. More spectacularly, *Cynara cardunculus* (Zones 6–9) (see page 57) has 20 in.

MAINTAINING PERENNIAL BORDERS

It used to be the practice for perennial borders to be heavily fed with well-rotted manure, cut back in fall, and dug over annually. With an eye to practicality (most people have to tend their own gardens today or manage with minimal help) and another to ecology, current practice is for borders not to be cut back until spring, for them to be fed sparingly, if at all, and for them to be mulched once a year in spring to improve the condition of the soil and suppress weeds. Fewer nutrients prevent the plants from getting too leggy and needing staking, and there is less disease. Also, the skeletons of plants in winter can be attractive.

At Little Court, Crawley, in Hampshire, England, there is a selection of English cottage-garden perennials, including sweet rocket (*Hesperis matronalis*), geranium (*Geranium psilostemon*), and forget-me-nots. There are also alliums (*Allium nigrum* and *Allium hollandicum*), plants that are great favorites with many of today's country gardeners. The modern shrub rose *Rosa* 'Constance Spry' covers the wall behind.

(50 cm) long, grayish green leaves, while those of **Acanthus spinosus** (Zones 5–8) are spiny, dark green and up to 3 ft. (1 m) long. In large borders, these dramatic "greens" could be planted at intervals to provide strong vertical accents. Adding more foliage plants, and including grasses as well, will make a planting look even more natural.

Large silver-leaved plants (in this case an onopordum) can soften a mixed-color planting as well as providing drama in their own right.

COTTAGE GARDENS

Mixed planting, in which woody plants are interspersed with perennials and bulbs, is very much the look of the traditional cottage garden, where plants are all jumbled together higgledy-piggledy fashion without much thought being given to their form or color.

It was in the latter half of the 19th century that Helen Allingham's and Myles Birket Foster's watercolors of cottage gardens opened the British public's eyes to their charms. Old cottage gardens were probably never quite as pretty as those in the paintings, but they were as crammed with plants of all kinds as we imagine.

For centuries English cottagers relied on homegrown vegetables for their staple diet, and any flowers in their gardens would have been wildflowers collected from hedgerows, including primroses and violets, or hand-me-downs from the local monastery garden or manor house. Every plant was

welcome; but before the days of modern medicine, those that could cure ailments or make life more comfortable were most prized. Many cottage garden flowers became so only because they were useful. For example, **scabious** (*Scabiosa*), **mullein** (*Verbascum*), **columbine** (*Aquilegia*), **mallow** (*Malva*), and **Saint John's-wort** (*Hypericum*) were grown for their medicinal properties. **Meadowsweet** (*Filipendula*), **wormwood** (*Artemisia*

Roses and geraniums were often found in traditional cottage gardens, the geranium's foliage helping to disguise "leggy" rosebushes.

89

Planting wild and cultivated plants together, in large informal plantings or in borders, is becoming increasingly popular. Here, the wild white valerian is mixed with cultivated grasses, white aquilegias, delphiniums, and dark-leaved fennel.

absinthium) and **southernwood** (*Artemisia abrotanum*) were valued for strewing, which kept flies and fleas at bay. **Hyssop** (*Hyssopus*), **lavender** (*Lavandula*), **sage** (*Salvia*), and **rue** (*Ruta*) were grown for their scent as well as medicinal properties, and tansy, woodruff, and sorrel for making toilet water. Primroses and cowslips were used for flavoring drinks, and the flowers of violets were put in salads.

Many plants arrived in British cottage gardens because they had gone out of fashion in grander circles, which may explain how more "exotic" plants such as **lilies, peonies, roses, delphiniums, oriental poppies, dahlias,** and **pelargoniums** first arrived on the scene. Unlike their grander neighbors, cottage-garden owners seldom threw out plants and so, unwittingly, became the conservers of strains of the best-loved, old-fashioned flowers: plants such as **sweet Williams, pinks, double primroses, gold-laced polyanthus, old ranunculus,** and **shrub roses**.

During the 17th century, Huguenot émigrés to Britain started the cultivation of "florist's" flowers—**anemones, auriculas, carnations, hyacinths, pinks, polyanthus, ranunculus,** and **tulips**—and, in time, these too found their way into cottage gardens, adding to the colorful mixture.

WILDFLOWER MEADOWS

Increasing development on the fringes of towns and cities, combined with modern farming methods, means that many beautiful wildflowers have been lost. This may be the reason why meadows and prairies have become such a cherished countryside image, and why so many contemporary country gardeners want to try to create them within their own boundaries. The plants for wild meadows vary in different parts of the world, depending on the nature and pH of the soil, but when making a meadow in a garden, there is no reason not to "cheat" and add plants from different areas, as well as introduced species and cultivars. Purists may balk at including plants that are not native to their part of the world, especially larger-flowered cultivars, but "meadow" is a loose term.

CUTTING WILDFLOWER MEADOWS

While meadow-style plantings look natural, they cannot be left entirely to their own devices. It was the custom for traditional meadows to be cut down from early summer to midsummer, and animals grazed on them afterward. However, this is too early for the seed of plants such as cowslips and fritillaries to set, and many summer-flowering plants are at their peak.

Today, the advice is to cut in mid- to late summer and to leave the hay *in situ* to allow the early-flowering plants to seed. Cutting then also allows summer-flowering perennials to make new leaf and flower again later.

A second cut in early fall is a good idea if there are spring-flowering bulbs in the meadow. A thick thatch left in place through the winter would prevent them from bursting through in spring and should be removed.

PLANTING PARTNERS FOR SHADE

British native lady's smock, *Cardamine pratensis* (1) (Z. 3–9), thrives in dampish shade and could fit into plantings of shade lovers, such as hellebores or epimediums like *Epimedium* × *versicolor* 'Sulphureum' (2) (Z. 3–8). It also goes with *Corydalis flexuosa* 'Père David' (3) (Z. 5–8) and *Dicentra spectabilis* 'Alba' (Z. 4–7) (see page 139).

Poppies in Claude Monet's garden at Giverny, in France. Wildflower meadows are the inspiration for some contemporary garden designers who interweave perennials into their plantings. Making a simple wildflower meadow is more difficult than it appears.

For those country gardeners who haven't the inclination or space for a meadow, an alternative is to plant drifts of small bulbs for spring color. Masses of **snowdrops** (*Galanthus*) mingled with **winter aconites** (*Eranthis*) and **crocuses** will give an early "meadow effect." *Narcissus pseudonarcissus* (Lent lily; see pages 121 and 178) or a smaller daffodil cultivar such as *Narcissus* 'Topolino' (Zones 3–8),

which has creamy yellow petals and lemon trumpets could be added. Later in the spring, the **checker lily** (*Fritillaria meleagris*) (Zones 4–8) naturalized in grass is a delight, and drifts of tulips under trees can look "meadowlike"—especially the smaller species, perhaps the scarlet-flowered *Tulipa sprengeri* (Zones 5–8) or *Tulipa orphanidea* **Whittallii Group** (Zones 5–8), which produces tangerine flowers tinged with

a color similar to that of tarnished brass. Gardeners with space and patience might like to try to create drifts of *Lilium martagon* (Turk's-cap lilies) (Zones 4–7) in the dappled shade of large trees. At Iford Manor, Wiltshire, and at Spetchley Park, Worcestershire, these charming lilies, with their deep pink flowers, come out in their thousands in early summer and never fail to steal the show.

Fritillaria meleagris, the checker lily, is a wildflower of the British Isles but can be naturalized in a garden easily, bringing touches of the countryside into a country garden. In Oxford, Magdalen College gardens and Christchurch Meadows are famous for their checker lilies in late spring.

Fritillaria meleagris

Coastal gardens

A flower-filled garden that looks out over a dramatic seascape is the dream of many would-be coastal gardeners. The great advantage of a situation near the sea, in addition to the view, is that temperatures are higher than inland, and there is little or no risk of frost. Also, in hot sunshine bright colors don't seem out of place, which means the gardener can be more adventurous with color, inventing plantings that might not look right in a town or country setting.

Despite these attractions, anyone gardening on the coast has to battle against the ravages of wind, salt, and, sometimes, very poor soil. The wind strips plants of moisture and "wind prunes" them, so they appear lopsided. Salt draws water out of plants when it lands on their leaves and shoots. Salt damage may even be a problem for gardens a few miles inland, too—in a storm, salt may be carried as far as 15 miles (24 kilometers).

Most plants resent being exposed to strong winds, so the first thing to consider when making a coastal garden is the provision of some protection from wind. Contouring the land, building screens, or planting tough, wind-resistant plants as the garden's "outer defenses" (see box, right) will all help to minimize its effects. However, implementing any of these may obscure a wonderful view, so it may be necessary to protect only part of the

WIND-RESISTANT PLANTS

Trees that withstand strong winds and are suitable for outer defenses in a coastal garden include the evergreen oak *Quercus ilex* (Z. 7–9), *Cupressus macrocarpa* (Monterey cypress) (Z. 8–9), and pines. Wind-resistant shrubs include the mountain pine, *Pinus mugo* (1) (Z. 3–8), an architectural conifer with a spreading, irregular habit, and *Griselinia littoralis* (2) (Z. 8–9), a glossy-leaved shrub with unusual ocher stems and round, medium green leaves.

SPRING BULBS IN SAND

Many bulbs thrive best in gritty, freely draining soil with scarce nutrients, so they grow happily in sand. This is especially useful for those who garden by the sea. Here grape hyacinths and chionodoxa flower profusely in a coastal setting.

In this coastal garden a low wall gives the plants in its lee some shelter against wind and salt without obscuring the view of the sea.

garden and leave the rest exposed so the view can be enjoyed. If hedges are to be included, keep them trimmed below eye level; alternatively, cut "windows" through them to allow glimpses of the panorama beyond the garden. An arbor draped with climbing plants will help to filter the wind around a sitting area—roses, clematis, passion flowers (*Passiflora*), and *Solanum crispum* (Zones 8–10) all thrive in the milder temperatures around the coast.

Once the outer defense plants have become established, the other plants that are not so wind resistant can be planted within their lee—for example,

trees such as **hawthorns** (*Crataegus*), **whitebeams** (*Sorbus aria*) (Zones 5–6) and poplars, in particular *Populus alba* (Zones 3–8) and *Populus tremula* (Zones 2–5). Other plants that grow well in these situations are evergreens with leathery leaves, such as **hollies** (*Ilex*), *Phillyrea latifolia* (see page 61), *Arbutus unedo* (Zones 8–10), cultivars of *Escallonia* (Zones 8–10), *Choisya ternata* (Zones 8–10), and *Euonymus fortunei* (Zones 5–8).

Silver-leaved plants seem especially well suited to coastal gardens, as is demonstrated by the beauty of the Mediterranean coast. All **santolinas** thrive in coastal regions, and *Atriplex halimus* (tree purslane) (Zones 6–9), with its attractive leathery, silvery gray leaves, copes with sea winds; it reaches 6 ft. (2m) and makes a good hedge.

Crambe maritima, sea kale (Zones 5–9), comes from coastal regions, and has bluish green leaves and clusters of tiny, star-shaped, white flowers in early summer. It makes mounds up to 30 in. (75 cm) tall and mixes well with other white- and yellow-flowered plants, such as **evening primroses** (*Oenothera*), **mulleins** (*Verbascum*) and many of the **daylilies** (*Hemerocallis*), particularly *Hemerocallis lilioasphodelus* (Zones 4–10). *Centranthus ruber* (Zones 4–8) has white, pink, or red flowers.

Centranthus ruber

Crambe maritima

PROSPECT COTTAGE, DUNGENESS

The late Derek Jarman's garden at Prospect Cottage, near Dungeness, Kent, in England, is a fine example of how to garden successfully beside the sea. Displaying an artist's skill, Jarman arranged plants such as poppies, santolinas, and *Crambe maritima* (sea kale) (Z. 5–9), which are happy in the almost pure shingle of the site, among an eclectic mix of driftwood, fishing floats, and other weathered objects, to produce a garden that complements the unpretentious cottage and fits seamlessly into its stark surroundings.

GOOD COMPANIONS

In coastal gardens, jazzy colors are never out of place. A simple but effective way of making a colorful planting is to scatter seeds of poppies (*Papaver*) and eschscholzias (1) among clumps of lavender (*Lavandula*), *Mesembryanthemum* (2), and sea hollies (*Eryngium*)—for example, the violet-blue-flowered *Eryngium maritimum* (3) (Z. 5–9).

Woodland gardens

Woods are atmospheric and beautiful, especially in late spring, when shafts of sunlight, filtering through unfurling leaves, gild tree trunks and small plants growing on the woodland floor. Woodland gardening can be the most pleasurable kind of gardening, and the good news is that it is not necessary to possess a wood in order to indulge in it. A single small, spreading tree planted in a garden can, when mature, provide shade for about a hundred woodland plants.

Erythroniums (here *Erythronium californicum*) are some of the most beautiful of spring-flowering woodland plants. They like fertile, rich soil that does not dry out and dappled light or partial shade.

In temperate regions, the flowers of native trees are mostly in muted, recessive colors; so are many shade-loving plants found on the woodland floor. However, woodland in other parts of the world is far more colorful. When creating a woodland garden, the choice is between making one similar in character to your own native woodland (using indigenous or introduced species, or a mixture of both), or a much more colorful garden containing exotic plants with vibrant-colored flowers, such as **Asiatic rhododendrons, azaleas,** and **camellias.**

PLANTS FOR WOODLAND GARDENS

Many herbaceous and bulbous plants that thrive in woodland have a refined charm. The great boon of a woodland garden is that lots of these flowering plants bloom at a time when the rest of the garden has not yet sprung back into life. Even in a small area, it is possible to have a wide selection of simple but beguiling flowers from the middle of winter until late spring. *Cyclamen coum* (see pages 51 and 168–69), *(Continued on page 97.)*

Some woodland plants (here *Helleborus foetidus*) flower long before many other plants.

TREES FOR WOODLAND GARDENS

The perfect trees for a woodland garden are those with deep roots, such as oaks (*Quercus*), or those with canopies that allow shafts of sunlight to reach the ground, for example larches (*Larix*) and the Scots pine, *Pinus sylvestris* (1) (Z. 2–8). However, it isn't necessary to plant large trees when making a woodland garden. There is a range of trees and shrubs better suited to smaller gardens that will provide dappled shade within a relatively short time. Among the best are magnolias, maples (*Acer*), whitebeams (*Sorbus aria*), and crab apples (*Malus*), all of which are eye-catching in more than one season. For example, *Magnolia wilsonii* (2) (Z. 6–8) has red-purple shoots, dark green leaves, which have felted reddish brown undersides, and white cup-shaped flowers with a prominent boss of bright red stamens in early summer. The snake-bark maples *Acer capillipes* (3) (Z. 5–7) and *Acer davidii* (Z. 5–8) color intensely in fall and have attractive green- and white-striped bark, which shows up beautifully in winter. *Sorbus hupehensis* var. *obtusa* (4) (Z. 6–8) has attractive pinnate, bluish green leaves, white flowers in late spring, and creamy white berries flushed with pink in fall. *Malus toringo* ssp. *sargentii* (Z. 4–7) produces masses of white flowers in spring and dark red fruits that stay on the tree for weeks in fall.

COLORFUL AND SUBTLE WOODLAND GARDENS

With the introduction of many Asiatic trees and shrubs in the latter part of the 19th century and early 20th century, many beautiful and highly colorful gardens were created in the United States and Britain—for example, the Arnold Arboretum, in Massachusetts and, in Britain, the Sir Harold Hillier Gardens, Hampshire (above), and Savill Garden, Windsor. More recently, there has been a move toward more naturalistic woodland gardens, such as the one created by Beth Chatto in Essex, England. Here, shade-loving species from around the world produce a garden of mixed but subtle colors in which foliage plays the principal part.

One of the most attractive features of a woodland garden is the way the leaves and branches of the trees create dappled light that changes throughout the day. Here the young leaves of the fern *Matteuccia struthiopteris* are gilded by early morning sunlight and appear a luminous yellow.

Anemone nemorosa

Lilium martagon var. album

Trillium grandiflorum

Hyacinthoides non-scripta

Dicentra 'Stuart Boothman'

Digitalis ferruginea

PLANTS FOR DRY SHADE

In very dry, shady areas, ivies (*Hedera*), *Helleborus foetidus* (see page 94), *Iris foetidissima* (Z. 6–9), silver dollar (*Lunaria annua*) (above) (Z. 7–9), comfreys such as *Symphytum caucasicum* (see page 127), and dead nettles (*Lamium*) (Z. 4–7) can be relied upon to perform consistently.

IMPROVING CONDITIONS FOR WOODLAND PLANTS

When creating a woodland garden under mature trees, it may be necessary to "lighten" the shade. Cutting out some lower branches to raise the trees' canopies and removing branches to thin out their crowns will allow more light to reach the ground, making it easier for plants beneath to flourish. It is also a good idea to try to create some patches where there is little or no shade, as this will permit a wider range of plants to be grown.

The soil under mature trees is often dry and poor in nutrients, especially on the sides facing north and east, and so it is good practice to mulch the ground with organic matter, preferably leaf mold, each spring—this will provide a reservoir of moisture for the plants' developing roots. A balanced slow-release fertilizer applied regularly in spring will make the soil less impoverished.

winter aconites (*Eranthis*), and snowdrops (*Galanthus*) will start the show by flowering in midwinter and late winter, and are followed by **Lenten roses** (*Helleborus orientalis*) (Zones 5–8) and **lungwort** (*pulmonarias*). **Primroses** (*Primula*), **navelworts** (*Omphalodes*), **wood anemones** (*Anemone nemorosa*) (Zones 4–8), **erythroniums**, **tiarellas**, **trilliums**, **epimediums**, small **narcissi**, and **bluebells** (*Hyacinthoides*) will ensure that there is a continuous display from early spring to mid-spring, while **Solomon's seal** (*Polygonatum*), **dicentras**, and **lily of the valley** (*Convallaria*) will carry the flowering period through into late spring. If you intersperse these flowering wood species with foliage plants such as **hostas**, **asarums**, and *Arum italicum* ssp. *italicum* 'Marmoratum' (see page 124), you will enrich the plantings and highlight the flowers' jewel-like colors.

By midsummer, when the trees are covered in new leaves, there may not be sufficient light for many plants to flower. So, just when the rest of the garden is resplendent with color, a woodland garden will be at its most green. However, some plants will go on flowering in deep shade—*Geranium macrorrhizum* (Zones 4–7) and *Geranium phaeum* (Zones 7–8), for example. In the less shady areas, *Alchemilla mollis* (lady's mantle; see page 154), **sweet woodruff** (*Galium odoratum*; see page 124), and cultivars of **periwinkle** (*Vinca*) (Zones 5–8) will bloom. In areas of lighter shade where the soil is moist, **foxgloves** (*Digitalis*) and **bugbanes**, such as *Actaea simplex* (Zones 3–8), with its bottlebrush white flowers, will enliven the scene. **Lilies** add real class to woodland plantings, especially the giant lily *Cardiocrinum giganteum* (Zones 7–9); but patience is needed, as it takes several years to reach maturity.

SHRUBS FOR WOODLAND PLANTINGS

While it is possible to create beautiful woodland plantings of small bulbs and perennials under trees, in larger spaces it is good to create an understory by including shrubs as well. Shrubs bring more contrast of leaf form and texture and, if evergreens are included, year-round interest. Hollies (*Ilex*) are perfect candidates for woodland planting, especially those with all-green leaves. *Ilex aquifolium* 'J.C. van Tol' (Z. 6–9) is a self-fertilizing holly with dark purple stems, dark green, non-prickly, leaves and scarlet berries. (The variegated cultivars produce the best leaf color if planted in sun.) *Lonicera pileata* (Z. 6–7) is a handsome evergreen with small, shiny green leaves; it grows little more than 2 ft. (60 cm) tall but spreads to 8 ft. (2.5 m) and is happy in poor soil. *Daphne laureola* (Z. 7), the spurge laurel, is another small shrub that flourishes in deep shade; it has shiny dark green leaves and small, scented green flowers in winter. Also small but widespreading, the glossy-leaved *Daphne pontica* (1) (Z. 8–9) has fragrant yellow flowers in spring. Sarcococcas are excellent shrubs for woodland, as they have attractive evergreen leaves and fragrant flowers in winter; plant them beside a path so their scents may be enjoyed. *Sarcococca confusa* (Z. 6–8) has tapering dark green, shiny leaves and highly scented white flowers. It grows up to 4 ft. (1.2 m) tall with a spread of 3 ft. (1 m). *Sarcococca hookeriana* var. *digyna* 'Purple Stem' (see page 173) has narrower leaves and young shoots flushed with purple-pink; it grows up to 5 ft. (1.5 m) high, and its sweetly scented flowers are white tinged with pink.

Among the deciduous shrubs, *Forsythia* × *intermedia* (2) (Z. 5–9) and most deutzias are happy in light dappled shade, as is the enchanting *Exochorda* × *macrantha* 'The Bride' (see page 123), which grows into a mound 6 ft. (2 m) by 10 ft. (3 m) and has abundant, white, cup-shaped flowers on its racemes in late spring and early summer. Golden-leaved and variegated shrubs can help to lighten dark areas in a wood. The golden-leaved privet *Ligustrum* 'Vicaryi' (Z. 4–8) is a semi-evergreen that has golden yellow leaves, and panicles of white flowers in summer. *Philadelphus coronarius* 'Aureus' (Z. 4–8), the golden mock orange, has yellow leaves, which become light green as they age and the bonus of sweetly scented flowers. *Sambucus racemosa* 'Plumosa Aurea' (3) (Z. 3–7) is an elder with finely cut golden leaves.

Water gardens

Ancient Egyptian and Persian gardens always contained pools, because gardens were considered to be sanctuaries from the harsh conditions of the desert. Today, gardeners value water not only for its soothing qualities but also because even a small pond or pool can bring huge ecological benefits, providing havens for wildlife, such as frogs, toads, and dragonflies. In addition, water offers opportunities to experiment with some beautiful aquatic and moisture-loving plants.

When creating a naturalistic water garden, it is important to grow aquatic and moisture-loving plants with leaves in varying shapes and textures. Here, the giant leaves of *Gunnera manicata* (on the far side of the pond) provide a dramatic contrast to those of water lilies and irises.

Whatever the situation, it is always important not to obscure the water totally and to have a range of foliage forms, textures, and sizes, as leaves will be present for far longer than flowers.

NATURAL SCHEMES

Naturalistic plantings may, of course, be constructed by selecting only indigenous species, but this may be too restrictive for some gardeners. For those who want to try growing non-native plants, it is possible to create natural-looking plantings by mixing indigenous species with carefully selected introduced ones. Grasses always bring an air of informality, and moisture-loving

When thinking about the colors for watery situations, consider whether the water feature is natural or artificial. If the body of water is a natural asset, perhaps a boggy area, stream, or pond, try to construct plantings that appear part of the immediate surroundings. Green should be the predominant color, while flowers should be mostly on the small side, and their tones should be muted. However, if a water feature is artificial, there is no reason for not embellishing it with plantings that are both dramatic and highly colorful,

especially if it is the centerpiece of its own area within a garden. Here, one could experiment with hot harmonies, mixing plants with flowers in reds, oranges, and yellows—for example, **cannas**, and interspersing them with large, highly textured and colored leaves. Try the giant rhubarb cultivar *Rheum* **'Ace of Hearts'** (Zones 5–7), bronze-leaved ligularias like *Ligularia dentata* **'Desdemona'** (Zones 3–8) or *Ligularia* **'Zepter'** (Zones 3–8), and large-leaved **hostas** such as *Hosta* **'Sum and Substance'** (Zones 4–8).

Ligularia 'Zepter'

The damp ground surrounding a naturalistic pool is the perfect place to grow moisture-loving perennials. In the boggy ground around this pool, candelabra primulas, irises, hostas, rodgersias, and billowing foliage plants provide a lush and tranquil setting for the water, even though the flowers' colors are mixed.

ones, such as **molinia**, can be used successfully in association with plants with pastel-colored flowers. The cultivar of the purple moor grass *Molinia caerulea* ssp. *arundinacea* 'Karl Foerster' (Zones 5–9) has purple flower heads on 4-ft. (1.2-m)-tall stems, and a graceful habit. It blends well with meadowsweet, *Filipendula ulmaria* (Zones 2–8), which has fluffy cream flower heads in summer, and the water plantain *Alisma plantago-aquatica* (Zones 5–8), with its gypsophila-like, pinkish white flowers in mid- to late summer (it flowers best when planted in 6 in. [15 cm] of water). A lovely addition would be the beautiful Eurasian flowering rush *Butomus umbellatus* (Zones 5–11); this has bluish pink flower heads, somewhat like those of an allium, which appear in late summer.

PONDS AND POOLS

In artificial ponds or pools, plants should be grown in containers—either troughs built into the sides of the pond or removable baskets filled with heavy clay soil and covered with gravel to prevent the soil from floating away. In the past, formal pools were usually accompanied by formal plantings, which featured a few species in recurring patterns. A much more relaxed approach is in vogue today, and many formal pools now include random, bold plantings of plants such as bamboos, ferns, hostas, rushes, and grasses.

WATER LILIES

The aristocrats of aquatic plants, water lilies are both beautiful and useful, as their large flat leaves help to provide essential shade for the water, thus preventing algae from developing.

Water lilies come in sizes to suit any expanse of water, from a large tub to a lake. Pygmy cultivars grow in less than 12 in. (30 cm) of water, while the largest need a depth of about 40 in. (1 m).

There are subtle contrasts of form and color between the yellow flowers of *Primula florindae* and *Iris ensata* in this waterside planting.

Common cotton grass, **Eriophorum angustifolium** (Zones 4–7), could be added to naturalistic plantings in peaty soil, as it thrives in or beside shallow water in acid conditions. Its silky white flower heads are carried on stems 12–18 in. (30–45 cm) long.

For a natural-looking planting that features creams and yellows, the statuesque umbellifer **Angelica archangelica** (Zones 4–8) (often grown as a biennial), with its domed flower heads of greenish yellow flowers, is hard to beat. It would make a handsome companion for **Caltha palustris** (marsh marigold) (Zones 3–7), with its egg-yolk yellow flowers, or perhaps a creamy colored cultivar such as **Trollius × cultorum** 'Cheddar' (Zones 5–7) or **Euphorbia palustris** (Zones 5–8), which has deep yellow bracts on 3-ft. (1-m) stems. For elegant foliage one could include the little South American perennial **Gunnera magellanica** (Zones 8–9), which has kidney-shaped, glossy

TENDER MARGINAL AQUATIC PERENNIALS

There are some highly decorative, subtropical aquatic plants that will add much to water's-edge plantings, but because they are too tender to withstand frost, they must be brought indoors for winter in colder zones.

Cyperus papyrus (Z. 10), the Egyptian paper rush, is a graceful plant, which can grow to over 6 ft. (2 m) in the right conditions. Its three-angled stems, which were flattened out by ancient Egyptians to make paper, carry globes of thin threads, on the end of which are tiny brown flowers. It grows best in 4–6 in. (10–15 cm) of water.

Thalia dealbata (Z. 9–10) is an elegant North American perennial found in the southern states and Mexico; it has evergreen lance-shaped or ovate grayish green leaves, 20 in. (50 cm) long, and violet flowers that are carried in slender panicles on stalks, up to 10 ft. (3 m) tall, in summer. It should be grown either in an aquatic basket or in fertile, loamy mud in water up to 6 in. (15 cm) deep.

The buttercup family contains perennials that thrive at the margins of pools. *Trollius chinensis* is one, here growing beside a pink astilbe.

Some umbellifers, like *Angelica archangelica*, thrive in damp soil and can be used to add height and structure to a waterside planting.

dark green leaves, 2–3½ in. (5–9 cm) across, carried on 3–6-in. (7–15-cm) stalks. **Nymphoides peltata** (Zones 6–10) would also make an attractive and useful addition to this kind of planting, as its rounded leaves form a floating carpet on water. By shading the water surface, the leaves help to keep the water clean and free from algae. In addition to attractive leaves, it has funnel-shaped, bright yellow flowers, carried on long stalks in summer.

DRAMATIC FOLIAGE PLANTINGS

The obvious choice for dramatic foliage plantings beside water would be *Gunnera manicata* (Zones 7–10); however, many gardeners may decide this South American giant, with its massive leaves, 6 ft. (2 m) in diameter, on stems up to 8 ft. (2.5 m) tall, is far too large. **Rodgersias** have much smaller leaves than this gunnera, but

The South American perennial *Gunnera manicata* makes an impressive architectural plant beside a pool or stream, but its huge leaves need plenty of room to look their best. Here they provide a sumptuous backdrop for *Primula florindae*.

brownish red. ***Rheum palmatum*** (Zones 5–7) is a colorful foliage plant. It has leaves with reddish stems and veins, and cream or pinkish flowers. ***Rheum palmatum*** 'Atrosanguineum' (see page 65) has leaves with plum red undersides and pink flowers.

Plants with spiky leaves always add drama, and **phormiums** (Zones 8–10), with their sword-shaped leaves, are suited to moist waterside plantings because they thrive in damp soil. There is now a wide choice of cultivars with very attractive foliage. ***Phormium*** 'Sundowner' has leaves that are up to 5 ft. (1.5 m) long, in brownish green with deep rose-red margins. Its spikes of yellowish green flowers are carried on stems up to 6 ft. (2 m) tall. ***Phormium cookianum*** ssp. *hookeri* 'Tricolor' has arching, light green leaves with clearly defined cream and red margins, which grow as long as 5 ft. (1.5 m). Another dramatic foliage plant is ***Lysichiton americanus*** (skunk cabbage) (Zones 6–7), a native of the western states, where it is found beside streams. Despite its musky smell, this perennial is worth growing for its vivid yellow spathes, which appear in early spring, as well as for its thick, shiny leaves, which can grow up to 4 ft. (1.2 m) long.

Rodgersia podophylla

long on stems 4 ft. (1.2 m) tall. ***Rodgersia podophylla*** (Zones 3–8) has leaves 16 in. (40 cm) long, which are purplish and wrinkly when young but become smoother with age. Its greenish cream flowers appear in late summer, carried in long plumes on stems up to 5 ft. (1.5 m) tall; in fall its leaves turn rich

they are still striking plants with large, dramatic leaves. Since they enjoy damp positions, they make good waterside plants. ***Rodgersia pinnata*** 'Superba' (Zones 5–8) has glossy, dark green, deeply veined leaves, up to 30 in. (1 m) long, which are purple or bronze when young. Its flowers, which appear in mid- to late summer, are tiny bright pink stars in tapering clusters up to 28 in. (70 cm)

Rheum palmatum

Lysichiton americanus

Hardscaping

The debate about the most important constituents of a garden has raged among the gardening fraternity for a long time. Some think that plants should always take precedence, while others believe that design incorporating hardscaping is all-important and that plants are incidental. In fact, it takes both to make a good garden; and just as the plants we choose affect the character and mood of our gardens, so, too, does the hardscaping.

The term "hardscaping" refers to a garden's walls, fences, dividers, paths, and paving, as well as structures such as arbors, arches, raised beds, garden buildings, and any decorative elements such as pots, fountains, and statuary. Today, hardscaping elements are made from a bewildering selection of different-colored stones, woods, metals, plastics, and composite materials, and there are numerous outdoor paints and wood stains available in a kaleidoscope of colors. It can be difficult to decide which will look best in your garden.

The secret of good garden design is simplicity and appropriateness, and this applies particularly to hardscaping. Remember to limit the number of materials and to select those with a color, texture, and finish that suit your garden's setting and character. Owners of wooden dwellings should therefore be choosing gravel or paving stones whose color mirrors that of their building material, whereas owners of redbrick houses will be aiming to match the texture, color, and finish of the house bricks. Materials indigenous to an area should be used whenever possible, and if you are restoring an old garden, any new materials should match what is already there. This applies as much to paving and gravel as it does to walls, screens, and arches. A garden near the sea might include decking, local pebbles, shingle, shells,

The hard landscaping in this 2004 Chelsea Flower Show garden shows how inventive one can be. The wall in the background is made from sawn logs, held in a wire frame. Green- and gray-leaved plants, some with flowers picking out the colors in the hard landscaping, soften the whole effect.

sand, and driftwood. These materials, normally found along the coast, would look somewhat out of place in a town garden. In the same way, contemporary concrete pavers would make a stylish surface for a high-tech modern house but would not sit well in a traditional rural garden.

Choosing the hard landscaping to suit a particular situation is important. Weathered wood decking makes the perfect foil for the moisture-loving perennials in this water garden.

Garden designer Christopher Bradley-Hole chose a rich crimson red for the walls in this contemporary garden and, very cleverly, mirrored it in the planting by including the perennial *Cirsium rivulare* 'Atropurpureum'.

WALLS AND FLOORS

Traditionally, a garden's boundaries are made from natural or reconstituted stone, brick, concrete, metal, or wood. However, some garden designers are now making walls of stone or timber encased in steel mesh. Plastic and glass are also being used.

Walls are a garden's most important piece of hardscaping and give a feeling of security and permanence. Both boundary walls and retaining walls should be made from the same materials as the house. This not only makes the house and garden seem like a single entity, but can also set the property in its wider landscape. Walls made from natural materials, such as brick and stone, get more beautiful as they age, because they acquire a patina that adds to their character. For this reason, it is important not to obscure them totally with climbers or shrubs.

Placing painted trellis on walls will produce different effects, depending on the color of the wood and of the wall itself.

WALLS IN URBAN GARDENS

Marylyn Abbott, in her book *Thoughts on Garden Design*, recommends painting walls in urban gardens in bright colors. She suggests deep Pompeian red as a backdrop for a series of pale-colored urns or a row of yuccas, and recommends paint the color of thunder clouds, marketed as 'Thunderclap', for a backdrop to terra-cotta and sandstone items. At her garden at West Green House, in Hampshire, England, she has replicated the intense Islamic blue of the Majorelle Gardens in Marrakesh, Morocco, in her fragrant herb garden.

This old stone wall with its terra-cotta coping provides the perfect backdrop for a pink-flowered hollyhock.

103

The color of garden furniture, as much as walls and other hard surfaces, will influence a garden's mood. Here old artifacts and the soft grayish green color of the chair and table contribute to the peaceful, timeless air of this tranquil, "old-fashioned" garden.

Walls made of concrete or concrete blocks can be greatly improved by painting them or rendering them with colored cement. A perimeter wall painted a pale color will reflect light, giving a dark garden a more cheerful atmosphere. Similarly, laying a light-colored paving in a dark corner instantly makes it seem less somber. Since most plants do not thrive in dark, shady conditions, using hardscaping to lighten spaces often enables the gardener to grow a wider, more interesting and colorful range of plants.

Walls painted white or pale cream will make the garden seem smaller. But this need not necessarily be a disadvantage. In fact, light colors are a perfect foil for dark evergreen foliage, making the leaves seem even greener. Trees or shrubs with finely dissected foliage look beautiful in front of pale walls, especially when the sun throws their shadows onto the walls. *Acer japonicum* (the Japanese maples) (Zones 5–8), *Acer palmatum* cultivars (Zones 6–8), and

Rhus typhina 'Dissecta' (Zones 3–8) have beautifully shaped leaves. These all sit happily in smaller gardens, as they never get too large.

White walls can seem cold and stark in cool northern climates, where in winter the light is often gray. Cream, pale yellow, or sand will cast a warmer feel than white.

Painting a garden's perimeter walls in a vivid color, from the warm side of the spectrum, will instantly bring a feeling of heat. For example, a garden surrounded by burnt orange or terra-cotta walls will seem to be bathed in perennial sunshine, and the feeling will be reinforced if Mediterranean-style terra-cotta pots and paving tiles are used as well. Placing plants with bluish green or glaucous foliage and plants with blue flowers (blue and orange are complementary colors) in such a garden will provide a sharp contrast to the walls, pots, and paving. In areas where there is little risk of frost, planting Mediterranean-style plants will emphasize the garden's mood, especially

The color of a garden's paving should never be so obtrusive that it overshadows any planting. Rocks and shingle (top) are a good foil for sempervivums; brick pavers (middle) complement the pink sedum; and large, pale apricot-colored concrete slabs blend in well in a contemporary water garden (bottom).

as many of them have bluish green or gray foliage. An **olive tree** (*Olea*) could be the centerpiece of a planting of **cistus**, **lavender**, **teucrium**, blue grasses such as *Helictotrichon sempervirens*, (Zones 5–9), and succulents like **echeveria**.

FENCES AND FEATURES

Fences used as garden boundaries are of two kinds—solid, which make complete barriers, and open, which

Painting garden structures such as fences, railings, arches, or obelisks a dark color, perhaps black or dark green, will lessen their impact and may even make them "disappear" into the surrounding greenery. The arches in the rose tunnel shown here are almost invisible when they are covered with the foliage of rambler roses.

Painting garden structures in subtle colors (top) will allow pale-colored flowers growing against them to show up well. A strong color, like the purplish blue of the door shown above, will draw the eye but will harmonize well with green plantings placed in front.

allow you to see the landscape beyond. Open fences are especially useful for rural settings, where a garden sits in a beautiful landscape, whereas solid fences come into their own in urban settings, providing privacy and hiding unsightly surroundings. The painting of fences and trellis, as well as garden buildings and other wooden features such as arbors and arches, can also affect the mood and feel of a garden. Painting them in light colors, say cream or white, has the effect of drawing the eye to them, thereby lessening the effect of what lies around them. This can be useful if the view beyond a fence is dull, or if a structure is helping to mask an eyesore. On the other hand, painting wooden structures in muted, cool colors lessens their impact, and paler-colored flowers growing against them seem even brighter.

Metal railings vary from the very simple to the highly ornate, and again, the choice should be based on what is right for the setting. Ornate wrought-iron railings do not look out of place as boundaries for the front garden of a grand town house but would be totally inappropriate on the balconies of ultra-modern apartments. In a country setting, a metal fence painted a dark color (black or dark green) will tend to disappear into the landscape. This is useful for disguising an unsightly fence or for drawing the eye to a landscape beyond it. It is also useful for disguising the metal netting around a tennis court, particularly against a green backdrop.

DUMBARTON OAKS

The garden at Dumbarton Oaks, in Georgetown, Washington D.C., designed by the famous landscape architect Beatrix Farrand, has exquisite elements of hardscaping, demonstrating Mrs. Farrand's meticulous attention to detail. Its steps, paths, pergola, fences, gates, pots, and handrails—even its water spouts—are beautifully crafted and reinforce the overall formality and Italianate feel of the garden.

105

Containers

Whatever the style and size of garden, it will be made more beautiful and more interesting by including pots and other containers. Container gardening is simply gardening in a different, and very practical way. It allows the gardener to play at being flamboyant, sophisticated, quirky, experimental, or just plain outrageous with plants. The beauty of a container is that if a planting doesn't match up to expectations, it can easily be dismantled and replanted. And it is mobile.

Perhaps the greatest advantage of containers is that they can bring color into the garden in every season. This is especially valuable for those with a very small garden, where there isn't sufficient room in beds and borders to grow plants for year-round interest. Another huge bonus of container gardening is that it allows gardeners to grow plants that are not suited to their particular soil type. For example, anyone with an alkaline soil can enjoy growing acid-loving plants such as **rhododendrons**, **camellias**, and **azaleas**, and exquisite woodlanders such as **trilliums** and **bloodroot** (*Sanguinaria*). In the same way, those gardening on heavy clay soil can raise plants, including **tulips**, that will succeed only in free-draining soil. For those gardening in cold areas, containers provide the chance to indulge in a little subtropical gardening, raising plants such as **citrus fruits**, **oleanders**, **aloes**, **agaves**, **echeverias**, and numerous others. Naturally, these tender creatures have to be brought into a frost-free environment in winter.

Containers can be used for all sorts of purposes: to disguise eyesores, lighten dark and dull corners, provide focal points, and embellish garden features such as doors, gates, seats, arches, or niches. They may also be popped into flower beds and borders that are looking past their best to give them a "lift" (Gertrude Jekyll used to put pots of lilies into her borders when she thought they

In this all-green composition, painted terra-cotta containers planted with boxwood add another dimension to the planting and provide color and structure when the flowers have ceased to bloom.

needed it) or to provide "movable" color. Sometimes simply shifting a container with flowers in full bloom to a position to catch the falling light, or to emphasize an area that is often overlooked, can transform a garden.

At its best, container gardening is an art form; and, like artists, container gardeners have to consider the style, form, texture, proportion, and, of course, color of the elements of their creations and how they relate to each other. Needless to say, the most successful container gardeners are those who can arrange a "happy marriage" between the container and its planting.

CHOOSING CONTAINERS

When choosing pots and containers, remember that, as with other elements of hardscaping, simplicity and appropriateness pay off; a few large pots look more effective than lots of small ones, and containers whose style matches that of the garden will never look out of place. So, large and ornate terra-cotta or stone pots that would look at home on the terrace of a grand country house would not meld well into a minimalist roof garden, and wooden containers might not look right in a classical parterre—unless, like the famous pots at the Palace of Versailles, they were designed and painted to match other features in the garden.

Of course, one does not have to choose conventional containers. A collection of old utensils, tools, pottery, and disused artifacts can make eye-catching planters and are a fun way of personalizing the garden, often in a unique way. A medley of old baskets hung from the branches of a tree near a sitting area can look attractive in a cottage garden and, if filled with fragrant annuals, would add to the

Placing containers near a seating area ensures that the plants will be admired at close hand, and you can vary the effect throughout the seasons. Individual pots, like the one shown below, can be given center stage as their flowers appear and then moved or replanted when they are over.

NATURAL OR SYNTHETIC?

When it comes to deciding between synthetic or natural materials, there is no right or wrong. The late David Hicks, whose garden in Buckinghamshire, England, is the epitome of good taste, removed all the terra-cotta pots from his garden and replaced them with plastic ones, which he had painted green. He was firmly of the opinion that no one ever noticed the difference. Synthetic materials have the advantage of being cheap and easier to lift and move. They also do not get damaged by frost; however, unlike natural materials, they do not acquire a patina as they age.

garden's atmosphere. In the same way, large tree stumps lying in a woodland garden can make interesting containers for shade-loving woodland plants such as **wood anemones** (*Anemone nemorosa*; see page 96), **primroses** (*Primula*) (Zones 6–7), and **violets** (*Viola*) (Zones 5–7). Old metal pots and pans that are no longer used in a kitchen would make quirky but practical containers for herbs in a vegetable garden, while old terra-cotta chimney pots filled with **grasses** always make an eye-catching feature on a roof garden or terrace.

For a stylish and eye-catching effect, match the color of the containers with that of the flowers or foliage of their plants. No one could ignore these bright orange pots and their early-flowering miniature tulips and daisies.

Many people use containers for bedding plants, bringing instant color in the summer months. Nurseries and garden centers are constantly expanding the range, and one can now buy plants with flowers in an array of both brilliant and subtle colors.

Growing hardy perennials in pots has the advantage that the plants can be left to grow to a size where they can be split and planted out in the garden. A planting for a shady area might include **ferns**, **pulmonarias**, and **Solomon's seal** (*Polygonatum*), while one for a sunny spot could include **daylilies** (*Hemerocallis*), **grasses**, and perhaps late-flowering daisies like **heleniums**.

PLANTS FOR CONTAINERS

Virtually any plant may be grown in a container, provided it is fed and watered regularly and grown in its ideal medium. However, most plants that are kept permanently in containers need to be re-potted from time to time. As a rule of thumb, shrubs need repotting every year or two in spring until mature, then they just need to be top-dressed in spring; trees need repotting every three to five years, either into the same container or into a larger one, and top-dressing each spring; however, bulbs need to be repotted only when they have become overcrowded.

Silver-leaved plants, such as eryngiums, do not need frequent watering, so they thrive in pots.

HOSTAS FOR POTS

Hostas (Z. 4–8) are exquisite foliage plants. Sadly, however, they are favorite fare for slugs and snails. Growing hostas in containers is one way of avoiding these pests and is especially effective if the pots are placed on a hard surface, some way away from flower beds and bare earth. An array of containers in all shapes and sizes filled with different varitieties of hosta can look very effective, and since most fare best in partial shade (yellow-leaved ones perform better in sun with some midday shade), a collection of them will give a lift to a dark corner of a garden. Copper strips and/or petroleum jelly placed around the perimeter of the containers provides extra defense.

Naturally, a container's position will determine the kind of plant that can be grown in it. A pot placed in shade, for instance, must be filled with shade-lovers, such as **hostas**. Containers in hot spots should be filled with sun-worshipers that are happy to be baked dry, as soil in containers dries out rapidly in warm weather. **Agaves**, **aloes**, **agapanthus**, **echeverias**, and silver-leaved plants thrive in hot, dry places.

All-foliage plantings are stylish, too; mixing spiky- or glossy-leaved plants with felted or ferny ones will emphasize their differences and attributes. Such a planting could feature the dramatic *Agave americana* (see page 56), with thick, fleshy, spiky, grayish green leaves, the delicate, hairy-leaved *Lotus hirsutus* (Zones 8–10), *Mentha suaveolens* (apple mint) (Zones 7–10), which has wrinkled, grayish green,

A tall pot with a spiky-leaved plant like this *Cordyline* 'Torbay Red' will make a dramatic focal point at the center of a small garden.

Containers do not have to be filled with flowering plants. A pot, or a group of pots, planted with a mixture of differently colored foliage plants can be very satisfying visually. And they do not need much maintenance to keep them looking good.

rounded or oblong ovate leaves, and the gray-leaved *Artemisia* 'Powis Castle' (see page 56).

Grasses look elegant in containers, either in mixed plantings or solo. A collection of grasses can be colorful in a subtle way. Those with bluish foliage include *Helictotrichon sempervirens* (Zones 5–9) and cultivars of *Festuca glauca* (Zones 4–8); yellows include *Milium effusum* 'Aureum' (Zones 6–9), *Hakonechloa macra* 'Alboaurea' (Zones 6–9), and *Carex elata* 'Aurea' (see page 45). *Carex oshimensis* 'Evergold' (see page 172) and *Holcus mollis* 'Albovariegatus' (Zones 5–9) have yellow-variegated and white-variegated foliage, respectively. For showy pinkish flowers choose *Pennisetum orientale* (Zones 7–9).

A large container filled with flowering plants looks good with a big foliage plant as its focal point. This might be a young shrub with dark leaves—perhaps a purple-leaved **cotinus**; a spiky-leaved specimen such as a **cordyline**; a handsome foliage plant like *Melianthus major* (Zones 8–9); or a plant with strikingly large leaves—for example, a **canna**, **datura**, or *Petasites japonicus* var. *giganteus* (Zones 4–10), whose kidney-shaped leaves may grow as long as 2 ft. (60 cm).

When it comes to choosing color combinations, one has to consider the container's position and the effect one wants to create—restful harmonies? vibrant harmonies? or high-octane contrasts? It may be that you are looking for a planting to stand out against a dark background, such as an evergreen hedge; here, use plants with red leaves or flowers, as red is the complementary color of green. Similarly, a mixture of yellow-flowering plants in a container will stand out against the backdrop of a blue fence or garden building.

Choosing containers and plants for a situation can be an art form. These simple unadorned steps have been much enhanced by the series of flat containers filled with grape hyacinths.

Inserting containers planted with flowers that come into their own in late summer or fall, like these agapanthus, offer an easy way to rejuvenate somewhat faded borders.

109

SEASONS

Clever gardeners make their gardens colorful all through the year, using plants whose hues are appropriate to the season. When selecting plants it is wise to follow nature's example, remembering that spring has a preponderance of yellows and blues, while summer offers an abundance of pastels in pinks and violets early in the season and a profusion of reds later on. Fall abounds with fiery oranges, golds, and reds, and winter is rich with grays, browns, silvers, whites, and numerous shades of green.

RIGHT: *Hyacinthoides non-scripta* in a spring woodland garden.

Narcissi come in all shapes and sizes but few have such elegant flowers as *Narcissus cyclamineus*.

Early spring

There is often a day in early spring when, as you stroll around your garden, you become aware that the restrained palette of winter, with its predominance of whites, silvers, grays, beiges, and browns, has been eclipsed by a brighter, jazzier one. Lemon yellow and greens may dominate, but there may also be some blues and the occasional splash of red, orange, pink, and purple.

The freshness and cool clarity of many of early spring's colors are intoxicating. Every day, the garden reveals something new—perhaps a group of crocuses opening their flowers wide in the sun, or a favorite shrub suddenly showered in blossom, or a crown of fresh young leaves peeping above ground; this is a time of incomparable excitement for a gardener. For me, it is the time to revel in whatever nature has to offer, and so, for the most part, I am happy to let the colors that emerge intermingle to produce kaleidoscopes of pure color.

YELLOW FLOWERS

The predominance of yellow in the early part of the year comes for the most part from early-flowering bulbs and shrubs such as **witch hazels** (*Hamamelis*, see pages 177–79), **forsythias**, and some kinds of **berberis**.

Daffodils reign supreme in the spring garden, and many begin flowering now (a few flower in fall and winter). Some are real gems—tiny narcissi, such as the dwarf species *Narcissus cyclamineus* (Zones 5–7), whose flowers have swept-

back petals and long, narrow trumpets, and *Narcissus minor* (Zones 5–8), whose pure yellow flowers grow on stems only 4 in. (10 cm) tall. Also, elegant cultivars such as *Narcissus* **'February Gold'** (Zones 5–7), (see pages 115, 120), with its welcome early, bright yellow flowers on long stems, and *Narcissus* **'Jenny'** (Zones 5–7), whose flowers have creamy white petals and lemon yellow trumpets. There are narcissi to suit every taste, but for me, it is the smaller species and cultivars that steal the show (see pages 120–21).

Some of the earliest **tulips** also have yellow in their flowers. The short-stemmed *Tulipa kaufmanniana* (Zones 4–8) has creamy yellow and pink flowers that open wide in the sunshine, and some of its cultivars also feature yellow—for example, *Tulipa* 'Berlioz', which has yellow petals flushed red. (For other early spring tulips, see page 117.)

We find yellow in the flowers of several early spring flowering shrubs, the most popular being **forsythias** (Zones 5–9), which are easy to grow and not too choosy about soil. However, some other yellow-flowered, early spring flowering shrubs may be more of a challenge but are more rewarding, because they have more subtly beautiful flowers. **Corylopsis**, for instance, are deciduous shrubs related to witch hazels and, like them, produce their flowers before the young leaves emerge. They need fertile, moist, acid soil, and being woodland shrubs, they prefer a semi-shaded site. *Corylopsis pauciflora* (Zones 6–8) has sweetly scented, bell-shaped, primrose yellow flowers arranged in hanging clusters, up to 3 in. (8 cm) long, on a spreading shrub, 5 x 8 ft. (1.5 x 2.5 m) when mature. *Corylopsis glabrescens* (Zones 5–8) grows to 1.5 x 1.5 ft. (5 x 5 m) and its flower clusters are only 1 in. (2.5 cm) long. The flowers of *Corylopsis sinensis* (Zones 6–8) (see page 44) are lemon yellow and 3 in. (8 cm) long. This vigorous species becomes a bushy shrub, 12 x 12 ft. (4 x 4 m) when mature.

Stachyurus (Zones 6–8) is another genus of unusual but delightful early-flowering woodland shrubs. They produce pendent clusters of flowers on bare branches. Like corylopsis, they need acid soil that is fertile, humus-rich and well-drained, but they grow happily in either sun or light shade and look especially effective when trained against a wall. *Stachyurus praecox* (see page 178) is a deciduous species with arching

Magnolia 'Elizabeth'

stems bearing pale greenish lemon flowers in hanging clusters, up to 7 in. (18 cm) long. It grows into a widely spreading shrub. Those gardeners who like variegated foliage may prefer to plant *Stachyurus* 'Magpie', which has medium green leaves with a wide edging of cream; it is less vigorous than *Stachyurus praecox*, a mature specimen grows to only 5 ft. (1.5 m) with a spread of 6 ft. (2 m).

Corylopsis pauciflora

Magnolia 'Elizabeth' (Zones 4–9) is a mid-spring flowering magnolia with pale yellow flowers that open before or just as the leaves emerge. It is conical in habit, reaching 30 x 20 ft. (10 x 6m) and making a fine specimen tree, given the space. (For more magnolias, see pages 118–19.) If space is limited, use a smaller shrub, such as *Forsythia × intermedia* 'Weekend' (Zones 5–9) or *Forsythia suspensa* (Zones 5–8).

Forsythia × intermedia 'Weekend'

Because the ground is only just starting to warm up in early spring, there aren't yet many perennials in flower, especially those with yellow flowers. An exception is *Lysichiton americanus* (skunk cabbage, see page 101) (Zones 6–7), a marginal aquatic perennial that produces bright yellow spathes up to 40 in. (1 m) tall before the leaves appear. The somewhat curious *Valeriana phu* 'Aurea' (Zones 4–8) is another perennial that appears yellow in early spring, but here it is the intricately divided, fernlike leaves that are a pale yellow as they emerge above ground. Their yellow color is short-lived, however, as they become a greener shade with age until, by midsummer, they are lime green.

WHITE FLOWERS

Although yellow explodes into our gardens in early spring, it is not, by any means, the only color that transforms them. White features prominently in the flowers of many early spring-blooming plants. We find it in the smallest bulbs, such as **crocuses**, the handsomest of shrubs, such as *Magnolia stellata* (Zones 4–9) (for other magnolias, see pages 118–19), and choice trees, like *Prunus incisa* (Fuji cherry) (Zones 5–7). However, none of these plants produces more beautiful flowers than the late-flowering **snowdrops** (Zones 4–8), which can still be in bloom now, for example *Galanthus* 'S. Arnott' and *Galanthus* 'Magnet' (see page 177). The **flowering quinces** also include a white-flowered cultivar, *Chaenomeles*

Chaenomeles speciosa 'Nivalis'

speciosa 'Nivalis' (Zones 4–8). This is less attention-grabbing than the red and pink cultivars (see page 117) but is a better color to use against brickwork.

Some **crocuses** have white and cream flowers, too, and mix well with smaller narcissi. *Crocus sieberi* 'Albus' (formerly *Crocus sieberi* 'Bowles' White', see Good Companions, opposite) (Zones 3–9) has flowers with pure white petals and orange stigmas, while the petals of *Crocus biflorus* 'Miss Vain' (Zones 3–9) are white with pale lemon yellow throats. *Crocus chrysanthus* 'Snow Bunting' (Zones 3–8) has ivory flowers with a hint of grayish blue inside the petals, but those of *Crocus vernus* ssp. *albiflorus* 'Jeanne d'Arc' (Zones 3–8)

are white with purple bases. Some **pulmonarias** also feature white, most noticeably those with spotted leaves, and the white-flowered *Pulmonaria* 'Sissinghurst White' (Zones 4–8).

Hellebores hybridize freely, and sometimes white-flowered types are produced. White *Helleborus* × *hybridus* flowers (Zones 5–8) may be pure white or embellished with pink spots at the base of their petals.

Crocus chrysanthus 'Snow Bunting'

Pulmonaria 'Sissinghurst White'

Magnolia stellata

Helleborus × hybridus

FRAGRANT PLANTS FOR EARLY SPRING *Acacia dealbata* • *Chimonanthus praecox* var. *luteus* •

Ajuga reptans 'Atropurpurea'

Pulmonaria 'Blue Ensign'

Scilla mischtschenkoana

Crocus chrysanthus 'Blue Pearl'

BLUE- AND PURPLE-FLOWERED PLANTS

The blues of early spring are especially welcome as a contrast to all the yellows now appearing, and they are found in the flowers of perennials and bulbs. Among the easiest to grow are the **bugleweeds**, perennials that are related to the blue-flowered *Ajuga reptans* (Zones 4–7), beloved by generations of cottage gardeners. There are many cultivars, some having bronze, green, or even variegated leaves, and some with white or pink flowers. *Ajuga reptans* **'Atropurpurea'** is a particularly fine cultivar, with dark bluish purple flowers and bronze-purple leaves.

GOOD COMPANIONS

The cheery, bright yellow flowers of *Eranthis hyemalis* (1) (winter aconite) (Z. 3–8) harmonize well with the white and orange flowers of *Crocus sieberi* 'Albus' (2) (Z. 3–9).

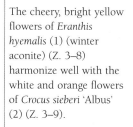

The silvery blue, darker-striped flowers of *Scilla mischtschenkoana* (3) (Z. 5–8) contrast with the flowers of the low-growing *Tulipa tarda* (4) (Z. 4–8), which are bright yellow when open.

Narcissus 'February Gold' (5) (Z. 5–7), with its golden flowers, makes a striking contrast to the blue-flowered *Anemone blanda* (6) (Z. 5–8).

Like ajugas, **pulmonarias** are easy to grow, and hybridists have produced some excellent cultivars with all-blue flowers; among them are the dark blue *Pulmonaria* **'Mawson's Blue'** (Zones 4–8) and *Pulmonaria* **'Blue Ensign'** (Zones 4–8), with violet-blue flowers. (See also page 62 and Good Companions, page 116.)

Among the most intense blues of early spring are the flowers of the bulbous perennial *Scilla siberica* (Zones 5–8), which are a deep, rich azure color. *Scilla mischtschenkoana* (see Good Companions, left) is pale silvery blue, and *Chionodoxa forbesii* (Zones 5–8) produces pale blue flowers with white eyes. *Anemone blanda* (see Good Companions, left) produces rich bright blue flowers whether planted in sun or in the shade of large trees. *Crocus chrysanthus* **'Blue Pearl'** (Zones 3–8) is a pale lavender-blue.

Daphne bholua 'Jacqueline Postill' • *Drimys winteri* • *Lonicera fragrantissima* • *Mahonia* × *media* 'Lionel Fortescue' •

Iris unguicularis

Crocus tommasinianus 'Ruby Giant'

Crocus tommasinianus

Ipheion uniflorum 'Wisley Blue'

Violet or purple may not be colors we instantly associate with early spring, but violet is the color of the wild *Viola riviniana* (wood violet or dog violet) (Zones 5–8) and of some early-flowering irises, such as *Iris unguicularis* (Zones 7–9), which produces mauve flowers with paler lilac standards, and *Iris unguicularis* 'Mary Barnard', with its dark purple falls and gold streaks. Purple also features in the flowers of some cultivars of *Anemone blanda* (Zones 5–8) and in some crocuses, for instance *Crocus tommasinianus* (Zones 3–8) and its darker-flowered cultivars: *Crocus tommasinianus* 'Ruby Giant', in violet-blue, and the reddish purple *Crocus tommasinianus* 'Whitewell Purple'.

Ipheions may not be as familiar as crocuses, but these South American bulbs are just as easy to grow and deserve to be much better known. Their principal flowering time is mid-spring, but milder weather will bring them into flower earlier. The cultivar *Ipheion uniflorum* 'Wisley Blue' (Zones 5–9) has lilac-blue flowers that sometimes appear as early as late winter.

Later in the season, these blue- and purple-flowered plants will be supplemented by many more, when perennials such as brunneras, forget-me-nots, gentians, omphalodes, mertensias, and bulbs, including bluebells all come into their own.

GOOD COMPANIONS

The blue flowers of *Muscari armeniacum* (Z. 3–8) appear in early spring, at the same time as the yellow trumpets of *Narcissus* 'Hawera' (Z. 4–9) (see also page 120).

The blue-violet flowers and dark green leaves of *Pulmonaria* 'Blue Ensign' (1) (Z. 4–8) serve as a perfect foil for the cream and yellow flowers of the early-blooming *Tulipa turkestanica* (2) (Z. 4–8).

116

OTHER EARLY SPRING FLOWERING SHRUBS *Azara microphylla* • *Berberis* 'Goldilocks' • *Daphne laureola* •

Viburnum × burkwoodii 'Anne Russell'

PINKS AND REDS

When it comes to pinks for early spring, we need look no farther than cultivars of *Helleborus orientalis* (Lenten rose) (Zones 5–8) and *Cyclamen coum* (Zones 6–8) (see pages 51, 168). Pink, cream, and white are also the colors of winter-flowering viburnums, such as the evergreen *Viburnum tinus* (Zones 8–9) (see page 82) and the deciduous *Viburnum bodnantense* 'Dawn' (Zones 6–8) (see page 180), which flower into early spring. Later, their flowers will be joined by others—for example, the evergreen *Viburnum × burkwoodii* 'Anne Russell' (Zones 4–8) (see also page 61), whose flowers are fragrant, pink in bud, but white when fully open.

Tulips bring a range of rich, dazzling colors to our gardens. By choosing carefully, it is possible to grow blooms in colors that range from darkest purple to the purest white, and to experiment with violets, reds, oranges, pinks, apricots, and yellows. In mild climates, the earliest tulips begin blooming at the end of winter, so by selecting some from each of the early-, mid-, and late-flowering groups, it is possible to enjoy these gorgeous flowers in the garden for about four months, until the end of spring.

Among the early-flowering kinds is *Tulipa turkestanica* (see Good Companions, opposite), a species that has as many as 12 star-shaped ivory flowers, striped with green, on each of its stems. The flowers have a somewhat unpleasant scent, but that should not put you off this understated tulip. Other early tulips include the free-flowering *Tulipa saxatilis* Bakeri Group 'Lilac Wonder' (above) (Z. 4–8), with lilac-mauve tepals, yellow at the base, and the elegant *Tulipa clusiana* (Z. 4–8). Its flowers are mostly white, but the tepals have dark purplish pink stripes on their outsides, and their bases are crimson or purple. The flowers are bowl shaped when they first appear, but as their tepals open wide they become flat stars. One or two flowers grow on each stem, which are up to 12 in. (30 cm) tall. *Tulipa biflora* (formerly *Tulipa polychroma*) (Z. 4–10) produces star-shaped fragrant flowers, which appear early; they are white, tinged with greenish pink, and when open reveal golden yellow centers. *Tulipa humilis* 'Eastern Star' (Z. 4–8) also has yellow centers, but its tepals are magenta with bronze green flames on their outer surfaces.

FLOWERING QUINCES

Early spring is the time when flowering quinces begin to reveal their captivating cup-shaped flowers, and among them there is an eye-catching array of colors—vermilion, scarlet, bright pink, and white. Among the most reliable performers are *Chaenomeles × superba* 'Nicoline' (Z. 4–8) and *Chaenomeles × superba* 'Knap Hill Scarlet' (Z. 4–8), both producing scarlet flowers (those of 'Nicoline' are sometimes semidouble). *Chaenomeles × superba* 'Crimson and Gold' (1) (Z. 4–8) produces darker red flowers and grows into a compact but spreading shrub (see also page 48), while *Chaenomeles × superba* 'Pink Lady' (Z. 4–8) has dark pink flowers, which appear earlier than most. *Chaenomeles speciosa* 'Moerloosei' (2) (Z. 4–8) is a paler cultivar, whose attractive soft pink and cream flowers could be mistaken for apple blossom.

Jasminium nudiflorum • *Prunus mume* 'Beni-chidori' • *Ribes sanguineum* 'Pulborough Scarlet' •

Magnolias

Magnolias are some of the most breathtaking trees and shrubs a gardener can grow, and they bring an air of distinction to any garden. With their magnificent goblet-shaped, cup-shaped, or star-shaped flowers, in pink, purple, white, cream, yellow, or green, they are perfect candidates for specimen planting, uncluttered by other plants. Many magnolias flower before the leaves appear, in winter or early spring, while others bloom later in spring, or in summer or fall.

There are both evergreen and deciduous magnolias among the 125 species (all those shown on these pages are deciduous), but among the most popular is *Magnolia × soulangeana* (Zones 4–9), which grows into a widely spreading shrub. As a mature specimen, it may have a diameter as wide as 20 ft. (6m), so is best suited to a larger garden. For those with smaller gardens, the good news is that there are lots of delightful magnolias that make ideal specimens for more restricted spaces. *Magnolia stellata* (Zones 4–9) is a beautiful white specimen shrub for a small garden (see page 114).

While they appear to be the epitome of sophistication, magnolias are, in fact, easy to grow, preferring soils that are moist, well drained, and humus-rich, with a neutral pH or a slightly acidic one. However, most species will tolerate a degree of alkalinity, especially *Magnolia × loebneri* (Zones 4–8) and *Magnolia stellata* and their cultivars. Magnolias should be planted in positions where they may grow to their full extent without pruning, which is unnecessary and destroys their elegant shape. The flowers of those types of magnolias that bloom in early spring are susceptible to damage from frost and wind, so it is important to select a spot for them that is as sheltered from the elements as possible.

Magnolia × soulangeana (Z. 4–9), 20 x 20 ft. (6 x 6 m), bears flowers with petals that have deep purplish pink bases and paler pink tips. Its flowers appear just before the leaves.

Magnolia × loebneri 'Leonard Messel' (Z. 4–8) has pale lilac-pink, star-shaped flowers with 12 petals, which appear before the leaves. It grows into a rounded shrub, 25 x 20 ft. (8 x 6 m).

Magnolia 'Susan' (Z. 3–8) has scented, slender, goblet-shaped flowers with narrow petals. The petals twist and are deep purplish pink on the outside and paler pink inside. It is relatively compact, at 12 x 10 ft. (4 x 3 m) when mature.

Magnolia campbellii (Z. 8–10) grows into a large spreading tree, eventually producing beautiful, big cup-and-saucer-shaped flowers in white, crimson, and rose pink. A magnolia for locations away from strong winds and hard frosts.

OTHER GOOD MAGNOLIAS

Magnolia 'Galaxy' (Z. 5–9) A cone-shaped deciduous tree, 40 x 25 ft. (12 x 8 m), with purplish pink, tulip-shaped flowers, 5 in. (12 cm) across, which appear on bare branches.

Magnolia 'Heaven Scent' (Z. 3–8) A large shrub, 30 x 30 ft. (10 x 10m), with fragrant flowers, flushed pink with a deeper stripe outside and white within; blooms well into early summer.

Magnolia wilsonii (Z. 6–8) A spreading shrub, 20 x 20 ft. (6 x 6 m). Exquisite white flowers hang from the branches, revealing a central boss of dazzling crimson stamens.

Magnolia stellata 'Centennial' (Z. 4–9) is a compact magnolia with decorative silky buds opening to reveal pure white, double, star-shaped flowers, up to 5½ in. (14 cm) in diameter, with as many petals in each bloom. They flower profusely before the leaves appear.

Dwarf and miniature narcissi

Narcissus **'February Gold'** (Z. 5–7) is a popular yellow daffodil, with slightly swept-back petals. (See Good Companions, page 115.)

Narcissus **'Thalia'** (Z. 4–9) is a mid-spring flowering daffodil with up to three exquisite pure white flowers per stem.

Narcissus **'Hawera'** (Z. 4–9) has pale lemon yellow, drooping flowers that sway in the wind. (See Good Companions, page 116.)

The garden daffodils, or narcissi, we all love to grow are descended from the 50 wild species found in areas of southern Europe and the Mediterranean region, North Africa, and western Asia. Narcissi grow from bulbs and are characterized by flowers that have six spreading perianth segments (petals) that surround the cup or corona, sometimes known as the "trumpet." The corona may be flat or prominent, widely flared, or long and thin. Wild daffodils have widely differing flower shapes, but few grow more than 12 in. (30 cm) tall. They are found in meadows in situations as diverse as mountain crags and coastal plains, and their colors are white, cream, and yellow.

Cultivars display a much wider selection of colors than wild narcissi, despite the fact that many of them—especially the dwarf and miniature varieties—are only one or two generations removed from their species ancestors. To distinguish between the many thousands of cultivars, horticulturists divide narcissi into 12 divisions, each of which has distinct characteristics. The species are placed in Division 10, and Division 12 includes daffodils not in any other division.

Narcissus pseudonarcissus (Lent lily) (Z. 4–9) has flowers with yellow trumpets and creamy white petals. Although it may take some time to get established, this charming daffodil is suitable for naturalizing in grass and woodland. (See Good Companions, page 178.)

Narcissus 'Canaliculatus' (Z. 5–10) is scented, with swept-back white petals and rounded yellow trumpets. It needs a well-drained site and good summer baking.

Narcissus 'Minnow' (Z. 4–9) has creamy petals and pale yellow cups. It reaches 7 in. (18 cm), with four or five blooms per stem.

Narcissus 'Jetfire' (Z. 4–9) is an early-flowering hybrid that produces neat plants with masses of flowers on 8 in. (20 cm) stems. The petals are bright golden yellow, and the long trumpets are bright orange.

USING NARCISSI IN THE GARDEN

Like their larger relatives, small narcissi may be grown in pots, borders, rock gardens, or naturalized in grass. *Narcissus triandrus* (Z. 5–8) and *Narcissus jonquilla* (Z. 4–8) hybrids thrive in borders and rock gardens and will add color early in the season. The bulbocodiums and tazettas are better grown in containers, raised beds, and frost-free greenhouses, where they can be given ideal growing conditions. The species *Narcissus pseudonarcissus* (Z. 4–9) and *Narcissus cyclamineus* (Z. 5–7) (see page 112) may be naturalized in grass (*Narcissus cyclamineus* flourishes only in damp acid soil), and so, too, the cultivar *Narcissus* 'Jack Snipe' (Z. 4–9). The latter has the advantage of not being too choosy about soil.

Narcissi grow best in moderately fertile, well-drained soil that is moist during the growing season. They should be planted in fall at one and a half times their own depth. Bulbs to be naturalized in grass should be planted slightly deeper.

Groups of pots, each containing a single dwarf or miniature narcissus, look effective, but narcissi in borders or beds associate well with later-flowering snowdrops, forget-me-nots, blue- or white-flowered pulmonarias and crocuses, and foliage plants such as asarums.

OTHER GOOD NARCISSI

Narcissus 'Baby Moon' (Z. 3–10), deep yellow, scented flowers, with up to six flowers on 6 in. (15 cm) stems.

Narcissus 'Fairy Chimes' (Z. 3–9), dark lemon yellow blooms on 8 in. (20 cm) stems.

Narcissus jonquilla (wild jonquil) (Z. 4–8), up to five golden yellow, scented flowers per 12 in. (30 cm) stem.

Narcissus 'Mite' (Z. 5–8), golden yellow flowers with long, straight trumpets and swept-back petals.

Narcissus 'Small Talk' (Z. 4–8), tiny golden flowers carried on 4 in. (10 cm) stems.

Narcissus 'Sundial' (Z. 4–9), one or two golden flowers on 8 in. (20 cm) stems.

Narcissus tazetta (Z. 8–9), up to 20 sweetly scented blooms with flat white petals and small yellow cups on each of its stems; these vary considerably in length.

Narcissus 'Tête-à-tête' (Z. 5–7), very early golden yellow flowers, 6 in. (15 cm) high, with slightly deeper trumpets.

Narcissus triandrus (angel's tears) (Z. 5–8), nodding creamy flowers with rounded cups and swept-back petals.

Prunus 'Shirotae', in full bloom.

Late spring

As the days lengthen and there is some warmth in the sun's rays, the atmosphere in the garden is one of luxuriant and abundant freshness, with color everywhere you look. Blossom has appeared on trees and shrubs, and an increasing number of perennials are producing flowers to add to those of bulbs.

As was the case earlier in the season, the principal colors of mid- to late spring tend to be yellows, whites, and blues, but now there are many more pinks, as the blossoms of trees such as **crab apples** (*Malus*), **magnolias**, and **cherries** (*Prunus*) reach their peak. Since this is the time when the majority of **tulips** flower, too (see pages 130–31), there is also much more apricot, orange, red, and purple, and gardeners can enjoy creating hot harmonies or striking contrasts with them. In gardens where the soil is acid, yet more exciting and

dramatic combinations are possible with **azaleas** and **rhododendrons**, which produce flowers in hot, vibrant yellows, apricots, pinks, and reds, as well as cooler pinks, violet, mauve, cream, and white. (See pages 132–33.)

WHITE-FLOWERED SHRUBS AND TREES

For those who prefer more subtle colors than those typical of rhododendrons, late spring is the time when many white-flowering shrubs and small trees

Viburnum plicatum f. tomentosum 'Mariesii'

produce their flowers; there are kinds to suit every situation. Some **viburnums** produce white flowers in late spring—for example, *Viburnum* × *carlcephalum* (Zones 6–9) and the widely spreading *Viburnum plicatum* f. *tomentosum* 'Mariesii' (Zones 5–8), whose flowers are carried in horizontal tiers. **Amelanchiers** are at their best now, producing masses of white

Cornus 'Norman Hadden'

Osmanthus delavayi

Fothergilla major

Exochorda × macrantha 'The Bride'

flowers, sometimes flushed with pink, and some crab apples also produce white blooms: *Malus toringo* (formerly *Malus sieboldii*) (Zones 4–7) and *Malus toringo* ssp. *sargentii* are choice shrubs or small trees that flower copiously in mid- and late spring. *Malus transitoria* (Zones 4–7) is an elegant larger tree, with pink buds that become white as the flowers open.

Many **dogwoods** are resplendent in white too, but prefer neutral or acid soil. *Cornus* 'Norman Hadden' (Zones 5–8) and *Cornus florida* (Zones 5–9) are excellent choices for smaller gardens. For those who love scent, now is the time to enjoy the fragrant flowers of shrubs such as *Osmanthus delavayi* (Zones 7–10), *Amomyrtus luma* (formerly *Myrtus lechleriana*), (Zones 9–10), and *Choisya ternata* (Mexican

---

WHITE-FLOWERING CHERRIES

Prunus glandulosa 'Alba Plena' (Z. 4–8)
Prunus 'Shirotae' (Z. 6–9)
Prunus avium 'Plena' (Z. 4–8)

---

orange blossom) (Zones 8–10). The tiny white flowers of North American native *Fothergilla major* (Zones 4–8) may not be heavily scented, but they are among the prettiest of the season.

Spiraea 'Arguta' (Zones 5–8) is an invaluable shrub that is easy to grow and flowers reliably. Its tiny, saucer-shaped white flowers, carried in clusters on short branches, are an asset to any garden in late spring.

Pieris are evergreen shrubs with handsome leaves, attractive colorful young shoots (pink, red, or bronze), and clusters of small, urnlike flowers. *Pieris*

japonica (Zones 5–8) and its cultivars, such as *Pieris japonica* 'Scarlett O'Hara', have white flowers carried in densely packed clusters.

Attractive as all these are, to my mind one of the most beautiful of all the white-flowered shrubs for late spring is *Exochorda × macrantha* 'The Bride' (Zones 5–7), with its profusion of flowers, like white apple blossoms. It grows into a spreading bush, up to 6 x 10 ft. (2 x 3 m) when mature. It needs fertile soil, so gardeners with poor, alkaline soil could grow it in a large pot.

123

WHITE WOODLAND PERENNIALS

Late spring is when more and more woodland perennials are bursting into bloom, and many have white flowers. Epimediums (Zones 5–8) are beautiful perennials that spread happily in shade and are useful for covering ground under trees and shrubs. They produce small, intricately shaped flowers in many colors including white. *Epimedium × youngianum* 'Niveum', *Epimedium pubigerum*, and *Epimedium grandiflorum* 'White Queen' all have white flowers and pretty young leaves. Sometimes old foliage completely hides the new flowers; to prevent this, cut back last year's leaves in early spring (taking care not to snip any new shoots). Some epimediums, such as *Epimedium grandiflorum* and its cultivars, have foliage that is bronze when young.

Arum italicum ssp. italicum 'Marmoratum' (Zones 5–8) produces beautifully marbled leaves, white on dark green, which emerge in late winter, so it makes the ideal foliage plant to accompany those woodlanders whose flowers appear in mid- and late spring, such as **erythroniums** (dogtooth

Trillium grandiflorum

violets) and **trilliums** (wood lilies). Some of the American species erythroniums have white or creamy white flowers, with pretty, backward-sweeping petals, on slender, upright stems. *Erythronium californicum* (Zones 4–8) shows up well in a shady corner; *Erythronium californicum* 'White Beauty' is a choice, large-flowered cultivar, which increases in suitable humus-rich soil, and *Erythronium oregonum* (Zones 5–6) is a similar, exotic-looking woodlander. All of these dogtooth violets are assets in any woodland or rock garden.

Smilacina racemosa

The trillium clan contains some beautiful white-flowered species, such as *Trillium grandiflorum* (Zones 5–7), *Trillium grandiflorum* 'Flore Pleno', which is even more captivating than the species, and the pretty, smaller-flowered *Trillium ovatum* (Zones 5–8). The flowers are three-petaled, and turn pink with age, but *Trillium chloropetalum* (Zones 6–9) has flowers that range from white to pink to purple. *Trillium cernuum* (Zones 6–9) has white flowers with maroon centers, sometimes hidden beneath luxuriant medium green leaves.

Some trillium species are also native to North America, the home of another

Arum italicum ssp. italicum 'Marmoratum'

GOOD COMPANIONS

An attractive all-white planting for woodland in late spring would include the dainty, bell-shaped flowers of the summer snowflake *Leucojum aestivum* (1) (Z. 4–8) among the saucer-shaped yellow and white blooms of the buttercup *Ranunculus aconitifolius* (2) (Z. 5–8). The star-shaped white flowers of *Asphodelus albus* (3) (Z. 5–10) and the scented sweet woodruff *Galium odoratum* (4) (Z. 5–8) add interest to the planting.

MORE WOODLAND PERENNIALS *Anemone nemorosa* • *Asarum splendens* • *Convallaria majalis* •

Polygonatum × hybridum

charming woodland plant, *Smilacina racemosa* (Zones 3–8), which carries elegant white "candles" of flowers in mid- to late spring. Somewhat similar are the **Solomon's seals** (*Polygonatum*), which produce their pendent, bell-like flowers on arching stems as spring progresses. *Polygonatum × hybridum* (common Solomon's seal) (Zones 4–8) has creamy white, green-tipped flowers that grow on stems up to 5 ft. (1.5 m) tall (see Good Companions, below), while its cultivar *Polygonatum × hybridum* 'Striatum' also has white flowers tipped with green, and its leaves are striped with creamy white.

One of the loveliest white-flowered bulbs is the curiously named summer snowflake, *Leucojum aestivum* (Zones 4–8), which produces its snowdroplike blooms on stems up to 2 ft. (60 cm) tall in mid- to late spring. It flowers best in full sun, and all-white plantings would benefit greatly from its presence. (See Good Companions, opposite.)

YELLOW IN THE GARDEN

Spring would not be spring without catkins, and late spring is when the **birches** and the **willows** produce them in large numbers. Most birches produce yellow or yellow and brown male catkins, but willows produce gray, silver, and green, as well as yellow ones; the males are always more striking than the females. Particularly stunning yellow male catkins are produced by *Salix lanata* (woolly willow) (Zones 2–9). They are golden and 2 in. (5 cm) long, while those of *Salix repens* (creeping willow) (Zones 2–9) are ¾ in. (2 cm) long in a silvery gray with yellow anthers.

Yellow is the color of many flowering shrubs, such as **kerrias** and **mahonias**, for example, the evergreen *Mahonia*

Mahonia aquifolium

Cytisus × praecox 'Warminster'

aquifolium (Oregon grape) (Zones 6–8), and some **brooms** (*Cytisus*). Brooms are magnificent when covered in their pealike flowers but need full sun and well-drained, moderately fertile soil to thrive. *Cytisus × praecox* (Zones 5–7) has pale yellow flowers, while those of its cultivar *Cytisus × praecox* 'Allgold' are dark rich yellow. Other yellow-flowered brooms include *Cytisus scoparius* 'Cornish Cream' (Zones 6–8), *Cytisus decumbens* (Zones 5–8), *Cytisus × beanii* (Zones 5–7), and *Cytisus × praecox* 'Warminster' (Zones 5–7).

GOOD COMPANIONS

A good planting for semishade would include Solomon's seals, such as *Polygonatum × hybridum* (1) (Z. 4–8), which look marvelous growing with the white tulips *Tulipa* 'Schoonoord' or *Tulipa* 'Purissima' (2) (Z. 4–8) (see also page 131). Both would be enhanced by the low-growing variegated *Euonymus fortunei* 'Silver Queen' (3) (Z. 5–8) mixed with blue-green hostas such as *Hosta* 'Frances Williams' (4) (Z. 4–8).

125

Hyacinthoides non-scripta • *Oxalis oregana* • *Tiarella wherryi* • *Trillium erectum* f. *luteum* • *Viola odorata* •

Uvularia grandiflora

Doronicum × excelsum 'Harpur Crewe'

There are many other late spring flowering perennials that could be included either in all-yellow plantings or in contrasting schemes of yellow and blue. *Uvularia grandiflora* (Zones 5–9), with its bell-shaped yellow flowers tinged with green, enjoys deep or partial shade, while *Asphodeline lutea* (yellow asphodel) (Zones 6–9), a native of the eastern Mediterranean, needs a sunny position to thrive. It has upright, narrow flower spikes, like tapering candles, which could be used as vertical accents for a planting of yellow-flowered perennials with rounded, daisylike flower heads such as doronicums. *Doronicum × excelsum* 'Harpur Crewe' (Zones 4–8) has golden yellow flowers on 2 ft. (60 cm) stems and attractive heart-shaped leaves. The **anemones** that produce yellow flowers in late spring are less imposing but make ideal carpeting plants in sun and partial shade. The small, refined *Anemone × lipsiensis* (Zones 4–8) has pale yellow flowers on stems 6 in. (15 cm) long and *Anemone ranunculoides* (Zones 4–8) produces deep yellow, buttercuplike blooms on 8 in. (20 cm) stems.

So much yellow in the garden could be overwhelming if it were not tempered by the emerging foliage of perennials and shrubs. **Hostas** and **geraniums** provide fresh green leaves in late spring, and some **spurges**

(euphorbias) produce their complex and curious-looking yellow, green, or lime green flower heads now. *Euphorbia amygdaloides* var. *robbiae* (Zones 7–9) and *Euphorbia cyparissias* (Zones 4–8) are lime green, *Euphorbia polychroma* (Zones 5–8) (see also page 66) and *Euphorbia myrsinites* (Zones 5–9) are bright yellow; and *Euphorbia seguieriana* (Zones 6–10) produces flower heads that are yellowish green.

For those with water gardens, late spring is when marginal plants really begin to make a show, and nothing could be more appealing than **marsh marigolds**, with their cup-shaped flowers. *Caltha palustris* (Zones 3–7) has golden blooms, and those of *Caltha palustris* var. *palustris* (giant marsh marigold) are twice the size of the species. *Caltha palustris* 'Flore Pleno',

with its double flowers, is especially beguiling. Just as beautiful are the **globeflowers** (*Trollius*), which produce buttercuplike flowers and thrive in damp sites. *Trollius × cultorum* 'Alabaster' (Zones 5–7) has primrose yellow flowers on 24 in. (60 cm) stems,

Trollius chinensis

Euphorbia polychroma

CLIMBERS FOR LATE SPRING *Actinidia kolomikta • Akebia quinata • Ceanothus impressus •*

while *Trollius* × *cultorum* 'Earliest of All' (Zones 5–7) bears intense yellow flowers on 18 in. (50 cm) stems and *Trollius chinensis* (Zones 5–8) has light orange-yellow blooms.

BLUE-FLOWERED PLANTS

As we have seen in the "blue" section of the book (see pages 40–41), blue-flowered plants are always treasured by gardeners, as true blues are few. Late spring is when some of the best reveal their wares—plants such as the gentians *Gentiana verna* (Zones 4–7), with bright blue, funnel-shaped flowers, and *Gentiana acaulis* (Zones 3–7), whose flowers are an intense blue. Less glamorous are **forget-me-nots** (*Myosotis*), which, once established in a garden, set seed indiscriminately. *Mertensia virginica* (Zones 3–7) will be familiar to many readers, as it grows wild in many woods. It produces violet-blue (sometimes white) flowers above

Brunnera macrophylla

Omphalodes cappadocica 'Starry Eyes'

Symphytum caucasicum

medium green leaves in late spring. Somewhat similar are the **brunneras** (Zones 4–8), perennials that produce flowers like forget-me-nots in airy clusters above heart-shaped leaves. *Brunnera macrophylla* 'Dawson's White' has bright blue flowers and white-edged leaves, while *Brunnera macrophylla* 'Jack Frost' bears attractive, green-veined silver leaves and pale blue flowers.

Navelworts (omphalodes) are related to mertensias and brunneras, and most produce flowers in mid- to late spring. *Omphalodes verna* (blue-eyed Mary) (Zones 6–9) produces vivid blue flowers with white eyes on 8 in. (20 cm) stems, while *Omphalodes cappadocica* (Zones 6–8) and its cultivars have azure flowers on 10 in. (25 cm) stems. The flowers of *Omphalodes cappadocica* 'Starry Eyes' are larger than those of the species, with a white margin to each petal, and *Omphalodes cappadocica* 'Parisian Skies' has very deep blue flowers. Also useful as ground cover for a shady border or a woodland garden is the bright blue comfrey *Symphytum caucasicum* (Zones 3–7).

GOOD COMPANIONS

Spurges such as *Euphorbia schillingii* (1) (Z. 7–9) look wonderful in all-green plantings; mixing them with *Hosta sieboldiana* var. *elegans* (2) (Z. 4–8) and ferns works well, and they also mix well with narcissi, such as the white and yellow *Narcissus* 'Surfside' (3) (Z. 4–9).

The silver foliage and pink flowers of *Lamium maculatum* (4) (Z. 4–7) combine beautifully with the pinkish leaves of the elephant's ears *Bergenia* 'Rosi Klose' (5) (see also page 129) and the crushed raspberry blooms of *Pulmonaria saccharata* 'Leopard' (6) (Z. 2–8).

127

Hydrangea anomala ssp. *petiolaris* • *Lonicera japonica* 'Halliana' • *Rosa banksiae* 'Lutea' • *Wisteria sinensis* 'Alba' •

Early-flowering clematis

One of the joys of mid- to late spring is watching the emergence of bell-shaped, nodding flowers on clematis of the alpina and macropetala types. They flower for about six weeks. Among them are cultivars with blue flowers, such as *Clematis* 'Frances Rivis' (Zones 3–9), whose medium blue flowers have twisted tepals, *Clematis* 'Columbine' (Zones 3–8), with powder blue flowers, and *Clematis* 'Frankie', (Zones 3–8) whose light Oxford blue flowers have white stamens like petals. *Clematis macropetala* (Zones 5–9) is similar to *Clematis alpina* (Zones 4–8), but its flowers appear to have double rather than single flowers.

Clematis montana (Zones 6–9) also blooms in late spring and into early summer, bearing masses of small white flowers. Its many cultivars include some with pink flowers, for example *Clematis montana* var. *rubens* 'Tetrarose' (see page 79). They are all very vigorous, so should be planted where they can scramble freely.

Clematis macropetala

(Z. 5–9) has blue or violet-blue, bell-shaped flowers from spring to early summer. Silver seed heads follow.

Clematis macropetala 'Blue Bird' (Z. 5–9) has drooping, mauve-blue flowers with cream colored stamens.

OTHER GOOD ALPINA AND MACROPETALA CULTIVARS

Clematis alpina 'Pamela Jackman' (Z. 4–8)
Clematis 'Jacqueline du Pré' (Z. 3–9)
Clematis 'Jan Lindmark' (Z. 3–8)
Clematis 'Markham's Pink' (Z. 3–8)
Clematis 'White Swan' (Z. 3–8)
Clematis 'Willy' (Z. 2–8)

ALPINA AND MACROPETALA CULTIVARS: CULTIVATION AND PRUNING

Clematis alpina (Z. 4–8) and *Clematis macropetala* (Z. 5–9) and their cultivars are easy to grow but prefer free-draining, fertile soil that is moisture retentive and does not dry out in summer. They should be mulched with well-rotted manure in spring and appreciate a liquid feed throughout the summer. A position in full sun produces the best flowers. Less vigorous than *Clematis montana*, they are good for small gardens.

Alpina and macropetala cultivars grown in pots should be fed regularly and hard-pruned annually after flowering. Those grown in the ground benefit from being pruned after their first flowering, as this will encourage new shoots to grow from the base and make training easier. After this initial flowering, they do not need regular pruning, but it is a good idea to cut them to the ground every few years after flowering, as otherwise they become a jumbled mass of stems with the newer ones covering the older ones.

Daphne tangutica Retusa Group

PINK-FLOWERED PLANTS

Those wanting to grow pink flowers for late spring have an assortment of **flowering cherries** (*Prunus*), **crab apples** (*Malus*), shrubs, perennials, and bulbs at their disposal. There are some aristocrats among these—for instance, **daphnes**, some of which produce lovely scented pink flowers at this time, namely *Daphne tangutica* (Zones 6–8), *Daphne tangutica* Retusa Group (Zones 6–8), *Daphne × burkwoodii* 'Somerset' (Zones 4–7), *Daphne* 'Valerie Hillier' (Zones 6–8), *Daphne arbuscula* (Zones 5–8), and *Daphne petraea* 'Grandiflora' (Zones 6–8). **Staphyleas** are intriguing shrubs, whose pink and white flowers make a welcome contribution to a late-spring garden. *Staphylea holocarpa* 'Rosea' (Zones 5–9) has bell-shaped, pale pink flowers and bronze young leaves, and *Staphylea pinnata* (Zones 6–8) has white flowers tinged with pink. Staphyleas are known as bladdernuts because they produce curious bladder-like, two- or three-lobed fruit.

Bergenias belong to the saxifrage family. With their handsome evergreen "elephant's ears" leaves and clusters of funnel-shaped or bell-shaped flowers, they are striking plants, which should not be overlooked when perennials with pink, red, or magenta flowers are required for a late-spring planting. *Bergenia* 'Rosi Klose' (Zones 5–9) has large, pink flowers in mid- to late spring

Bergenia 'Rosi Klose'

Lamium maculatum 'Beacon Silver'

and is one of the bergenias that look good in winter, as its foliage becomes glossy bronze-red. (See Good Companions, page 127.) *Bergenia cordifolia* (Zones 4–8) has dark pink or pale rose red flowers in late spring, and purple-flushed leaves in winter. *Bergenia* 'Morgenröte' (Zones 4–8) has reddish pink flowers that are carried on rigid red stems. Bergenias associate well with taller white, cream, or pink tulips (see pages 130–31).

The **dead nettles** (lamiums) may not be everyone's first choice when it comes to selecting perennials, but not all are invasive and some have prettily colored and mottled leaves. *Lamium maculatum* 'Beacon Silver' (Zones 4–7) is one of the more refined species; it is noninvasive and has attractive silver leaves with a narrow green margin, and pale pink, two-lipped flowers from late spring to summer. (See also Good Companions, page 127.)

FRITILLARIES

The fritillaries are bulbous plants that produce bell-shaped, tubular, or cup-shaped, pendulous flowers in spring and early summer. Some are suitable for raised beds or borders, while others look best in a woodland garden. They vary in size and color, and often the blooms are checkered. Flowers range from *Fritillaria meleagris* (see page 91), with its pinkish purple and white flowers on 12 in. (30 cm) stems, to the dainty maroon-purple, yellow-tipped *Fritillaria michailovsky* (1) at 8 in. (20 cm) high, the creamy *Fritillaria pallidiflora* (2) (Z. 5–8), at 16 in. (40 cm) high, and the imposing *Fritillaria imperialis* (crown imperial, see page 66), with yellow, orange, or red blooms, and a cluster of dark green bracts on stems up to 3 ft. (90 cm) tall.

OTHER GOOD FRITILLARIES

Fritillaria acmopetala (Z. 6–8)
Fritillaria persica (Z. 6–8)
Fritillaria persica 'Adiyaman' (Z. 6–8)
Fritillaria pontica (Z. 7–8)
Fritillaria raddeana (Z. 6–9)

Tulips

Tulipa 'Blue Diamond'   *Tulipa* 'Attila'

Left: *Tulipa* 'Orange Emperor'
Below: *Tulipa* 'Pink Impression'

Tulips are among the most captivating of spring flowers, and their blooms, which are composed of six petal-like tepals, come in various shapes and sizes. They may be cup-shaped, star-shaped, or goblet-shaped. Some are single and have tepals that open widely, while others are double with tightly packed tepals resembling old cottage-garden peonies. Some have fringed tepals, and others have complex shapes with twisted or elongated tepals. However, their principal appeal lies in the clarity and opulence of their colors. There are tulips in sumptuous reds, mouth-watering oranges, scintillating pinks, subtle mauves, cool whites, and some that are striped or whose colors are swirled together like different flavors of ice cream.

To distinguish between them, tulips are divided into 15 groups, which reflect their flowers' characteristics and, to a lesser extent, their flowering times. For example, the Rembrandt Group consists of single, cup-shaped flowers in white, yellow, or red, with other colors such as black, brown, bronze, purple, red, or pink superimposed as stripes or feathers. These were the kind of tulips that commanded enormous sums during the height of tulipomania in Holland in the 1630s. (Now we know that these so-called "broken" tulips owe their color variations to a virus.) Striped tulips are found in the Viridiflora Group and the Parrot

Group, and petals with fringed edges are placed in the Fringed Group. Many tulips are marked with strong, contrasting colors. The leaves of most tulips are medium green or gray-green, and they are variable in width; some have wavy edges.

When choosing tulips, the important factors to consider, apart from their shape and color, is their flowering time and whether they are suitable for tubs, beds, borders, or—in the case of the smaller species—a rock garden. Some are suitable for naturalizing in fine grass. Tulips dislike excessive wet, and almost all like to grow in fertile, well-drained soil in full sun in positions sheltered from strong winds. The species *Tulipa sprengeri* and *Tulipa tarda* (see Good Companions, page 115) prefer humus-rich, peaty soil. (For another selection of early-flowering tulips, see page 117.)

Tulipa 'Angélique'   Tulipa 'Purissima'   Tulipa 'West Point'   Tulipa 'Blueberry Ripple'   Tulipa 'Queen of Night'

APRICOT FLOWERS

Tulipa 'Apricot Beauty' (Z. 4–8) has cup-shaped flowers in salmon pink in early or mid-spring. The tepals' margins become orange as they age. Useful for bedding or mixed borders.

Tulipa 'Cape Cod' (Z. 4–8) has single, bowl-shaped, apricot-yellow flowers, with red central stripes, in early or mid-spring. Its leaves are bluish gray splashed with dark maroon. Good for the front of a border or a rock garden.

PINK FLOWERS

Tulipa 'Angélique' (Z. 4–8) bears peonylike flowers in pale pink in late spring. The tepals are suffused with paler and deeper pinks. The blooms may be damaged by rain, so provide shelter from wet. Suitable for bedding or a border.

Tulipa 'Attila' (Z. 4–8) has cup-shaped, purplish violet flowers

that appear in mid- to late spring. Suitable for bedding and as cut flowers (See also Good Companions, page 173.)

Tulipa 'China Pink' (Z. 4–8) bears goblet-shaped pink blooms in late spring. The flowers' tepals have swept-back, pointed tips, which makes them look very elegant. Makes a good bedding plant in a formal setting.

WHITE FLOWERS

Tulipa 'Purissima' (Z. 4–8) produces single, bowl-shaped, pure white flowers in mid-spring. Suitable for a border. (See also Good Companions, page 125.)

Tulipa 'Schoonoord' (Z. 4–8) produces fully double, bowl-shaped, pure white flowers in mid-spring. Good for bedding and containers.

VIOLET OR BLUE FLOWERS

Tulipa 'Blueberry Ripple' (Z. 4–8) has single, cup-shaped

flowers in late winter or early spring. The petals are violet or lavender with contrasting white or near-white markings. Suitable for cut flowers and for bedding.

Tulipa 'Blue Diamond' (Z. 3–8) has bowl-shaped flowers, full of dark bluish purple tepals, which appear in mid- to late spring. Suitable for use as bedding or for a border.

Tulipa 'Blue Parrot' (Z. 4–8) produces single, cup-shaped, bright violet-blue flowers with the characteristic "cut" tepals of parrot tulips, in late spring. The insides of the tepals are shaded with bronze. It is excellent for cutting and may also be grown in a border.

RED FLOWERS

Tulipa 'Apeldoorn' (Z. 3–8) has single, ovoid, cherry red flowers in mid-spring. The inside of the flower is orange-red with black and yellow marks and

prominent black anthers. Useful for bedding and cut flowers.

Tulipa praestans 'Fusilier' (Z. 4–8) has single, bowl-shaped, bright red flowers in early and mid-spring. Several blooms are produced on a single stem. Good for growing in a rock garden. Keep bulbs dry in summer.

YELLOW FLOWERS

Tulipa sylvestris (Z. 4–8) produces single, star-shaped yellow flowers in mid- and late spring. The flowers' outer surfaces are tinged with green, and the blooms are sweetly scented. Suitable for a rock garden.

Tulipa 'West Point' (Z. 4–8) produces clear yellow, goblet-shaped flowers in late spring. Makes a good bedding plant for formal settings.

GREEN FLOWERS

Tulipa 'Groenland' (Z. 4–8) produces single,

bowl-shaped green blooms with rosy pink margins in late spring. Good for using for cut flowers and for planting in mixed borders.

Tulipa 'Spring Green' (Z. 4–8) produces single, bowl-shaped flowers, marked with green on the outside, in late spring. Suitable for planting in mixed borders and also excellent for cutting.

PURPLE-BLACK FLOWERS

Tulipa 'Arabian Mystery' (Z. 4–8) has single, cup-shaped, deep purple flowers with white-margined tepals, in mid-spring. Ideal for bedding and also good for cutting.

Tulipa 'Queen of Night' (Z. 4–8) has single, cup-shaped, velvety dark purple or maroon flowers in late spring. The "blackest" tulip to date, it is good for cut flowers as well as bedding. (See also page 38.)

Rhododendrons and azaleas

The genus *Rhododendron* is one of the largest in the plant kingdom, with between 500 and 900 species. Within the genus there are plants as diverse as trees, growing up to 80 ft. (25 m) tall, and small prostrate shrubs, only a few inches high. Azalea is the common name given to all the deciduous species and hybrids and many of the small-leaved evergreens.

All rhododendrons produce spectacular blooms, and they flower between late autumn and late summer depending on the species or cultivar, and some are sweetly scented. The flowers occur singly or in racemes, known as trusses, and vary widely in size and shape. They may be tubular or trumpet-, funnel-, saucer-, or bell-shaped, or something in between. Some have hose-in-hose flowers, with one flower tube inside the other. Most rhododendrons produce lance-shaped, medium or dark green leaves, but they vary greatly in size from ⅛ in. (4 mm) to 30 in. (75 cm).

Rhododendrons must be grown in acid soil that is fertile and humus-rich with excellent drainage. Most prefer cool woodland conditions, but some dwarf ones thrive in more open positions. Many adapt well to being grown in pots and, once established, need feeding only occasionally and mulching annually.

Rhododendron 'Peste's Fire Light' (left) (Z. 7–9) is a compact hybrid evergreen rhododendron that reaches 5 ft. (1.5 m). The loose trusses of hose-in-hose flowers, the color of ripe peaches and flecked with coral and mahogany, appear in mid-spring.

WHITE FLOWERS

Rhododendron 'Cunningham's White' (Z. 6–8) is an old hybrid evergreen rhododendron with white flowers marked with yellow and brown. Although not the showiest of rhododendrons, it is hardy and tolerant of slightly alkaline soil.

Rhododendron 'Polar Bear' (Z. 6–9) is a hybrid evergreen rhododendron that makes a large shrub at least 12 ft. (4 m) tall. In late spring it bears large trusses of lilylike fragrant, white flowers delicately marked with green. Flowers are produced only on mature plants, but it's worth the wait.

Rhododendron 'Silver Slipper' (Z. 5–8) is a deciduous azalea that reaches 6 ft. (2 m) high and wide. The young leaves are coppery, the flowers white flushed pink with an orange flare in the throat. It flowers in mid-spring.

Rhododendron Loderi Group (Z. 8–10) has large, fragrant flowers. The colors are variable.

Rhododendron 'Irene Koster' (Z. 5–7), a deciduous azalea, has fragrant flowers of salmon pink marked with yellow and orange.

Rhododendron 'Mrs. Furnivall' (Z. 5–8) is a fine evergreen rhododendron at least 10 ft. (3 m) high and wide. The pale rose pink flowers are marked with crimson and sienna, and are carried in large clusters.

RED FLOWERS

Rhododendron 'Cynthia' (Z. 5–7) is a hardy, hybrid evergreen rhododendron that reaches 16 ft. (5 m) in height when mature. In mid- to late spring it bears big, pyramid-shaped clusters of rosy crimson flowers with darker markings. This is regarded as one of the easiest rhododendrons to grow.

Rhododendron 'Scarlet Wonder' (Z. 5–7) is a low-growing, compact evergreen shrub that reaches 40 in. (1 m) high and wide. The frilled trumpet flowers are ruby red and are freely produced even on young plants.

Rhododendron 'Fireball' (Z. 5–7), a deciduous azalea, up to 6 ft. (2 m), with coppery foliage and orange-red, fragrant blooms in early spring. Good autumn foliage.

MAUVE-BLUE FLOWERS

Rhododendron Blue Diamond Group (Z. 5–7) is a compact shrub that slowly reaches 40 in. (1 m) in height. In early spring open, lavender blue flowers appear in clusters against the small, neat leaves.

Rhododendron 'Blue Danube' (Z. 6–9) is an evergreen azalea; a spreading shrub, up to 3 ft. (90 cm) by 4 ft. (1.2 m). The large blooms are blue-violet—striking against the dark green leaves. It flowers in mid-spring.

YELLOW FLOWERS

Rhododendron luteum (Z. 5–8), is perhaps the loveliest deciduous azalea, an elegant shrub of open habit, at least 6 ft. (2 m) high. In mid- to late spring it bears delicate clusters of honeysuckle-scented, soft yellow flowers at the branch tips. It also has superb autumn foliage.

Rhododendron 'Hotei' (Z. 5–8) is a compact evergreen shrub, up to 40 in. (1 m) or more, with loose clusters of clear yellow, bell-shaped flowers in mid-spring.

PINK FLOWERS

Rhododendron calophytum (Z. 6–9) is a large-leaved evergreen rhododendron that reaches 16 ft. (5 m) or more. The loose cluster of large, bell-shaped flowers are pale pink with darker throat markings.

Rhododendron 'Homebush' (Z. 5–9) is a deciduous azalea that reaches 5 ft. (1.5 m) high and wide. Round clusters of double, strawberry pink flowers open at the tips of the upright branches in late spring.

Rhododendron 'The Hon. Jean Marie de Montague' (Z. 5–8) bears many red flowers in mid-to late spring.

Rhododendron 'Colonel Coen' (Z. 6–8) is a compact evergreen that has deep purple flowers in mid-spring.

Rhododendron 'Horizon Monarch' (Z. 5–7) is a hardy evergreen, with large soft yellow flowers opening from salmon-tinged buds early to mid-spring.

133

Early-summer plantings like this have a translucent, harmonious beauty, with pink, violet, silver, and white much to the fore.

Early summer

There is something magical about early summer. Queen Anne's Lace along the roadside, fresh, soft green leaves on the trees, and a feeling of lushness everywhere. The sap has risen, and suddenly we are seeing the results. In gardens, flowers of every description are appearing daily, and the color palette seems to have transformed into one where pinks are vying with purples, violets, and blues to be most numerous. White flowers add to the general feeling of airiness.

This is the time of year when harmonies seem to be more appropriate to the freshness of the season, and in those gardens that feature perennials these are easily created, especially when mixing pinks with mauves, violets, and blues. If these schemes seem to be too predictable, it can be fun to experiment with single-colored borders, random effects, or stark contrasts, perhaps of purples and yellows. Whichever color approach is taken, one thing is certain: There is an enormous amount of plant material to play with.

BLUE FLOWERS

While in spring many of the blues are found in the flowers of bulbous plants, in early summer it is mainly perennials whose flowers are blue—for example, *Anchusa azurea* 'Loddon Royalist' (Zones 4–8), a cultivar with clusters of gentian blue, tubular flowers on 3 ft. (90 cm) stems. It has the advantage of not always needing to be staked. (See Good Companions, opposite.)

Among the **veronica** (speedwell) clan there are also some that produce blue

Anchusa azurea 'Loddon Royalist'

flowers. Veronicas vary in habit from creeping, mat-forming plants to tall kinds over 40 in. (1 m) tall, but all produce tiny flowers in tapering spikes. *Veronica gentianoides* (see page 41) has pale blue, cup-shaped flowers in racemes up to 10 in. (25 cm) on stems up to 18 in. (45 cm) tall, and is an excellent plant for the front of a border. Its cousin *Veronica spicata* ssp. *incana* (silver speedwell) (Zones 5–8) may be used in similar situations, as it has very decorative silvered leaves and dark purplish blue flowers on 12 in. (30 cm) stems. Mat-forming veronicas, such as *Veronica prostrata* (Zones 5–8) and *Veronica peduncularis* (Zones 4–8), are

Veronica spicata subsp. incana

useful plants for carpeting in a rock garden and both produce blue flowers. The cultivar *Veronica peduncularis* **'Georgia Blue'** has deep blue flowers with white eyes that appear most abundantly in spring and occasionally until late summer or fall.

Traditional English gardens would not be complete without at least a few **delphiniums**. These magnificent plants cannot be ignored wherever they are planted, especially those whose flowers are an intense deep, rich blue. Among the best of the blue-flowering kinds are

Delphinium 'Kestrel'

Delphinium **'Kestrel'** (Zones 4–8), which is one of the earliest to flower and is a light gentian blue color with a black eye; *Delphinium* **'Oliver'** (Zones 4–8), which bears pretty semidouble, medium blue flowers with black eyes (see also Good Companions, below);

Delphinium 'Oliver'

Delphinium **'Blue Nile'** (Zones 4–7), with striking semidouble, rich blue flowers with white eyes; *Delphinium grandiflorum* **'Blue Butterfly'** (Zones 4–7), with azure blue flowers; and *Delphinium* × *bellamosum* (Zones 3–7), with deep purple-blue flowers.

While not possessing the stateliness of delphiniums, **campanulas**—so beloved of cottage gardeners—are worth growing for their pretty bell- or cup-shaped flowers, some of which are blue. One of the most exquisite of all is *Campanula persicifolia* **'Telham Beauty'** (Zones 4–8), which has pale powder blue, cup-shaped flowers in slender spires. (Continued on page 137.)

GOOD COMPANIONS

Anchusa azurea 'Loddon Royalist' (1) (Z. 4–8) complements pink-flowered geraniums and purple-red roses, for example *Rosa* 'Roseraie de l'Haÿ' (2) (Z. 2–7) (see also pages 69, 145).

Delphinium 'Oliver' (3) (Z. 4–8) provides a strong vertical accent, so it is ideal with clump-forming plants, such as *Paeonia lactiflora* 'Sarah Bernhardt' (4) (Z. 4–8) (see also page 142).

Ceanothus

Some clematis produce blue flowers in early spring and late summer, but it is to the California lilacs, or *Ceanothus*, that we must turn if we are looking for shrubs with blue flowers in early summer. Ceanothus may be grown in shrub borders, against walls, or, if they are prostrate or low-growing, as carpet-forming ground cover for borders or in rock gardens. A wall-trained shrub could provide the backdrop for an all-blue or mixed-color planting scheme featuring white, cream, pink, or violet. Ceanothus should be grown in fertile, well-drained soil in a site where they get full sun and are sheltered from cold winds. They do not fare well in shallow alkaline soils. The best time to prune evergreen kinds is after flowering; deciduous ones should be pruned in spring.

Ceanothus 'Blue Mound' (Z. 9–10), as you might expect, grows into a dome shape or mound, which reaches 5 x 6 ft. (1.5 x 2 m) when mature, so it may be grown as part of a shrub border. It is an evergreen shrub with glossy, dark green leaves, and its flowers, produced from late spring to early summer, are bright blue.

Ceanothus 'Concha' (Z. 9–10) is a dense, evergreen shrub, 10 x 10 ft. (3 x 3 m) when mature, with dark green leaves and reddish buds opening into deep blue flowers in tightly packed, rounded clusters. (See also page 69.)

Ceanothus arboreus 'Trewithen Blue' (Z. 9–10) is an evergreen that grows vigorously up to 20 x 25 ft. (6 x 8 m) if left unpruned, and so is a suitable candidate for a large shrub border; it has dark green, rounded leaves, and large deep blue, scented flowers.

Ceanothus thyrsiflorus 'Skylark' (Z. 8–9) has large glossy, evergreen leaves and masses of medium blue flowers carried in loose clusters; upright in form, it makes a good wall shrub, as it grows to 6 x 5 ft. (2 x 1.5 m).

Ceanothus impressus (Z. 8–10), a fast-growing California lilac, has soft blue flowers and dark green, rounded evergreen leaves; it makes an excellent wall shrub as it reaches only 5 x 8 ft. (1.5 x 2.5 m).

Ceanothus 'Cascade' (Z. 9–10) is well named, as its bright blue flowers tumble down from arching stems, which carry evergreen, dark green leaves; it is 12 x 12 ft. (4 x 4 m) when mature, and looks effective cascading over a bank or down a slope.

The flowers grow on tall stems, about 40 in. (1 m) high, above rosettes of bright green, lance-shaped leaves. Another excellent kind is *Campanula lactiflora* 'Prichard's Variety' (Zones 5–7), which has rich violet-blue flowers carried in conical clusters on 30 in. (75 cm) stems. On a considerably smaller scale, *Campanula cochlearifolia* (Fairies' thimbles) (Zones 6–8) is a

Campanula lactiflora 'Prichard's Variety'

Campanula 'Samantha'

charming, creeping, rock-garden campanula, whose slate blue flowers appear all through summer on short stems, only 3 in. (8 cm) long. *Campanula* 'Samantha' (Zones 5–9) is another low spreader, forming mats of blue-violet, upward-facing flowers.

There are also plenty of less well-known early-summer perennials with blue flowers that are well worth seeking out. *Cichorium intybus* (chicory) (Zones 3–8) is a captivating perennial, with toothed leaves and light blue or, occasionally, white or pink flowers reminiscent of dandelions, on branching

stems up to 4 ft. (1.2 m) tall. **Amsonias** (Zones 3–9) are perennials found in grassland and woods in central and northeastern United States, Japan, and southeastern Europe; they, too, deserve to be more widely grown. *Amsonia orientalis* has willowlike leaves and panicles of tiny, funnel-shaped, violet blue flowers on 12 in. (30 cm) stems, while *Amsonia tabernaemontana* has dense clusters of pale blue flowers from late spring to summer on taller stems, 24 in. (60 cm) high. Amsonias will grow in moist but well-drained soil in full sun.

Linum narbonense (flax) (Zones 5–8) produces beautiful saucer-shaped, rich blue flowers with white eyes; it needs well-drained, moderately fertile, humus-rich soil, and tends to be short-lived. *Myosotidium hortensia* (Zones 8–10) is an evergreen perennial from Chatham Island, New Zealand, with large, heart-shaped, glossy leaves; it bears forget-me-not, pale to dark blue flowers in dome-shaped clusters on 24 in. (60 cm) stems in early summer. The main disadvantage of this charming plant is that it is half hardy and so has to be lifted in winter if grown outdoors in frost-prone areas. A position in dappled shade, in moist but well-drained soil with added grit and humus suits it best.

WHITE FLOWERS

Plants from trees to mat-forming alpines provide the wealth of white available to gardeners in early summer. White-flowering trees include *Davidia involucrata* (handkerchief tree) (Zones 5–8), whose insignificant flowers are surrounded by prominent white bracts like fluttering handkerchiefs, and the elegant *Stewartia pseudocamellia* (Zones 4–8), with its roselike white flowers with creamy yellow stamens. *Cornus controversa* 'Variegata' (see page 42) is an elegant tree with tiered branches and attractive leaves with

wide, creamy margins; it looks its best in early summer. This is also the time when the leaves of the whitebeam *Sorbus aria* 'Lutescens' (Zones 5–6) appear at their most white; as summer wears on, they become greener.

Early summer is when shrubs such as **philadelphus**, the mock oranges, are flowering to perfection, too. Among them are shrubs that produce single or

Davidia involucrata

Stewartia pseudocamellia

Sorbus aria 'Lutescens'

Philadelphus 'Virginal'

Gillenia trifoliata

Geranium clarkei 'Kashmir White'

Cistus × obtusifolius 'Thrive'

Crambe cordifolia

lactiflora 'White Wings' (Zones 4–8), with fine, tissuelike white petals and prominent yellow stamens, is particularly appealing and is also fragrant.

Among white-flowering perennials for early summer, the choice is wide. *Gillenia trifoliata* (Zones 4–7) is a graceful perennial for semishade on soil with adequate moisture. Its pretty, divided leaves and reddish stems are the perfect background for the dainty white flowers, which open from red buds all summer. Some **cranesbills** have white flowers, such as *Geranium clarkei*

'Kashmir White' (Zones 5–7), *Geranium renardii* (Zones 5–7), and *Geranium sylvaticum* 'Album' (Zones 5–8). Any of these would mix well with the silver-leaved, daisylike *Anthemis punctata* ssp. *cupaniana* (Zones 3–9). For airy effects, there is *Gypsophila*

double, cup- or bowl-shaped flowers, most of which are scented. Some good performers are the double-flowered *Philadelphus* 'Virginal' (Zones 5–7) and *Philadelphus* 'Buckley's Quill' (Zones 5–8), the single *Philadelphus* 'Beauclerk' (Zones 5–7) and *Philadelphus* 'Burfordensis' (Zones 5–8), and the compact *Philadelphus* 'Manteau d'Hermine' (see page 62).

Cistus, such as *Cistus* × *obtusifolius* 'Thrive' (Zones 8–10), and **deutzias** also provide white flowers in early and midsummer, and there are white-flowered varieties of both tree and herbaceous **peonies**. The single-flowered herbaceous peony *Paeonia*

GOOD COMPANIONS

The yellow-centered flowers of *Tanacetum parthenium* (feverfew) (1) (Z. 4–9) harmonize beautifully with the lime green flowers and foliage of *Nicotiana* 'Lime Green' (2) (see also page 43).

The soft gray leaves of *Stachys byzantina* 'Big Ears' (3) (Z. 4–8) provide the perfect foreground for the stiff white spikes and feathery foliage of the monkshood *Aconitum* 'Ivorine' (4) (Z. 5–8).

MORE COTTAGE-GARDEN PLANTS *Aquilegia vulgaris • Centaurea montana • Digitalis purpurea •*

Dictamnus albus

Digitalis purpurea f. albiflora

paniculata 'Bristol Fairy' (Zones 4–8) or the much taller *Crambe cordifolia* (Zones 6–8), which reaches 6 ft. (2 m) and has large, dark green leaves. Both these perennials produce delicate branched stems with tiny white flowers in loose, spreading, cloudlike clusters.

Thalictrums have delicate, fernlike leaves and fluffy flowers; *Thalictrum aquilegiifolium* var. *album* (Zones 5–8) has white flowers in flat-topped clusters on 40 in. (1 m) tall stems. The pyramidal flower panicles found on **rodgersias**, statuesque moisture-loving

perennials from Asia, are much more solid and look like thick, tapering candles. Their flowers are star shaped, and *Rodgersia podophylla* (see pages 65, 101) produces white ones tinged with green in 12 in. (30 cm) panicles. *Rodgersia aesculifolia* (Zones 4–8), on the other hand, produces white or pink flowers in longer panicles (see page 143)

Plants that produce spires of flowers are always welcome in a planting, and *Dictamnus albus* (Zones 4–8), with its open racemes of five-petaled flowers in white or pink, and the white form of the common foxglove, *Digitalis purpurea* f. *albiflora* (Zones 4–8), add an elegant dimension to any planting scheme. (See Good Companions, below.)

Dicentra spectabilis 'Alba' (Zones 4–7) is a white-flowered form of

Dicentra spectabilis 'Alba'

bleeding heart, whose charming heart-shaped flowers dangle from arching stems in late spring and early summer. This perennial will grow happily in sun or light shade. *Hesperis matronalis* (sweet rocket, see page 89) is just as obliging. This old cottage-garden favorite is a vigorous self-seeder, but its sweetly scented, four-petaled, white or pale lilac flowers are so charming that they are always an asset. Its white double-flowered form, *Hesperis matronalis* var. *albiflora* 'Alba Plena' (Zones 6–8) is even lovelier. *Galium odoratum* (sweet woodruff) (Zones 5–8) has tiny, star-shaped scented flowers, which persist for weeks in late

GOOD COMPANIONS

Myrrhis odorata (1) (sweet Cicely) (Z. 5–8), with its umbels of white flowers on tall stems, goes with the white spires of the foxglove *Digitalis purpurea* f. *albiflora* (2) (Z. 4–8). Both suit a shady corner.

The dark foliage and clear white daisy blooms of *Leucanthemum* × *superbum* 'Esther Read' (3) (Z. 4–7) contrast with the white spikes of *Delphinium* 'Clear Springs White' (4) (Z. 4–7).

Galega officinalis • *Nepeta* 'Six Hills Giant' • *Paeonia officinalis* 'Rubra Plena' • *Polemonium caeruleum* •

Anemone rivularis

Trifolium ochroleucon

spring and summer. With its attractive emerald green leaves, it makes good ground cover for woodland or for under evergreen hedges. (See page 124.)

The easily grown *Anemone rivularis* (Zones 6–8) has saucer-shaped white flowers with blue undersides. It flourishes in sun or light shade, and the flowers grow on long, spreading 24 in. (60 cm) stalks. *Trifolium ochroleucon* (Zones 6–9) is a good clover reaching a similar height, with large, translucent cream green-tinged flower heads.

Lilium regale

Osteospermum 'Whirlygig' (Zones 9–10) needs much more cosseting, as it is only half hardy. In frost-prone areas, therefore, it has to be lifted and brought into a frost-free environment in winter. However, its daisylike flower heads, about 2 in. (5 cm) across, with petals like teaspoons, are very eye-catching, and since they appear from late spring until fall, the effort is worthwhile.

Osteospermum 'Whirlygig' has a cheery charm very far removed from the grandeur of **lilies**, the aristocrats of the summer garden in many people's eyes. None produces blooms more beautiful than the pure white trumpets of *Lilium candidum* (Zones 6–8) and the creamy white ones of *Lilium regale* (Zones 3–8).

PURPLE AND LAVENDER

When it comes to the violet shades of early summer, they range from the dark purples to the palest of lavenders, with numerous tones in between. Rich, dark purples are found in *Salvia* × *sylvestris*

Salvia × sylvestris 'Mainacht'

'Mainacht' (Zones 4–8) (see also page 159), which has thin spires of purple flowers and is effective in a wild planting of perennials and grasses, and *Baptisia australis* (Zones 4–8), or false indigo, whose dark purplish blue, pealike blooms appear in loose racemes on stems up to 4 ft. (1.2 m) tall. (See Good Companions, opposite.)

Some of the prettiest, palest violets are found in the **polemonium** clan, perennials that produce bell- or funnel-shaped flowers above finely divided, pinnate leaves. *Polemonium caeruleum* (Zones 4–7) is a tall variety, with light blue flowers; those of *Polemonium boreale* (Zones 3–9) vary from purple-blue to light blue. Low-growing *Polemonium carneum* (Zones 4–9) has flowers that vary from pale pink or yellow to dark purple and lavender, but the bell-shaped flowers of *Polemonium* 'Lambrook Mauve' (Zones 4–7) are always lilac-blue, on branching stems. While polemoniums make excellent border plants, the taller ones work just as well in a wildflower garden, and *Polemonium caeruleum* looks good naturalized in grass.

Baptisia australis

Centaurea montana

Reliable perennial performers with brighter purple or violet flowers are numerous. One of the easiest to grow is *Centaurea montana* (knapweed) (Zones 4–8), with its deep bluish purple flowers with hints of red, which appear consistently throughout summer; it can

OTHER GROUND-COVER PLANTS *Artemisia schmidtiana* • *Lamium maculatum* 'Beacon Silver' •

be effective in a wild planting or in a border. *Stachys macrantha* 'Superba' (Zones 5–7) is a fine plant for the front of a border, as it has striking pinkish purple, hooded, two-lipped blooms carried in dense spikes and downy green leaves. The flower spikes, on 24-in. (60 cm) stems, remain upright without support and appear for weeks from early summer to fall. Hardy **tradescantias**, distinguished by their flowers of three triangular petals and three sepals, also make excellent border plants, and grow in either sun or light shade. *Tradescantia* Andersoniana Group 'Concord Grape' (Zones 5–8) is a fine cultivar with rich purple flowers.

Scabious, with their pincushion flower heads, are charming plants for a wildflower garden or border. *Scabiosa caucasica* (Zones 4–9) is perhaps the most beautiful of all, and it has several excellent cultivars. Its large pale blue or lavender blue flower heads, 3 in. (8 cm) in diameter, grow on 18-in. (45 cm) stems from mid- to late summer. Besides looking good in a border, it makes an elegant container-grown plant. To fare well, plant scabious in full sun in well-drained, moderately fertile, neutral or alkaline soil.

Stachys macrantha 'Superba'

Tradescantia Andersoniana Group 'Concord Grape'

Scabiosa caucasica

Geranium pratense 'Plenum Violaceum'

Geraniums, also known as cranesbills, are very good, reliable, undemanding perennials with flowers in all the colors we associate with early summer: pinks, blues, and white, as well as violets and purples. Taller species and cultivars are excellent plants for including in perennial plantings or as ground cover under shrubs and roses (see Good Companions, left). They are equally happy in sun or partial shade, and interweave easily among other plants in a border. Once flowering is over, they respond well to being cut back hard and soon produce fresh new leaves and, occasionally, more flowers.

Among the violet- and purple-flowered cranesbills, *Geranium* × *magnificum* (Zones 4–7) produces lots of large, single blue flowers crisscrossed with darker violet-blue veins in densely packed cymes, and *Geranium clarkei* 'Kashmir Purple' (Zones 5–7) has single blooms in a rich lilac-blue with bright red veining and finely cut leaves. *Geranium pratense* 'Plenum Violaceum' (Zones 4–7) (see also page 63), a delectable cultivar of the meadow cranesbill, has

GOOD COMPANIONS

The medium to lavender-blue *Geranium* 'Johnson's Blue' (1) (Z. 4–8) is a perfect companion for low-growing pale pink-flowered roses such as *Rosa* 'Bonica' (2) (Z. 5–9).

The indigo blue *Baptisia australis* (3) (Z. 4–8) looks charming with *Rosa* 'Ballerina' (4) (Z. 4–9), which has mop-headed clusters of pale pink and white single flowers from summer to fall.

Myosotis sylvatica • *Saponaria ocymoides* • *Saxifraga* × *urbium* • *Vinca minor* 'Azurea Flore Pleno' •

Geranium pratense 'Cluden Sapphire'

PINK FLOWERS

When thinking of colors for early summer, the pinks cannot be ignored. This is the time of year when they are at their most numerous, for along with many pink-flowered perennials, most **roses** are at their best now. Descriptions of pink-flowered roses alone would fill many pages, and so it is not possible to discuss them in detail. However, a short list of garden-worthy roses, arranged by color, may be found on page 145.

fully double, violet flowers shaded with purple-blue in their centers, while *Geranium pratense* 'Cluden Sapphire' (Zones 4–7), a relatively tall cranesbill at 40 in. (1 m) or more high, has a dense inflorescence of single, deep blue flowers from early summer to midsummer. *Geranium himalayense* (Zones 4–7) has single blooms in violet-blue with white centers tinged red. They appear from early summer until late summer. *Geranium sylvaticum* 'Mayflower' (Zones 5–8), a choice cultivar of the wood cranesbill, has single flowers on 24 in. (60 cm) stems in a soft blue with pink veins. It flowers best in damp conditions, so may suit a planting beside a pool or stream, or in a bog garden.

Paeonia lactiflora 'Bowl of Beauty'

Peonies, with their showy flowers, add an air of glamour to any border in early and midsummer. There are shrubby tree peonies as well as herbaceous ones, and both kinds produce flowers in pink, white, red, or yellow. Pink-flowered herbaceous peonies include *Paeonia lactiflora* 'Sarah Bernhardt' (see also Good Companions, page 135) and *Paeonia lactiflora* 'Shirley Temple' (Zones 4–8), both of which have blowsy double blooms packed with rose pink petals.

Paeonia lactiflora 'Sarah Bernhardt'

The flowers of *Paeonia lactiflora* 'Bowl of Beauty' (Zones 4–8) resemble anemones, with reddish pink petals and creamy white centers; their centers are composed of many narrow petals packed together. Peonies may be included in shrub, mixed, or herbaceous borders, but once planted, they should not be disturbed, as they dislike being uprooted. Some have leaves that color beautifully in fall—a small compensation for their short flowering season.

Massed planting of peonies can look most effective, but teaming them with plants with spires of flowers emphasizes the plants' differing forms and flower shapes—particularly essential in single-color plantings. *Eremurus robustus* (Zones 5–8), with its imposing, foxtail-like

GOOD COMPANIONS

The buff-colored plumes of *Macleaya microcarpa* (1) (Z. 3–9) would make a good companion for apricot-pink plants, for example *Digitalis ferruginea* (2) (Z. 4–8).

The mauve-flowered *Dictamnus albus* var. *purpureus* (3) (Z. 4–8) is a perfect partner for cranesbills, such as the compact, pale pink *Geranium sanguineum* var. *striatum* (4). (Z. 4–8)

OTHER PINK-FLOWERED PERENNIALS *Campanula lactiflora* 'Loddon Anna' • *Erigeron* 'Charity' •

Rodgersia aesculifolia

Astilbe 'Venus'

Dictamnus albus var. purpureus

Geranium maderense

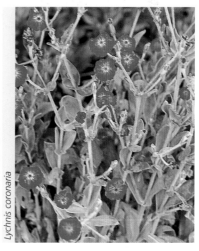

Lychnis coronaria

racemes of pale pink flowers, would mix well with pink-flowered tree peonies or taller herbaceous ones. Its racemes can grow up to 4 ft. (1.2 m), on stems reaching 10 ft. (3 m). *Macleaya microcarpa* (plume poppy) (Zones 3–9) is less imposing than *Eremurus robustus* as its buff flowers are arranged in loose, plumelike panicles. They grow on 6-ft. (2 m) stems. (See Good Companions, opposite.) The plumes of *Macleaya microcarpa* 'Kelway's Coral Plume' are soft coral pink. Macleaya is a fine plant but must be kept in check as it is invasive.

Rodgersia aesculifolia (Zones 4–8) is another plant with conspicuous inflorescences. It has large, fluffy pink or white panicles of tiny star-shaped flowers rising above leaves like those of a horse chestnut. It forms clumps up to 4 ft. (1.2 m) tall.

Astilbes are plumelike perennials that are ideal for semishade in moist soil. They look particularly effective en masse. *Astilbe* 'Venus' (Zones 4–8) has feathery panicles of pinkish flowers.

Dictamnus albus (burning bush or dittany) (Zones 4–8) is another imposing perennial with long, candlelike flower racemes. Its variant, *Dictamnus albus var. purpureus*, has mauve flowers with purple veining on stems up to 3 ft. (90 cm) tall, and it would make a fine companion for bushy purple- or pink-flowered **cranesbills** (geraniums). (See Good Companions, opposite.) Some pink-flowered cranesbills have good "shock" value: The magenta *Geranium psilostemon* (Zones 5–7) and *Geranium* 'Ann Folkard' (Zones 5–7) add drama to any planting, and *Geranium maderense* (Zones 5–8), which can grow to 4 ft. (1.2 m), has pinkish magenta flowers and finely dissected leaves, which add to its charm. Tender *Geranium × riversleaianum* 'Russell Prichard' (Zone 8), with its spreading, grayish foliage and magenta flowers, grows up to only 12 in. (30 cm).

Lychnis coronaria (Zones 4–8) is a gray-leaved perennial that bears pinkish magenta blooms on 3-ft. (90 cm) stems; it is best suited to growing in a border, perhaps with other silver-leaved plants. Its relative *Lychnis flos-jovis* (Zones 4–8) has less eye-catching, paler bluish pink, white, or red flowers, but is a fine border plant, with flowers on whitish stems that may grow to 24 in. (60 cm).

YELLOW FLOWERS

Perhaps the most beautiful yellow blooms produced in early summer are the lemon yellow blooms of *Paeonia mlokosewitschii* (Zones 5–8). They are

Incarvillea delavayi • *Liatris spicata* • *Persicaria bistorta* 'Superba' • *Rehmannia elata* • *Verbena* 'Sissinghurst' •

The star-shaped flowers of *Hemerocallis* 'Hyperion' with the tall spires of *Verbascum bombyciferum*.

and *Anthemis tinctoria* 'E.C. Buxton' (Zones 2–8) produce their daisylike, yellow flowers in early and midsummer. In an all-yellow planting, they could serve as a foil to *Thalictrum lucidum* (Zones 5–8), with its fluffy flower heads and fernlike foliage. *Achillea filipendulina* 'Gold Plate' (see page 154) has flat, platelike, golden flower heads, which mix well with grasses and other, smaller-flowered perennials.

Funnel-shaped, rounded, trumpet-, or star-shaped flowers are features of **hemerocallis**, (daylilies; see page 69) and there are many garden-worthy cultivars with yellow flowers. But certain species, such as *Hemerocallis lilioasphodelus* (Zones 4–10), with its lemon yellow, star-shaped flowers, and *Hemerocallis citrina* (Zones 3–8), with its pale greenish yellow, star-shaped flowers, have enduring appeal. Good cultivars include *Hemerocallis* 'Hyperion' (Zones 4–10) and *Hemerocallis* 'Marion Vaughn' (Zones 4–10), with fragrant, lemon yellow, star-shaped nocturnal flowers.

Anyone who grows **verbascums** (mulleins) will know that they produce tall spires of flowers. *Verbascum* 'Gainsborough' (Zones 6–8) has creamy yellow flowers on 4-ft. (1.2 m) stems and grayish green leaves, and the taller *Verbascum bombyciferum* (Zones 6–8) bears sulfur yellow flowers on towering stems up to 6 ft. (1.8 m) high. This verbascum also has attractive white, woolly, semi-evergreen leaves. **Phlomis** have decorative foliage and flowers, and *Phlomis russeliana* (Zones 5–8) is an attractive perennial, with pale, soft yellow flowers in whorls around the 3-ft. (90 cm) flowering stems. The winter seed heads are most attractive.

The occasionally invasive perennial wildflower *Thermopsis rhombifolia* (Zones 3–8) has charming, pale yellow, lupinelike flowers on 3-ft. (90 cm) stems, but here the leaves are finely divided, hairy, and silvery in color.

single, with oval petals that open to reveal a boss of pale yellow stamens. (See page 45.) The scented, double blooms of *Paeonia lactiflora* 'Laura Dessert' (Zones 4–8), which have creamy white outer sepals and canary yellow inner ones, are captivating too.

Most yellow-flowered daisies appear in late summer, but *Argyranthemum* 'Jamaica Primrose' (Zones 9–11/ann.)

Argyranthemum 'Jamaica Primrose'

Hemerocallis lilioasphodelus

A SHORT SELECTION OF RECOMMENDED ROSES

WHITE FLOWERS

Rosa 'Albéric Barbier' (Z. 4–9)

Rosa 'Blanc Double de Coubert' (Z. 3–7)

Rosa 'Iceberg' (Z. 4–9)

Rosa 'Margaret Merril' (Z. 6–10)

Rosa 'Nevada' (1) (Z. 5–10)

Rosa 'Seagull' (Z. 5–10)

YELLOW FLOWERS

Rosa 'Arthur Bell' (Z. 6–10)

Rosa 'Golden Celebration' (2) (Z. 5–10)

Rosa 'Golden Wings' (Z. 4–8)

Rosa 'Goldfinch' (Z. 4–9)

Rosa 'Grandpa Dickson' (Z. 7–10)

Rosa 'Harrison's Yellow' (Z. 3–9)

Rosa pimpinellifolia 'Dunwich Rose'
(Z. 4–8)

BLUISH PINK FLOWERS

Rosa 'Constance Spry' (Z. 5–9)

Rosa 'Fantin-Latour' (Z. 7–9)

Rosa 'Hansa' (Z. 3–8)

Rosa 'Königin von Dänemark' (Z. 4–9)

Rosa 'Mary Rose' (Z. 5–10)

Rosa 'Président de Sèze' (3) (Z. 4–8)

Rosa 'The Fairy' (Z. 4–9)

APRICOT-PINK FLOWERS

Rosa 'Alchymist' (4) (Z. 4–9)

Rosa 'Bonica' (Z. 5–9)

Rosa 'Desprez à Fleurs Jaunes' (Z. 7–10)

Rosa 'Gruss an Aachen' (Z. 6–10)

Rosa 'Martin Frobisher' (Z. 3–9)

Rosa 'Mrs. Oakley Fisher' (Z. 6–10)

Rosa × *odorata* 'Mutabilis' (Z. 6–10)

RED FLOWERS

Rosa 'Etoile de Hollande' (Z. 5–9)

Rosa 'Fragrant Cloud' (Z. 7–10)

Rosa 'Geranium' (Z. 5–9)

Rosa 'Henry Kelsey' (Z. 3–9)

Rosa 'Tess of the d'Urbervilles' (5) (Z. 4–9)

Rosa 'Tuscany Superb' (Z. 4–9)

Rosa 'Zigeunerknabe' (Z. 5–10)

PURPLISH FLOWERS

Rosa 'Cardinal de Richelieu' (Z. 4–8)

Rosa 'Madame Isaac Pereire' (Z. 6–10)

Rosa 'Nuits de Young' (Z. 4–9)

Rosa 'Roseraie de l'Haÿ' (6) (Z. 2–7) (see also page 69 and Good Companions, page 135)

Rosa 'Veilchenblau' (Z. 5–9)

PLANT PROFILE

Penstemons

Penstemon 'Burgundy' (Z. 7–10) has large, deep wine purple flowers from midsummer to early or mid-fall, on stems approximately 30 in. (75 cm) high, and relatively large leaves.

Penstemon 'Andenken an Friedrich Hahn' (Z. 7–10), also known as *Penstemon* 'Garnet', bears small, wine crimson flowers from midsummer to mid-fall and narrow leaves. Its flower spires reach about 30 in. (75 cm).

Penstemons have become increasingly popular in recent years as gardeners have come to recognize the value of their elegant, foxglovelike flowers in a range of subtle and bright colors, from white to dusky purple, and encompassing pinks, mauves, and blues. Some have flowers with white throats, and others have blooms streaked with contrasting colors. The flowers may go on appearing week after week throughout summer, especially when they are deadheaded regularly.

There are about 250 species in the *Penstemon* genus, all of which are found in North and Central America. The genus includes deciduous, semi-evergreen, and evergreen perennial species and sub-

shrubs, and they are found in a variety of situations from open plains to alpine regions. While some of the species are garden-worthy plants, it is the arrival on the garden scene of some excellent cultivars that has led to their becoming such sought-after plants. The cultivars grow vigorously and flower prolifically, and some are semi-evergreen with leaves that persist throughout the winter months.

Penstemons produce their tubular flowers in racemes or panicles. Individual flowers are composed of two lips, the upper usually with two lobes, the lower with three. Some cultivars bear small leaves, which are linear or lanceshaped, while others have larger elliptic or ovate leaves.

The taller penstemons are superb perennials for borders, where they should be grown in sun or partial shade and in any good soil, as long as it is well-drained. In areas where frost is prevalent in winter, it is a good idea to mulch the soil around them for protection. The shrubby and dwarf species must have full sun and prefer less fertile, very free-draining soil.

All of the penstemons described on these pages are perennial unless otherwise stated.

Penstemon 'Evelyn' (Z. 7–10) is a narrow-leaved penstemon, with small pale pink flowers from midsummer to early or mid-fall on stems up to 2 ft. (60 cm) tall.

Penstemon 'Stapleford Gem' (Z. 6–9) has lilac flowers with white throats from midsummer to early or mid-fall, and dark leaves. It grows to 3 ft. (90 cm) high.

Penstemon 'Alice Hindley' (Z. 7–10) is a tall, large-leaved penstemon. Its large pale mauve flowers with white throats are tinged purple on the outside and are borne from midsummer to early or mid-fall on stems up to 40 in. (1 m) tall.

OTHER GOOD PENSTEMONS

Penstemon 'Apple Blossom' (Z. 7–9) Small pale pink flowers with white throats from midsummer to early fall; narrow leaves. Height 30 in. (75 cm).

Penstemon isophyllus (Z. 8–10) Evergreen sub-shrub with medium-size, deep pink and red flowers, from early to late summer; lance-shaped leaves. Height 28 in. (70 cm).

Penstemon 'King George V' (Z. 6–9) Small flowers, bright red with red-veined white throats, from midsummer to early or mid-autumn; narrow leaves. Height 2 ft. (60 cm).

Penstemon 'Sour Grapes' (Z. 7–10) Big, lilac-blue flowers, tinted purple, from midsummer to early or mid-autumn; large leaves. Height 3 ft. (90 cm).

Penstemon 'White Bedder' (Z. 6–9) Large pure white flowers, from midsummer to early fall; large leaves. Height 2 ft. (60 cm).

Penstemon heterophyllus 'Catherine de la Mare' (Z. 8–9) is an evergreen sub-shrub, 12–20 in. (30–50 cm) high, with medium-size blue flowers in summer, and linear to lance-shaped leaves.

Penstemon barbatus (beardlip penstemon) (Z. 5–8) is sometimes more than 4 ft. (1.2 m) tall. It has pendent, narrow flowers, red with yellow "beards," from early summer to early fall.

Penstemon 'Raven' (left) (Z. 7–9) is an excellent border perennial, with deep purple flowers with white-veined throats, on stems about 40 in. (1 m) high. The flowers bloom from early summer to mid-fall.

The color of late summer: *Crocosmia* 'Lucifer' and *Lilium* Pink Perfection Group, with *Rosa glauca* and *Sambucus nigra*.

Late summer

Even in zones where summers can be cool and wet, there are days in late summer when the sun shines in all its glory, ripening fruit, and bringing a host of later-flowering perennials and shrubs into flower. On these dry, hot days the fresh, cool colors of early summer seem to melt away, as an array of rich, warm hues starts to appear. Late summer is the time when scintillating reds, oranges, and yellows and some penetrating pinks, purples, and blues hold sway.

Canna indica

In late summer, with so many vividly colored perennials at their best, vibrant hot harmonies featuring reds, oranges, and yellows can be breathtaking. But darker, more sumptuous and, perhaps, more mysterious color schemes can also be made by adding coppers, bronzes, deep pinks, purples, and blues to the mix. With such a rich palette at hand, gardeners can throw caution to the wind and make some of the boldest plantings of the year, remembering that vibrant-colored schemes work best if they have lots of dark green foliage, as well as flowers.

HOT REDS

When constructing hot plantings for late summer it would be hard to ignore plants with large, bright red flowers, such as the dramatic *Dahlia* 'Bishop of Llandaff' (see page 47), with its scarlet, semidouble blooms and almost black leaves; the elegant *Crocosmia* 'Lucifer' (Zones 7–9), with its tomato red flowers in arching sprays among pleated, sword-shaped leaves; and the stately *Canna indica* (Zones 8–11), which bears orange-scarlet, gladiolus-like blooms and has brownish purple leaves.

148

These plants have a weighty presence, so it is a good idea to contrast them with lots of foliage and plants with small flowers, such as potentillas, fuchsias, or grasses. There are several **potentillas** with red flowers. The herbaceous perennial *Potentilla* **'Gibson's Scarlet'** (Zones 5–8) (see also page 48) produces scarlet blooms; the shrubby *Potentilla* **'Etna'** (Zones 5–8) has semidouble, dark red blooms like velvet; and *Potentilla fruticosa* **'Red Ace'** (Zones 2–7) has vermilion, saucer-shaped flowers with yellow-backed petals. Shrubby potentillas flower from late spring to mid-fall.

Fuchsias, too, bloom from summer to fall. Semi-hardy kinds should be grown in pots and popped into borders

Potentilla 'Gibson's Scarlet'

when needed. *Fuchsia* **'Mrs. Popple'** (Zones 7–9) is one of the hardier cultivars, with single scarlet and violet flowers; bushy in habit, it grows up to 40 in. (1 m), with a similar spread.

In an all-red planting, the perennial *Lobelia tupa* (Zones 8–10) can be used to provide height, as its spires of brick red, two-lipped flowers grow on 6-ft. (2 m) stems. This Chilean lobelia will not survive a hard frost, so in cooler areas it should be lifted or mulched in winter. Its elongated flower spires would form a striking contrast to the rounded, shaggy-looking flowers of monardas.

Monarda **'Cambridge Scarlet'** (Zones 3–7) has scarlet flowers with brown calyxes, and *Monarda* **'Mahogany'** (Zones 5–9) has wine red flowers. The flowers of both cultivars grow on 3-ft. (90 cm) stems. Monardas prefer moist, well-drained soil in sun or light shade.

With their bright, showy flowers, which resemble small gladioli, the South African perennials **schizostylis** (Zones 6–8) make fine companions for monardas at the front of a planting, but they do need sun. *Schizostylis coccinea* **'Major'** has scarlet flowers carried on 2-ft. (60 cm)- tall stems. Its cousins, *Schizostylis* **'Viscountess Byng'** and *Schizostylis* **'Sunrise'**, have pale pink and salmon pink flowers respectively, and all three make excellent cut flowers.

Fuchsia 'Mrs Popple'

Schizostylis coccinea 'Major'

SMOKE BUSHES

Late summer is when smoke bushes (*Cotinus*) produce their small, inconspicuous flowers in light, airy panicles, which resemble puffs of smoke. In addition to their highly decorative flowers, smoke bushes also have attractive rounded, purple, or green leaves that turn glorious shades of orange and red in fall. They are easy-to-grow shrubs, faring well in any moderately fertile, moist but well-drained soil, and may be grown in sun or light shade. However, the purple-leaved varieties, such as *Cotinus coggygria* 'Notcutt's Variety', with its deep red leaves and pinkish flower panicles, perform best in sun. A particularly striking cultivar for autumn is *Cotinus coggygria* 'Royal Purple' (above), whose dark wine red foliage turns bright scarlet. The light green leaves of *Cotinus* 'Flame', on the other hand, become orange-red or flame in fall, and those of *Cotinus* 'Grace' (see pages 69, 162) go a deeper cardinal red. With their brilliant leaves, smoke bushes can be used either as specimens or as constituents of shrub borders. At The Courts, the National Trust's garden near Melksham, in Wiltshire, England, cotinus form the centerpieces of the magnificent large late summer/autumn borders featuring reds, oranges, yellows, and bronze foliage.

Tropaeolum speciosum

Where a red planting is backed by an evergreen hedge, it is fun to allow the attractive Chilean climber ***Tropaeolum speciosum*** (Zones 7–9), with vermilion flowers and medium green, palmate leaves, to tumble over it. However, to perform well this perennial nasturtium needs moist, humus-rich, neutral to acid soil, and its roots must be in cool shade.

DUSKY REDS

Reds with orange in their makeup, such as scarlet, always command attention, while those with brown or violet in their composition are less eye-catching. However, their rich, sultry quality makes them very satisfying to use in plantings. These dusky reds are found in the flowers of plants such as ***Cirsium rivulare* 'Atropurpureum'** (Zones 5–8) (see also page 103), with its dark, wine red, thistlelike blooms, and ***Knautia macedonica*** (Zones 6–9) and its cultivars, such as ***Knautia macedonica* 'Mars Midget'**, whose deep, purple-red flowers resemble those of a small scabious. Perennials such as these, with small, dark flowers, not only have great charm but can be useful in schemes to provide dots of color. Set amid larger, paler masses of color, they highlight textures and enliven a planting. The same is true of the Mexican perennial ***Cosmos atrosanguineus*** (Zones 7–10), with its rich, velvety, brownish red, saucer-shaped flowers, with a distinctive chocolate scent, and are borne on reddish brown stems, 30 in. (75 cm) long, amid dark green leaves. In cold areas, the tubers have to be lifted in winter and kept frost free.

If bright bluish red, tall, fluffy panicles are desired for a late-summer planting, then you need look no further than

Cirsium rivulare 'Atropurpureum'

Knautia macedonica 'Mars Midget'

PHYGELIUS

These late summer flowering, evergreen South African shrubs and sub-shrubs produce attractive tubular flowers in pink, magenta, red, yellow, and orange. They mix well with perennials in borders or in front of a sunny wall. Good cultivars include *Phygelius* × *rectus* 'Winchester Fanfare' (above) (Z. 8–10), with coral red flowers, *Phygelius* × *rectus* 'Salmon Leap' (Z. 8–10), with orange flowers; *Phygelius* × *rectus* 'Devil's Tears' (Z. 8–10), with deep, reddish pink flowers; *Phygelius* × *rectus* 'Moonraker' (Z. 8–10), with creamy yellow flowers; and *Phygelius aequalis* 'Yellow Trumpet' (Z. 8–9), with light yellow flowers. As they are susceptible to cold weather, they should be mulched in winter in frost-prone areas.

Filipendula purpurea (Zones 5–8), which bears carmine flower plumes carried on purple stems to 4 ft. (1.2 m) tall, or *Filipendula rubra* 'Venusta' (Zones 2–8), which has rosy red plumes, which become paler with age. They are easy to grow and thrive in damp sites.

Eupatoriums (Zones 5–8) also prefer moist soil, and suit the back or middle of the border. *Eupatorium purpureum* ssp. *maculatum* 'Atropurpureum' has purplish green leaves, deep pinkish red, domed flowers on stems 6 ft. (2 m) high and, in fall, good seed heads.

MORE DUSKY PLANTS *Buddleia davidii* 'Black Knight' • *Dahlia* 'Mount Noddy' • *Imperata cylindrica* 'Rubra' •

Lilium henryi

Crocosmia × crocosmiiflora 'Jackanapes'

ORANGE-FLOWERED PLANTS

The range of orange-flowered plants for late summer offers a gardener the chance to create high drama by selecting large, showy flowers, such as **cannas**, **lilies**, **dahlias**, and **kniphofias** (see page 152), or to play it somewhat safer by choosing smaller-flowered plants such as **crocosmias**, **heleniums**, and **potentillas**.

Cannas (Zones 8–11), with their paddle-shaped leaves and large, asymmetrical, three-petaled flowers, are stars of late-summer plantings. The most glamorous are *Canna* 'Striata', with green leaves striped with yellow veins and bright orange flowers, and *Canna* 'Wyoming', which bears dark brownish purple leaves and frilly orange flowers. There are many orange-flowered **lilies**, but *Lilium henryi* (see Good Companions, right) is particularly elegant, producing its characteristic Turk's-cap blooms on tall stems of six or more well-spread flowers in late summer and early fall. Another good orange lily is *Lilium* **African Queen** (Zones 3–9), a vigorous grower with fragrant, trumpet-shaped flowers on 6-ft. (2 m) stems, appearing from midsummer onward.

Crocosmias (Zones 7–10), or montbretias, do not have the grandeur of lilies or cannas, but they are undemanding plants that are useful for late-summer plantings, because their funnel-shaped flowers, which are carried on arching spikes, open over a long period. *Crocosmia × crocosmiiflora* 'Jackanapes' produces brilliant light and dark orange flowers on 2-ft. (60 cm) stems, and *Crocosmia × crocosmiiflora* 'Solfatare' has flowers that are apricot tinged with yellow.

Daisy-flowered perennials are always popular, and some of the best flower in late summer. Among the best orange-flowered ones is *Helenium* 'Moerheim Beauty' (Zones 3–8), with burnt orange petals and dark brown centers. The flowers grow on branching stems up to 3 ft. (90 cm) tall and stay for weeks. Other handsome heleniums have red, yellow and bronze flowers. All make good border plants, suitable for growing in sunny spots. *Helenium* 'Blütentisch' (Zones 3–8) has rich yellow flowers flecked with brown; *Helenium* 'Butterpat' (Zones 3–8) has butter-yellow flowers; and *Helenium* 'Bruno' (Zones 3–8) has rusty-red blooms.

Dahlias were out of fashion for a long time, but now many are being grown again, especially those in rich, vibrant colors. *Dahlia* 'David Howard' (Zones 9–11) is a stunning cultivar, whose flowers are crowded with apricot orange petals, which are darker in the center. It grows on 30-in. (75 cm) stems and has dark green leaves tinged with black. (*Continued on page 153.*)

GOOD COMPANIONS

The striking orange, Turk's-cap flowers of *Lilium henryi* (1) (Z. 5–8) stand out among golden, tufted grasses, such as *Stipa gigantea* (2) (Z. 8–10) (see also page 67).

The deep red flowers of *Penstemon* 'Port Wine' (3) (Z. 6–9) (see also page 49) look very striking set against the bronze-chocolate foliage of *Eupatorium rugosum* 'Chocolate' (4) (Z. 5–8).

151

Lysimachia atropurpurea 'Beaujolais' • *Penstemon* 'Raven' • *Phlox paniculata* 'Amethyst' • *Potentilla atrosanguinea* •

Kniphofias

Red-hot pokers, or kniphofias (Zones 6–9), are statuesque plants with torchlike flower heads carried on rigid stems above grass- or straplike leaves; they are much loved by bees. The species, both evergreen and deciduous, are denizens of tropical and southern Africa, but because they have been extensively hybridized, there are numerous elegant and interesting cultivars. Their small flowers are tubular or cylindrical, in colors varying from red and orange to yellow, cream, white, and greenish white, and they are grouped together in long racemes—these are the characteristic torches. The torches vary enormously in shape and size; they may be long and thin, short and rounded, tapering, bulbous, or straight-sided, and in every size, from 2–16 in. (5 to 40 cm). Some are two-toned in shades of red and yellow. The majority bloom in late summer or fall, although some flower from late spring and early summer.

Red-hot pokers add an aura of drama wherever they are planted, in groups in large plantings or individually in meadow-style plantings. They thrive in sun or partial shade, in any good, humus-rich and well-drained soil. Young plants are vulnerable in their first winter, so should be mulched.

The orange-red flower heads of *Kniphofia rooperi* are borne on robust stems, 4 ft. (1.2 m) tall. They later turn to orange-yellow.

Kniphofia 'Erecta' has coral flowers, which turn upward once the buds have opened; it reaches 3 ft. (90 cm) high.

Kniphofia 'Victoria', which is one of the taller cultivars at up to 6 ft. (1.8 m) high, bears a lemon yellow flower spike.

Kniphofia 'Royal Standard', the classic, up to 40 in. (1 m) tall, has pale yellow buds and red flowers.

OTHER GOOD KNIPHOFIAS

Kniphofia 'Bees' Sunset' has yellowish orange flowers; 3 ft. (90 cm) high.

Kniphofia 'Green Jade' is evergreen, with pale creamy green flowers that fade to white; 5 ft. (1.5 m) high.

Kniphofia 'Little Maid' has white flowers that are yellow in bud; 2 ft. (60 cm) high. (See also page 44.)

Kniphofia 'Percy's Pride' has canary yellow flowers; 4 ft. (1.2 m) high.

Kniphofia thomsonii var. *thomsonii* has fewer flowers than most varieties on each "poker," in coral or yellow-orange; 3 ft. (90 cm) high.

Dahlia 'Nargold'

Helianthus 'Loddon Gold'

Rudbeckia fulgida

Achillea 'Walther Funcke'

Dahlia 'Nargold' (Zones 9–11) (see also page 65) is a spiky dahlia with pinkish orange, double flowers with slightly pointed petals. In an all-orange planting, its rounded shape would contrast well with the thick, upright flower spikes of the exotic red ginger lily *Hedychium coccineum* 'Tara' (Zones 8–11), which produces racemes of pale orange flowers with darker stamens and styles. The flowers grow on stems that may reach 5 ft. (1.5 m), but are usually much shorter. This ginger lily withstands temperatures down to about 23°F (–5°C) but, like all ginger lilies, needs protection from cold winds. Ginger lilies like any good, well-drained soil, and are happy in sun or partial shade.

The flattened, disklike flower heads of **yarrows** are great foils for ginger lilies, grasses, and tall flower spires. Two attractive orange cultivars are *Achillea* 'Terracotta' (see page 47) and *Achillea* 'Walther Funcke' (Zones 3–8).

YELLOW-FLOWERED PERENNIALS

While we associate spring with an explosion of yellows, late summer is also a yellow season, as this is when many daisylike, yellow-flowered perennials bloom. None are more imposing than annual sunflowers, with their large flower heads that resemble miniature suns. Today, thanks to plant breeders, there are also annual sunflowers with orange, red, brown, and bronze flowers. But for those who prefer to grow perennials, there are some good cultivars, such as *Helianthus* 'Lemon Queen' (Zones 4–9), whose flowers have lemon yellow petals and darker centers; the flowers, which appear from late summer to mid-autumn, grow on 5½-ft. (1.7 m) stems above dark green, heavily veined leaves and may not need staking. *Helianthus* 'Loddon Gold' (Zones 4–8) has double, golden yellow flowers on 5-ft. (1.5 m) stems.

Many late-summer, daisy-flowered perennials are natives of North, Central, and South America and have become denizens of North American gardens. In addition to helianthus, **rudbeckias**, **heleniums**, **heliopsis**, and **echinaceas**, have all become firm favorites. *Rudbeckia laciniata* 'Herbstsonne' (Zones 4–9) has attractive flowers with sunny yellow petals that curve backward and green centers gathered into a dome; the flowers grow on 6-ft. (2 m) stems. *Rudbeckia fulgida* (black-eyed Susan) and its cultivars (Zones 4–8) are always popular. *Rudbeckia fulgida* var. *sullivantii* 'Goldsturm' has golden flowers with blackish brown centers borne on 2-ft. (60 cm) stems. The flower heads of the double-flowered *Rudbeckia laciniata* 'Goldquelle' are packed with lemon yellow petals and grow on stems 3 ft. (90 cm) high.

The daisylike flowers of **heliopsis** (oxeyes) (Zones 4–8) resemble those of sunflowers, and their normally yellow, solitary blooms grow on stiff, branching stems. *Heliopsis helianthoides* var. *scabra* 'Sommersonne' bears single or semidouble flowers with brown centers and dark gold-yellow petals, which may be tinged with orange-yellow; the stems are 3 ft. (90 cm) high. *Heliopsis helianthoides* var. *scabra* 'Light of Loddon' has semidouble, bright yellow

Heliopsis helianthoides var. scabra 'Sommersonne'

YELLOW-FLOWERED SHRUBS

Although it is yellow-flowered perennials that steal the show in late summer, there are some shrubs with yellow flowers that are also worth growing. *Potentilla fruticosa* 'Primrose Beauty' (1) (Z. 2–7) is a great standby, as it has grayish green leaves and pale primrose flowers. Like potentillas, shrubby hypericums can be relied upon to provide flowers over a long period. *Hypericum* 'Hidcote' (2) (Z. 6–7) has cup-shaped flowers and is a dense evergreen, which grows up to 4 ft. (1.2 m); *Hypericum* × *inodorum* 'Elstead' (Z. 7–9), a deciduous cultivar, has small, star-shaped flowers followed by large pinkish red fruits; *Hypericum calycinum* (Z. 6–9) has bright yellow flowers and dark green leaves and makes attractive ground cover in shady sites, as it grows up to only 16 in. (40 cm).

A warm wall or a sunny, sheltered spot is needed to grow *Cytisus battandieri* (3) (Z. 8–9) successfully. This late summer-flowering deciduous broom has decorative silvery gray leaves and candles of bright yellow flowers with a strong pineapple scent. A mature specimen can reach 15 x 15 ft (5 x 5 m).

Oenothera fruticosa (Zones 4–8) is an evening primrose with deep yellow, saucer-shaped flowers, which appear during daylight from late spring to late summer, and *Achillea filipendulina* 'Gold Plate' (Zones 2–9) and *Achillea* 'Moonshine' (Zones 2–9) both have the disklike flower heads of the yarrows, in dark gold and pale yellow, respectively.

Euphorbia schillingii (see Good Companions, page 127), *Euphorbia sikkimensis* (Zones 7–9), *Alchemilla mollis* (Zones 4–7), and its much smaller relative *Alchemilla conjucta* (Zones 3–7) all produce airy clusters of yellow flowers into late summer and are perfect for growing among daisies and other perennials at the front of plantings.

For scent, grow the late summer flowering lily *Lilium* Golden Splendor Group (Zones 5–10), which has large, trumpet-shaped flowers on sturdy 6-ft. (2 m) stems. This lily is a stately plant, as is *Angelica archangelica* (Zones 4–8), an umbellifer, like a huge Queen Anne's Lace, with greenish yellow flowers on thick stems, also 6 ft. (2 m) tall. This perennial dies after flowering, so many grow it as a biennial. (See page 100.)

Achillea filipendulina 'Gold Plate'

flowers with domed, yellow centers, on 3½-ft. (1.1 m) branched stems. The leaves are a darker green than most cultivars'. *Heliopsis helianthoides* var. *scabra* 'Incomparabilis' (Zones 4–8) has double orange-yellow flower heads.

Inulas (Zones 4–8) also have yellow flower heads, but their daisies are flat with narrow petals. *Inula magnifica* has bright yellow flower heads on 6-ft. (1.8 m) stems, and those of *Inula hookeri* are a paler yellow on shorter stems, 30 in. (75 cm) high. All these daisylike flowers look enchanting among grasses and other perennials whose flowers have different shapes. In an all-yellow planting, **evening primroses** and **yarrows** would make attractive companions for them.

Alchemilla mollis

BLUE-FLOWERED SHRUBS *Caryopteris* × *clandonensis* • *Ceanothus* × *delileanus* 'Gloire de Versailles' •

Geranium wallichianum 'Buxton's Variety'

Echinops ritro

Eryngium bourgatii Graham Stuart Thomas's selection

Agapanthus 'Blue Giant'

BLUE-FLOWERED PLANTS

Some blue-flowered perennials flower for long periods in late summer. The beautiful deep blue- and white-flowered *Geranium wallichianum* 'Buxton's Variety' (Zones 7–8), and *Geranium* 'Rozanne' (Zones 5–8), with its purplish blue flowers, both flower for long periods, and the undemanding *Echinops bannaticus* (Zones 3–9) and *Echinops ritro* (globe thistle) (Zones 6–7) display their drumstick flower heads in grayish blue and steel blue, respectively, for weeks in late summer. Attractive as these are, the pinhead flowers of **eryngiums**, with their decorative spiny bracts and rosettes of basal leaves, are even more eye-catching. The degree of blueness of their flowers and bracts varies: *Eryngium giganteum* (Miss Willmott's Ghost, see page 57) has silver bracts surrounding a core of steel blue flowers, while in *Eryngium × oliverianum* (Zones 5–8) the flowers and bracts are both silvery blue. *Eryngium alpinum* (Zones 4–8) has similarly colored flowers and bracts but its bracts are finely divided and soft to the touch. *Eryngium × tripartitum* (Zones 5–7) produces very much smaller, lavender blue flowers

with fine, linear, grayish blue bracts, and *Eryngium bourgatii* Graham Stuart Thomas's selection (Zones 3–8) has veined foliage and silver-blue flowers and bracts, carried on 18-in. (45 cm) stems (the other eryngiums grow up to 3 ft./90 cm). Eryngiums keep their color when dried, and mix well with the lavender-blue, cloudlike flower panicles of *Limonium latifolium* (sea lavender) (Zones 4–8), which appear in late summer on branching, wiry stems. Most geraniums, eryngiums, and limoniums are medium-sized plants, so are best in the front or middle of a bed. In contrast, *Cynara cardunculus* (cardoon) (Zones 6–9) is a giant perennial with large, silvered, lobed leaves and thistlelike, violet-blue flower heads, which grow on stems 6 ft. (1.8 m) tall in late summer. With its architectural lines and stature, it makes a fine specimen or focal point for a large planting. (See page 57.)

Intensely blue flowers, such as those of *Salvia patens* (Zones 8–10) and *Salvia uliginosa* (Zones 6–9), are always welcome in a garden in late summer. The Australian perennial *Parahebe perfoliata* (Zones 7–10) also has rich blue flowers that appear at this time of year; tiny and saucer-shaped, they are carried in spikes on 30-in. (75 cm) stems and nestle among its

glaucous, rounded leaves. As it has a cascading habit, this is a perfect plant for tumbling over walls or for planting in a gravel bed. It prefers full sun in well-drained, poor to moderately fertile soil.

Agapanthus, one of the stars of the late-summer garden, also need sun to flourish, but need fertile, well-drained soil to produce their spherical clusters of bell-shaped or tubular, blue or white flowers. The species *Agapanthus inapertus* (Zones 8–9) has the darkest, midnight blue blooms. Many good deciduous agapanthus cultivars are available, such as *Agapanthus* 'Blue Giant' (Zones 7–9) and *Agapanthus* 'Midnight Blue' (Zones 7–9), all of which are hardier than evergreen kinds such as *Agapanthus africanus* (Zones 9–10). Agapanthus grow particularly well in pots, but the less hardy ones may need to be overwintered indoors.

• *Ceratostigma willmottianum* • *Hibiscus syriacus* 'Oiseau Bleu' • *Perovskia* 'Blue Spire' •

PINK-FLOWERED PLANTS

The pinks of late summer are not as numerous as those of early summer, but there are some first-rate perennials, shrubs, and bulbs among them. **Astrantias** are perennials with an understated but elegant charm. Their first flush of pincushion-like flower heads comes in early to midsummer, but they perform right through to the end of

Astrantia 'Hadspen Blood'

summer. *Astrantia maxima* (Zones 5–7) has pointed, rich pink bracts surrounding slightly paler pink tiny flowers. Its flower clusters grow on 2-ft. (60 cm) stems above medium green, deeply lobed leaves. Its cousin *Astrantia major* (Zones 5–8) grows up to 2 ft. (60 cm) and has whitish pink bracts that form a collar for the green, pink, or purple flowers. (See pages 54, 70.) *Astrantia* 'Hadspen Blood' (Zones 5–8) has deep red flower heads, and *Astrantia major* ssp. *involucrata* 'Shaggy' (Zones 5–8) has elongated bracts. Astrantias, with their small, rounded flower heads, make good foils for plants with spiky flowers, such as

those of **liatris**, which have tubular flowers tightly packed into spires. These North American perennials are unusual in that their flower spikes open from the top downward. *Liatris spicata* (see page 74) has bluish pink or white flowers, but its cultivars may be white, purple, or bluish purple.

Physostegias (obedient plants) are also North American perennials from moist, sunny sites; the "obedient" sobriquet refers to the flowers' property of remaining in a new position if they are moved on the stalks. *Physostegia virginiana* (Zones 4–9) has deep purple, lilac-pink or white flowers carried in small, pointed spires; *Physostegia virginiana* 'Vivid' is a striking cultivar with purplish pink flowers carried on 2-ft. (60 cm) stems. **Linarias** are grown for their snapdragon-like flowers in a range of colors and *Linaria purpurea* (Zones 4–7) produces slender spires of violet-purple flowers from early summer to early fall; its popular cultivar *Linaria purpurea* 'Canon Went' has pale pink flowers. Both physostegias and linarias mix well with daisies, and in a pink planting, these could be the flowers of *Echinacea purpurea* (see Good Companions, below, and page 75), with

Echinacea purpurea 'Rubinstern'

purplish pink petals and golden brown, domed centers, on 2 to 3-ft. (60 cm to 1 m) stems. It has some good cultivars, such as the deep pink to carmine red *Echinacea purpurea* 'Rubinstern'.

Chelones also flower in late summer and have two-lipped, pink, white, or purple flowers. A dark pink species is *Chelone obliqua* (Zones 3–8), which is borne on strong 2-ft. (60 cm) stems. Both chelones and echinaceas are good partners for *Verbena bonariensis* (Zones 8–9), a perennial from South America with lilac or purple flowers, which appear over a long period from midsummer to early fall; the flowers are in little domed clusters and are carried on long, thin stems, up to 6 ft. (2 m) tall. (See Good Companions, below.)

GOOD COMPANIONS

The showy, tubular dark pink or purple flowers of *Chelone obliqua* (1) (Z. 3–8) are complemented by the lighter, lilac-purple flower heads of *Verbena bonariensis* (2) (Z. 8–9).

Linaria purpurea (3) (Z. 4–7), with its erect spires of purple flowers, is a foil to the solitary, daisylike, purplish pink flowers of *Echinacea purpurea* (4) (Z. 4–8) (see also page 75).

PINK-FLOWERED SUMMER BULBS *Crinum* × *powellii* • *Colchicum alpinum* • *Lilium speciosum* •

Some striking pink-flowered shrubs for late summer can be used to add interest and height to large plantings. **Abelia × grandiflora** and its cultivars (Zones 6–9) flower over a very long period, and their leaves color well, too. **Hibiscus** flower for weeks at the end of summer and add a touch of the exotic. **Hibiscus syriacus** 'Woodbridge' (Zones 5–8) has clear, rich pink flowers with darker centers, and grows slowly into a mature specimen of 10 × 6 ft. (3 × 2 m). The

Escallonia 'Iveyi'

Abelia × grandiflora

Romneya coulteri

Chamerion angustifolium 'Album'

Hibiscus syriacus 'Woodbridge'

indigoferas also come from exotic climes, and **Indigofera heterantha** (Zones 6–10) is an elegant shrub with deep purplish pink, pealike flowers, which appear from early summer to early fall. It looks marvelous growing among perennials and makes a pretty backdrop for later-flowering violet or purple-flowered clematis, such as **Clematis** 'Etoile Violette' (Zones 5–9).

WHITE-FLOWERED PLANTS

Anyone looking for white-flowered plants for late summer will not be disappointed, as there are some gems among them: trees as beautiful as **eucryphias** (Zones 8–10), with their white, saucer-shaped, fragrant flowers, and **Franklinia alatamaha** (Zones 5–9), with its scented blooms; and various elegant shrubs, such as the evergreen **Escallonia** 'Iveyi' (see also page 61) and **Luma apiculata** (Zones 9–10), with its peeling brown and cream bark and cup-shaped flowers. Some splendid yuccas, including **Yucca gloriosa** (Zones 6–9), **Yucca flaccida** 'Ivory' (Zones 4–9) and **Yucca whipplei** (Zones 8–10), produce their towers of blooms above dramatic, swordlike leaves in late summer. In total contrast, **Romneya coulteri** (tree poppy) (Zones 7–8) has an ethereal beauty, with fragile, tissue paper, cup-shaped flowers and finely divided, grayish green leaves.

Among the perennials, the white willowherb **Chamerion angustifolium** 'Album' (formerly called *Epilobium angustifolium* f. *album*) (Zones 2–9), with its spires of saucer-shaped flowers, is a beautiful addition for a large planting where its wandering ways can be accommodated. Another useful plant is **Eupatorium rugosum** (Zones 5–8), a North American perennial that produces clusters of flowers, looking like cotton balls, from midsummer to early fall. **Sanguisorba canadensis** (Canadian burnet) (Zones 3–7) has spiky, bottlebrush-like flower heads on 6-ft. (1.8 m) stems, while the somewhat rampant **Lysimachia clethroides** (Asian loosestrife) (Zones 4–8) is a shorter plant with flowers in curving spires, which resemble shepherds' crooks. Its cousin **Lysimachia ephemerum** (Zones 6–8), which is better behaved, produces thin spires of flowers on 40-in. (1 m) stems in midsummer. These loosestrifes should be grown in moist, humus-rich, but well-drained soil that does not dry out at all.

157

Salvias

Culinary sage will, no doubt, be familiar to many readers, but there are lots of other kinds of sage (*Salvia*) that are well worth growing, too. Salvias have brilliantly colored flowers in reds, blues, purples, pinks, cream, and white, and are highly valuable to gardeners, as they grow happily in various situations, from sunny borders to dappled woodland and wild-style meadow plantings. There are about 900 species in the genus, which includes annuals, biennials, herbaceous and evergreen perennials, and shrubs. Most flower in summer or fall, but there are also salvias that flower in spring and even winter.

The leaves and stems of salvias may be hairy, woolly, or silver, and many species are aromatic. Leaf shapes vary, but a characteristic of all species is that their tubular, bell- or funnel-shaped flowers open out into two lips at the tip. The flowers' upper lip is hooded and upright, and the lower one, with two lobes, is flatter. Although most species produce colorful flowers, some also have colorful, leaflike bracts. Some species produce flowers in clusters, known as panicles, and others in whorls around the flowering stems. The hardy salvias should be grown in light, moderately fertile, humus-rich, moist, but well-drained soil. Those with silver or hairy leaves need full sun and sharp drainage and require protection from cold winds and from excessive wet in winter.

Annual sages, or perennials grown as annuals—for instance, *Salvia splendens* and its cultivars—have brilliant clear colors and so bring a dazzling quality to borders and containers. The more tender species and cultivars—for example, *Salvia* × *jamensis* 'La Luna' (Zones 7–10), which has creamy yellow flowers but is not always frost-hardy—fare well when grown in pots. The hardy annual *Salvia viridis* (clary) has pink, purple, and white bracts, and there are some excellent cultivars with even more pronounced bract colors, which make excellent cut and dried flowers.

Salvia sclarea var. *turkestanica* white-bracted is a biennial whose white flowers appear from spring to summer. It grows to 40 in. (1 m). (See also page 55.)

Salvia lavandulifolia, known as lavender sage or Spanish sage (Z. 5–9), as it is the only sage used in cooking in Spain, is a perennial with blue-violet flowers in summer and gray to white, furry leaves. (See also page 53.)

Salvia farinacea 'Victoria' (mealy cup sage) (Z. 8–10), a perennial that is usually grown as an annual, has whitish stems and deep blue flowers carried in long, tapering, but densely packed spikes on 2-ft. (60 cm) stems from summer to fall. Its leaves are glossy, medium green, and lance shaped.

OTHER GOOD SALVIAS

Salvia argentea (Z. 5–8) is an attractive biennial or short-lived perennial that is worth growing for its leaves alone; they grow in rosettes and are woolly and distinctly silvered. Its white or pale pink flowers, on 3-ft. (90 cm) stems, appear in midsummer and late summer.

Salvia fulgens (syn. *Salvia cardinalis*) (Z. 9–10) is a woody perennial or sub-shrub that produces bright red flowers in short spikes in summer. The lower lips of the flowers are particularly downy. The flowers grow on 40-in. (1 m) stems.

Salvia guaranitica 'Blue Enigma' is (Z. 8–10) a sub-shrub or perennial that produces fragrant, rich royal blue flowers with striking green calyxes, arranged in spikes on 5-ft. (1.5 m) stems, from late summer until late autumn.

Salvia involucrata 'Bethellii' (Z. 9–10) is a perennial with rich crimson flowers in late summer and mid-autumn. The dark green leaves are velvety and hairy, and the flowers grow on 5-ft. (1.5 m) stems.

Salvia microphylla var. *microphylla* (Z. 7–9) is an evergreen shrub or shrubby perennial with soft green leaves and cherry red flowers, which appear in fall and grow in racemes on 4-ft. (1.2 m) stems.

Salvia patens (Z. 8–10) is a perennial with hairy, medium green leaves and pure blue flowers in loosely arranged racemes on stems up to 2 ft. (60 cm) tall. The flowers appear from midsummer to mid-fall. *Salvia patens* 'Cambridge Blue' has paler blue flowers than the species.

Salvia pratensis Haematodes Group (Z. 4–8) is a short-lived perennial that produces rosettes of dark green, wavy-margined leaves, from which its bluish violet flowers, with paler throats and hairy upper lips, emerge. The flowers grow on 3-ft. (90 cm) stems in early and midsummer.

Salvia uliginosa (bog sage) (Z. 6–9), a perennial sage, produces short racemes of clear, medium blue flowers on thin, branching stems up to 5 ft. (1.5 m) tall, from late summer to mid-fall. It needs moist soil and full sun.

Salvia nemorosa 'Ostfriesland' (Z. 5–8) is a neat, clump-forming perennial. From summer to fall it carries densely packed, deep blue-purple flower heads on erect, branching stems, 18 in. (45 cm) high.

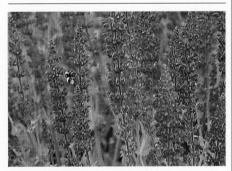

Salvia × *sylvestris* 'Mainacht' (Z. 4–8) is an erect, branching perennial with large, indigo blue flowers in long, tapering spires, on stems up to 28 in. (70 cm) tall. The flowers appear from early to midsummer. (See also page 140.)

The glorious yellow-orange foliage of the Japanese maple *Acer japonicum* 'Vitifolium'.

Fall

Trees weighed down by fruit, early morning mist hovering above the landscape, cobwebs festooning hedges, and a chill in the air confirm that summer is drawing to a close and autumn is under way. Nature may be pulling in its horns with temperatures falling and days shortening, but gardens are glorious, with stunning reds, golds, and oranges, complemented by rich browns and evergreen shrubs. Inevitably, the drama will come to an end, so enjoy it while you can.

Fall is when trees show off their swansong finery, and shrubs smothered with berries take center stage. There are perennials and bulbs that start blooming now, but most color in the garden is supplied by late summer flowering perennials that go on producing flowers well into autumn, and by ornamental grasses (see pages 170–71). Fall may be the season of decay, but it is also the most brilliant season in the garden.

AUTUMN REDS

The reds of autumn are numerous, but none are more glorious than those of the leaves of **Acer rubrum** (red or scarlet maple) and its cultivars (Zones 3–9). This maple is a native of eastern North America, and is one of the trees that contribute to the breathtaking autumn color of the woods in New England. Good cultivars include **Acer**

Acer rubrum 'Schlesingeri'

rubrum 'Schlesingeri', with foliage that turns dark red in early fall; *Acer rubrum* 'Scanlon', which produces orange-red autumn leaves; and *Acer rubrum* 'October Glory', which has shiny leaves that turn a rich red shade in early fall. These striking maples can reach 50–70 ft. (15–20 m) tall, with a spread of 15–30 ft. (5–10m), so a large garden is needed for them.

By contrast, *Acer palmatum* and its cultivars (Zones 6–8) are well suited to small spaces. *Acer palmatum* 'Bloodgood' is a choice cultivar with beautiful dark red, deeply incised leaves that become rich bluish red in fall. It seldom grows larger than 15 x 15 ft. (5 x 5 m) and so would make a good specimen for a small garden, if sheltered from cold winds. (See also page 49.) Another elegant Japanese maple with dark red leaves in fall is *Acer japonicum* 'Vitifolium', a spreading tree that reaches 30 x 30 ft. (10 x 10 m), with big, fan-shaped leaves.

Acers do not hold the patent for fine red foliage in fall. *Liquidambar styraciflua* (sweet gum) (Zones 5–9), a largish tree of about 80 x 40 ft. (25 x 12m), has leaves that turn bright red, orange, and purple, and there are cultivars with other permutations of autumn color. Liquidambars grow and color best in acid or neutral soil in full sun. Acid soil is also needed to grow *Quercus coccinea* (scarlet oak) (Zones 4–8) successfully. This North American oak is a rounded tree, similar in size to *Liquidambar styraciflua*. Its shiny dark green leaves have whiskered lobes and turn scarlet in fall; those of its cultivar *Quercus coccinea* 'Splendens' become darker and richer than the species.

Nyssa sylvatica (black gum or tupelo) (Zones 3–9) is another elegant, large tree, which is splendid for a large garden. It comes into its own in fall, when the leaves turn gorgeous shades of red, orange, and gold.

Acer palmatum 'Bloodgood'

Quercus coccinea 'Splendens'

Liquidambar styraciflua

Nyssa sylvatica

Whereas oaks, liquidambars, and black gums are beautiful trees for larger gardens, *Sorbus aucuparia* (European mountain ash) (Zones 3–7) suits smaller gardens, as it seldom grows taller than 40 x 20 ft. (12 x 6 m); its leaves turn red or yellow after its reddish orange berries ripen. *Sorbus commixta* (Zones 6–8) is a particularly dramatic feature in fall, as its pinnate leaves, 10 in. (25 cm) long, turn rich red, then yellow and purple, and it produces numerous bright red

berries. Crab apples also produce large numbers of fruits, and some of these are gleaming red. Some of the most eye-catching belong to *Malus pumila* 'Cowichan' (Zones 4–8), which produces round, deep bluish red fruit, about 1½ in. (4 cm) in diameter. *Malus × robusta* 'Red Sentinel' (Zones 4–7) has smaller dark red rounded fruit and *Malus* 'John Downie' (Zones 4–8) has egg-shaped scarlet and orange fruits, which make excellent crab-apple jelly.

Sorbus commixta

There are also some shrubs that are worth growing for their red autumn leaves alone. *Euonymus alatus* (Zones 3–8) has dark green leaves that turn a breath-taking rich dark red in fall. This euonymus is a bushy, dense shrub, which is rarely taller than 6 x 10 ft. (2 x 3 m), whereas *Euonymus europaeus* 'Red Cascade' (Zones 3–7) is a larger, more spreading shrub. It has scalloped leaves that turn red in fall, providing an eye-catching backdrop for its dazzling deep pink fruits with their bright orange seed arils. *Euonymus latifolius* (Zones 6–9) has finely scalloped leaves that turn crimson in late fall, and pendent red fruits with prominent wings and orange seed arils. Since it grows to 10 x 10 ft. (3 x 3 m), it is ideal for a large shrub border.

A large border or a woodland setting is perfect for the larger **cotoneasters**, many of which produce striking berries. *Cotoneaster frigidus* 'Cornubia' (Zones 7–9), a semi-evergreen shrub, is particularly handsome, producing masses of scarlet berries in large clusters and dark green leaves; left to its own devices, it reaches 20 x 20 ft. (6 x 6 m). Cotoneasters are easy to grow, and there are cultivars to suit every taste.

Berberis are also adaptable plants, and some have good autumn color—for example, *Berberis thunbergii* f. *atropurpurea* 'Dart's Red Lady'

RED CLIMBERS FOR FALL

One of autumn's pleasures is watching climbers, such as *Parthenocissus tricuspidata* (Boston ivy) (1) (Z. 4–8) and *Parthenocissus quinquefolia* (Virginia creeper) (Z. 3–10) acquire their magnificent fall colors. Despite its common name, Boston ivy is a native of China, Japan, and Korea, and its bright green, 8 in. (20 cm) long, lobed leaves turn scarlet to purple in fall. Its cultivar *Parthenocissus tricuspidata* 'Veitchii' is more restrained than the species, and its leaves become a dark, sultry reddish purple before they fall.

Rich red is the color of the leaves of the Virginia creeper in fall. Characteristically, they are 5 in. (12 cm) long and composed of five ovate leaflets with toothed edges. Even more spellbinding autumn color is found in the large, textured leaves of the vine *Vitis coignetiae* (2). They are heart-shaped, 12 in. (30 cm) long, dark green with felted undersides, and have attractively roughened upper surfaces caused by the indentations of the veins. When they turn bright orange-red in fall they are a magnificent sight, especially if this climber is allowed to reach its full height of 50 ft. (15 m). *Vitis vinifera* 'Purpurea' (Z. 6–8), which climbs to 22 ft. (7 m), has more discreet charms, as its 6-in. (15 cm) plum-colored, lobed leaves turn dark purple in fall.

(Zones 4–8), with very dark reddish purple leaves that turn bright red in fall. **Smoke bushes** are also excellent for autumn color—for example, the bushy shrub *Cotinus* 'Grace' (Zones 5–8) (see also pages 69, 149) turns bright, translucent red in late fall.

Sedums are very welcome in late summer and fall, as their disklike flower heads are decorative, and some, such as *Sedum spectabile* (Zones 4–8), attract bees and butterflies. One fine cultivar is *Sedum telephium* ssp. *maximum* 'Atropurpureum' (Zones 3–8), with dark purple leaves and stems and bluish red flower heads or cymes (see Good Companions, opposite).

Handsome as this perennial is, for sheer shock value it can't compete with the moisture-loving perennial *Darmera*

peltata (Zones 7–8). This plant undergoes a metamorphosis when its huge, rounded and lobed, dark green leaves carried on 6-ft. (2 m) stems, turn bright red in fall. It looks spectacular growing beside a stream or pond.

Cotinus 'Grace'

Sedum telephium ssp. maximum 'Atropurpureum'

TREES WITH RED, YELLOW, AND ORANGE AUTUMN LEAVES *Acer circinatum* • *Aesculus flava* •

ORANGE LEAVES AND FRUIT

Celebrate fall with the quintessential color of the season: orange. Many trees boast foliage that turns orange as autumn arrives. The maple *Acer triflorum* (Zones 4–8), which grows to 30 x 25 ft. (10 x 8 m), carries medium green leaves, which become discernibly orange in fall, and *Acer saccharum* (sugar maple) (Zones 3–8) has fall leaves in burnt orange, red, or yellow. It reaches 75 x 45 ft. (23 x 14 m).

Perhaps the most spectacular orange autumn leaves belong to *Sorbus sargentiana* (Zones 5–7). They are pinnate, 14 in. (35 cm) long, and turn bright orange. This sorbus also has attractive, crimson, sticky buds in fall. It grows up to 30 x 30 ft. (10 x 10 m) and performs best in acid or neutral soil.

Orange fruits are less common than red, but some trees and shrubs produce them, although they are often tinged with red or yellow. Some crab apples produce orange fruit, namely *Malus × zumi* var. *calocarpa* 'Professor Sprenger' (in dark orange-red) (Zones 4–7), *Malus tschonoskii* (Zones 4–8) (yellowish green flushed with red), and *Malus* 'Butterball' (orange-yellow) (Zones 4–8). Other good plants include *Cotoneaster simonsii* (Zones 5–7), with egg-shaped, orange fruit in fall, and *Pyracantha* 'Golden Charmer' (Zones 6–9) and *Pyracantha* 'Golden Dome' (Zones 6–9), with orange-red and orange-yellow berries respectively.

Attractive as all these fruits are, perhaps none is as showstopping as those of the popular, though invasive, perennial *Physalis alkekengi* (Zones 4–7), known as Chinese lantern. With its bright orange or scarlet berries, encased in papery orange-red bracts or "lanterns," this cottage-garden favorite needs no introduction; and the color of its lanterns makes it a good candidate for an autumn planting scheme. (See Good Companions, left, and page 46.)

Sorbus sargentiana

Malus × zumi var. *calocarpa* 'Professor Sprenger'

Pyracantha 'Golden Charmer'

Physalis alkekengi

GOOD COMPANIONS

The bright orange berries and bracts of *Physalis alkekengi* (Chinese lantern) (1) (Z. 4–7) complement the purple-leaved *Sedum telephium* ssp. *maximum* 'Atropurpureum' (2) (Z. 3–8) and the grass *Panicum virgatum* 'Heavy Metal' (3) (Z. 6–8) (see also page 171), with purple leaves in fall and orange plumes in winter.

Pink-flowered Japanese anemones, like *Anemone hupehensis* var. *japonica* 'Prinz Heinrich' (4) (Z. 6–9), mix well with *Actaea simplex* Atropurpurea Group (5) (Z. 3–8), which has thin spires of white flowers.

• *Cercidiphyllum japonicum* • *Parrotia persica* • *Rhus typhina* 'Dissecta' • *Sorbus* 'Joseph Rock' • *Zelkova serrata* •

Acer cappadocicum

Ginkgo biloba

AUTUMN YELLOWS

There are some glorious yellows to be enjoyed in fall in the form of leaves, berries, fruits, and flowers. Moreover, numerous ornamental grasses have flower spikelets that turn yellow as they ripen (see pages 170–71).

Especially fine yellow autumn leaves are found on the two trees *Acer cappadocicum* (Caucasian maple) (Zones 6–8) and *Ginkgo biloba* (maidenhair tree) (Zones 3–9). *Acer cappadocicum* is a spreading tree that grows up to 70 x 50 ft. (20 x 15 m) and has broadly ovate, light green leaves that become bright yellow before they fall. *Ginkgo biloba* has beautiful fan-shaped, yellowish green leaves, 5 in. (12 cm) across, that turn golden yellow in fall. Ginkgos are large and columnar, and make good landscape trees.

Some of the best yellow berries of the season are produced by *Cotoneaster salicifolius* 'Rothschildianus' (Zones 6–8), an evergreen cotoneaster with narrow, lance-shaped, pale green leaves, that grows to 15 x 15 ft. (5 x 5 m). It carries spherical, golden yellow berries that are produced for weeks in large clusters. The deciduous *Cotoneaster frigidus* 'Fructu Luteo' (Zones 7–9) bears creamy yellow berries and dull green leaves with wavy edges. It needs room to spread, as it grows up to 30 x 30 ft. (10 x 10 m) when mature.

Much less space is needed for *Viburnum opulus* 'Xanthocarpum' (Zones 3–8), though this appealing cultivar of the guelder rose is quite a vigorous shrub. It has attractive, maplelike leaves and, in fall, produces clusters of fleshy, glowing yellow berries.

Yellow crab apples, which resemble small golden eggs, are produced by *Malus* × *zumi* var. *calocarpa* 'Golden Hornet' (Zones 4–7). They brighten the

Malus × zumi var. calocarpa 'Golden Hornet'

Cotoneaster salicifolius 'Rothschildianus'

autumn garden and last for weeks after the leaves have fallen. This crab apple grows into a rounded tree, about 30 x 25 ft. (10 x 8 m), when mature.

If yellow flowers are required, there are some beautiful shrubs that start blooming in fall and may flower into winter. **Mahonias** produce sweetly scented yellow flowers—for example, *Mahonia* × *media* 'Buckland' (Zones 6–9), which has bright yellow flowers in long, arching racemes, and *Mahonia* × *media* 'Charity' (Zones 6–9), which has similarly colored flowers. Its racemes are upright when they first appear but spread as they mature. These mahonia hybrids, hardier than some of the species, are very useful for winter color. Though large if left unpruned, they can be cut back in spring if they become too tall and leggy. (See also pages 177–78.)

Witch hazels make truly excellent specimen shrubs for a winter garden, as they have decorative, spiderlike, fragrant flowers, which appear on the bare branches in winter. *Hamamelis virginiana* (Zones 3–10), although not the showiest of the family, has yellow flowers, which start appearing in fall at the same time as its leaves turn yellow; it grows slowly and is best left unpruned. (See also pages 177–79.)

The narrow, rich dark green leaves and pretty flowers of the beguiling small bulb *Sternbergia lutea* (Zones 3–9) appear simultaneously in fall. The flowers resemble rich yolk yellow

Mahonia × media 'Charity'

MORE BERRIES FOR FALL *Arbutus* × *andrachnoides* • *Cotoneaster salicifolius* 'Exburyensis' •

goblets on 6-in. (15 cm) stems. This bulb is perfect for growing in a sunny rock garden or at the front of a border that has free-draining, moderately fertile soil.

BLUES AND VIOLETS

Late summer flowering shrubs with blue or purplish blue flowers, such as *Perovskia* 'Blue Spire' (Zones 5–8), *Caryopteris* × *clandonensis* 'First Choice' (Zones 7–8), and *Ceratostigma willmottianum* (Zone 8), as well as blue- or purple-flowered perennials, such as *Salvia patens* (Zones 8–10/ann.), *Salvia uliginosa* (Zones 6–9), and *Aster* × *frikartii* 'Mönch' (Zones 5–7), continue to flower well into fall. However, some plants start producing flowers only now. *Ceanothus* 'Autumnal Blue' (Zones 9–10), an evergreen California lilac, flowers profusely in fall. It has deep sky-blue flowers and glossy, bright green leaves, and it grows to 30 ft. (10 m).

Callicarpa bodinieri var. giraldii 'Profusion'

Aster × frikartii 'Mönch'

Caryopteris × clandonensis 'First Choice'

Ceratostigma willmottianum

Aconitum carmichaelii

Aconitum carmichaelii (Zones 4–8) is a good early autumn flowering perennial, with leathery, dark green, lobed leaves and upright, densely packed spikes, which may be up to 2 ft. (60 cm) long, of blue or violet, hooded flowers carried high above the leaves, on tall stems. This monkshood has some very attractive cultivars, such as *Aconitum carmichaelii* 'Arendsii', which has rich blue flowers on branching stems, and the lavender blue *Aconitum carmichaelii* Wilsonii

Group 'Kelmscott'. Monkshoods like partial shade in moist, fertile soil.

Shade is also preferred by *Liriope muscari*, an evergreen, autumn-flowering perennial from China and Japan, but it needs acid soil that is light and moderately fertile. It has straplike leaves, up to 12 in. (30 cm) long, in rich dark green, and tiny rounded mauve or violet flowers packed into short, thick spikes on 12-in. (30 cm) stems. Liriopes make excellent ground cover under shrubs and trees. The flowers are long-lasting, and large drifts are a lovely sight.

Fall is when the deciduous shrub *Callicarpa bodinieri* var. *giraldii* 'Profusion' (Zones 6–8) looks its best, as this is when its clusters of unusual violet, beadlike berries appear. They give a new dimension to this somewhat bland shrub, with its rather dull leaves and little pink flowers in summer. This plant grows happily in sun or partial shade in a good, fertile, well-drained soil, and a mature specimen can reach 10 x 8 ft. (3 x 2.5 m).

Gentians are never bland, as most of them have quite large and very distinctive flowers in beautiful deep blues. *Gentiana sino-ornata* (Zones 6–8) is an autumn-flowering species with trumpet-shaped flowers, deep blue around their rims but striped inside with deep purplish blue and outside with greenish cream. Its flowers grow on

Gaultheria mucronata • *Hippophae rhamnoides* • *Rosa rugosa* • *Sorbus commixta* 'Embley' • *Viburnum opulus* •

3-in. (7 cm) stems amid slender dark green leaves. *Gentiana septemfida* (Zones 5–8) also flowers in fall, and has bright or purplish blue, narrow, bell-shaped flowers on 6- to 8-in. (15–20 cm) stems. The white-throated blooms are striped with darker blue. Gentians can be tricky, normally needing non-alkaline soil that is well drained but never dries out. Like most gentians, *Gentiana sino-ornata* needs protection from hot sun, while *Gentiana septemfida* prefers sun.

When it comes to blue-flowered bulbs for autumn we turn to **crocuses**, which typically flower when the ground becomes damp after rain. *Crocus speciosus* (Zones 3–8), which naturalizes well in grass, and *Crocus pulchellus* (Zones 4–8) produce prettily veined violet-blue and lilac-blue flowers, respectively. *Crocus sativus* (saffron crocus) (Zones 6–9) has dark lilac flowers with dark purple veins; it does not set seed so has to be increased by division.

AUTUMN WHITES

White is not normally associated with fall, but *Sorbus cashmiriana* (Zones 4–7) and *Sorbus prattii* (Zones 6–8)

Camellia sasanqua 'Narumigata'

Anemone × hybrida 'Honorine Jobert'

Sorbus cashmiriana

Symphoricarpos albus

both bear round white berries, and *Symphoricarpos albus* (snowberry) (Zones 3–7) also produces fleshy white berries at this time. The latter is really a plant for the wild garden, forming dense thickets with its running roots. It is extremely hardy and tolerant of poor soil conditions, but, unlike some of its more compact and refined relatives, it is not attention-grabbing.

Sasanqua camellias (Zones 7–10) produce flowers in fall and with their glossy, dark green leaves and waxy, cup-shaped blooms, have all the glamour that most snowberries lack. *Camellia sasanqua* 'Narumigata' has beautiful, single white, fragrant flowers, 1½ in. (4 cm) across, tinged with pink. Generally, camellias must be grown in acid soil that is moist and humus-rich, in positions sheltered from cold winds. Sasanqua camellias, unlike other types, will grow in sun, once established. In colder areas, this camellia would make a lovely specimen for a large container.

Just as lovely, and considerably less fussy about their growing conditions, are the **Japanese anemones**. They produce their flowers over a long period in late summer and into fall, but none are prettier than the single white blooms of *Anemone × hybrida* 'Honorine Jobert' (Zones 6–8), whose flowers are 3½ in. (9 cm) across and grow on wafting 40-in. (1 m) stems set above its medium green basal leaves. In addition to white, there are also pink Japanese anemones (see opposite).

MORE FLOWERING PLANTS FOR FALL *Aster* 'Coombe Fishacre' • *Colchicum byzantinum* •

AUTUMN PINKS

The perennial and bulb fraternities contribute most of the pinks of autumn. There are hundreds of cultivars of **chrysanthemums**, **Michaelmas daisies**, and **asters** in every tone of pink, so it is worth seeking out specialist growers when selecting them. One fine cultivar is *Aster novae-angliae* 'Pink Victor' (Zones 2–8), a sturdy, clump-forming New England aster, which produces pink flowers with yellow centers between late summer and mid-fall.

Among the **Japanese anemone** clan, there are now many cultivars with both pale and dark pink, single, semidouble, and double flowers. *Anemone hupehensis* var. *japonica* 'Prinz Heinrich' (Zones 6–9) and *Anemone hupehensis* 'Hadspen Abundance' (Zones 6–9) are fine single varieties with darker pink flowers, and *Anemone × hybrida* 'Königin Charlotte' (Zones 5–7) has semidouble, rich pink flowers, while those of *Anemone × hybrida* 'September Charm' (Zones 5–7) are single and pale pink. Japanese anemones like these grow on stems from 24–40 in. (60 to 100 cm) tall. (See Good Companions, page 163.)

We tend to think of bulbs as flowering in spring, but there are some that bloom in fall and of these, some have pink flowers. Nerines are bulbs from southern Africa, with wavy-

Nerine bowdenii

Anemone hupehensis var. japonica 'Prinz Heinrich'

Aster novae-angliae 'Pink Victor'

edged, lilylike flowers that appear in fall with, or before, their strap-shaped leaves. *Nerine bowdenii* (Zones 9–10) has exotic, funnel-shaped, shocking pink flowers grouped on 18-in. (45 cm) stems and is one of the hardier nerine species. It thrives if grown in front of a sunny, warm wall in well-drained soil.

Amaryllis belladonna (Zones 8–10) is another southern African, autumn-flowering bulb that has blowsy, showy flowers resembling large-flowered lilies. The flowers are funnel-shaped, usually in a rich rosy pink, and are scented. They are arranged in umbels with six or more blooms in each, and are carried on sturdy, upright stems, 2 ft. (60 cm) tall. *Amaryllis belladonna* may be grown in front of a warm wall, and thrives best in moderately fertile, well-drained soil. It can withstand temperatures only down

Amaryllis belladonna

to about 23°F (–5°C), so it must be grown inside in colder areas.

There are **colchicums** (autumn crocus or naked ladies; Zones 3–9) that flower in late summer, winter, and spring, as well as the more numerous autumn-flowering ones. Their flowers are similar to those of crocuses, but usually taller, in pink, lilac, and white, and most open long before the leaves; hence the reference to nakedness in their common name. *Colchicum speciosum* has pinkish mauve, goblet-shaped flowers, with yellow anthers. A beautiful white form, *Colchicum* 'Waterlily', has double, pinkish lilac blooms, and *Colchicum autumnale* (meadow saffron) bears goblet-shaped, lavender-pink flowers, and some cultivars have white. All these colchicums should be planted in full sun. They can sometimes be successfully naturalized in grass.

Colchicum autumnale

Fuchsia 'Mrs Popple' • *Indigofera heterantha* • *Kniphofia* 'Prince Igor' • *Salvia uliginosa* • *Schizostylis coccinea* 'Major' •

Cyclamen

Cyclamen grow from tubers and come from a variety of habitats, from the Mediterranean region to Iran in the east and Somalia in the south. They bear elegant, nodding flowers, between ⅜ and 1 in. (8 mm and 2.5 cm) long, on stems 2–6 in. (5–15 cm) high, depending on the species. The flowers have five twisted petals, which curl back on themselves to reveal the openings of their perianth tubes. These tiny openings look like little rounded mouths, and are often highly colored. Some flowers' petals are white, others are shades of pink, and some are carmine red. Their leaves are rounded, triangular, or heart-shaped, some with distinctive silver and gray mottling and marbling; the leaves of autumn-flowering cyclamen remain through winter into spring.

There are cyclamen flowers for every season of the year. After flowering is over, most species' flower stalks coil on the soil surface to release the seeds. The cyclamen sold around Christmas time are cultivars of *Cyclamen persicum* (Zones 9–10) that have larger and more varied colors than the species. Hardy species cyclamen may be grown in raised beds, rock gardens, or borders, and some fare well naturalized under tall trees.

CULTIVATION DETAILS

The various species have different growing requirements.

Cyclamen cilicium (Z. 7–9), *Cyclamen purpurascens* (Z. 6–7), *Cyclamen repandum* (Z. 7–8) —Plant tubers in light shade about 1–2 in. (3–5 cm) deep, in any good soil that is well drained and enriched with compost, or in an alpine house or bulb frame in loam-based compost mixed with grit and leaf mold.

Cyclamen coum (Z. 6–8), *Cyclamen hederifolium* (Z. 7–9)—Plant tubers about 1–2 in. (3–5 cm) deep, in any good soil that is well drained and enriched with compost. Grow in light shade, in positions that are dry and warm in summer.

Cyclamen graecum (Z. 7–8)—Thrives best if it is grown in containers, in a loam-based compost with added grit and leaf mould.

Cyclamen pseudibericum (Z. 6–8)—Plant tubers about 1 in. (2.5 cm) deep or at the soil surface, in loam-based compost mixed with sharp sand and leaf mold.

Cyclamen hederifolium (above)
(Z. 7–9) has large, flat tubers and
produces attractive flowers, sometimes
faintly perfumed, mostly in shades of
pink but some white, with deep red
blotches around the mouth. The flowers
appear in mid- to late fall, before the
heart-shaped leaves emerge. The
foliage is dark green and patterned
with purple undersides.

AUTUMN-FLOWERING CYCLAMEN

Cyclamen cilicium (Z. 7–9) produces
flowers in white or pink, with carmine
staining around the mouth. They appear
in fall, at the same time as the leaves.
The foliage is medium green, rounded
or heart-shaped, with distinct and
attractive silver patterning.

Cyclamen graecum (Z. 7–8) has
flowers in various pinks and carmine
red, with maroon marks around the
mouth. The flowers appear in fall, just
before the leaves, which are deep green
and heart-shaped and patterned with
silver and pale green.

WINTER- AND SPRING-FLOWERING CYCLAMEN

Cyclamen pseudibericum (Z. 6–8)
bears fragrant, magenta-red flowers,
darker at the mouths with white rims,
from winter to spring. The foliage,
which is borne at the same time as the
flowers, is heart-shaped in a silvery
dark green, and may be mottled with
silvery gray or silvery green.

Cyclamen repandum (Z. 7–8)
produces fragrant, slender bright pink
flowers together with the dark green,
heart-shaped, or triangular leaves in
mid- to late spring.

SUMMER-FLOWERING CYCLAMEN

Cyclamen purpurascens (Z. 6–7)
has strongly scented, pale and dark
carmine flowers, with broad mouths,
borne at the same time as the leaves
in midsummer and late summer. The
dark green, rounded, or heart-shaped
leaves have purplish red undersides
and are generally evergreen.
Sometimes there is faint mottling on
their upper surfaces.

Cyclamen coum (left) (Z. 6–8) produces flowers in a variety of colors, mostly shades
of pink, but including white and deep carmine red, with carmine stains around the
mouth. The flowers appear in winter and early spring, at the same time as the
handsome rounded, dark green leaves, which show variations in their markings.
(See also page 51.)

Ornamental grasses

We are surrounded by native grasses, but it is only in fairly recent times that they have become the must-have plants for many gardeners, who have recognized they are easily cultivated, reliable plants with a long season of interest.

Grasses are always elegant and bring movement into any planting of which they are a part. Their leaf and flower colors are subtle and so they are useful for all kinds of schemes, but perhaps look best when planted with those perennials that flower in late summer and fall. Echinaceas, heleniums, and rudbeckias with daisylike flower heads complement them well, and grasses provide a perfect foil for those perennials with large composite flower heads carried on stiff stems, such as eupatoriums, achilleas, sedums, and verbenas.

Miscanthus sinensis 'Morning Light' (Z. 5–9) is a clump-forming deciduous grass with panicles of pale gray, silky spikelets tinted pink in early fall on 4-ft. (1.2 m) stems. The arching foliage is finely textured green and cream. (See also page 74.)

Other suitable companions for grasses include pincushion-flowered perennials, such as astrantias, sanguisorbas, and knautias. Dotting these throughout a grass planting produces dark spots of color in the neutral colors of the grasses' flowers and foliage.

Most grasses are happy growing in average garden soils and prefer open, sunny sites. Some with blue leaves thrive in very dry conditions, for example *Festuca* 'Elijah Blue' (Zones 4–8), and many sedges and rushes tolerate very damp conditions. Sedges also tolerate some shade.

Panicum virgatum 'Heavy Metal' (Z. 6–8) has deciduous, blue-gray upright leaves, 2 ft. (60 cm) long, that turn yellow in fall and light brown in winter. It has broad panicles, 20 in. (50 cm) long, of tiny, purple-green spikelets on 40-in. (1 m) stems in fall. (See Good Companions, page 163.)

OTHER GOOD GRASSES

Briza media (Z. 4–8) This common quaking grass is a short-lived perennial with blue-green leaves and delicate purple and green flower heads that dance in the breeze. The flower heads, on 2- to 3-ft. (60–90 cm) stems, turn buff in fall.

Carex buchananii (Z. 7–9) Evergreen sedge with arching, copper-bronze leaves characteristically curled at the tips. Brown flower spikes, 1¼ in. (3 cm) long, appear on bending 20-in. (50 cm) stems in midsummer and remain until late summer.

Deschampsia cespitosa 'Goldschleier' (Z. 4–9) Evergreen grass with arching dark green leaves, 2 ft. (60 cm) long and a cloud of airy, silver-tinted, purple flower heads from early to late summer on 6-ft. (2 m) stems. The flowers change color as they age, so in fall are bright silvery yellow.

Molinia caerulea ssp. *caerulea* 'Moorflamme' (Z. 5–9) Deciduous perennial with medium green leaves that have purple hints in fall. Narrow, dense flower heads appear from spring to fall on erect 18-in. (45 cm) stems. These dark purple spikelets turn orange in winter.

Stipa tenuissima (Z. 8–9) produces dense tufts of erect, bright green, deciduous leaves. Throughout summer it bears panicles of feathery, greenish white spikelets on 2-ft. (60 cm) stems. In fall the spikelets become straw-colored. (See also page 43.)

Calamagrostis × *acutiflora* 'Overdam' (Z. 5–9) is a striking, deciduous perennial grass that has medium green linear leaves with cream edges. The leaves fade in fall to pink flushed with white, and complement the pinkish brown plumes of flowers that first appear between mid- and late summer. The seed heads last well through the winter.

Miscanthus 'Yakushima Dwarf' (Z. 5–9) is a tufted, mound-forming grass, up to 40 in. (1 m) high, which is ideal for the front of a border. The foliage is pale green with white midribs, and small pinkish buff, fluffy plumes emerge from the center of the clump from late summer on; the plumes fade to silver with age and persist well into winter.

The red stems of *Cornus alba* 'Sibirica' with the variegated foliage of *Carex oshimensis* 'Evergold'.

Winter

Winter can be cold, frosty, and even snowy. Faced with this unprepossessing picture, it is tempting to retreat indoors until the first shoots of spring appear—and in some regions, the weather requires that response. Whatever your zone, you can outfit your garden to yield great pleasure in winter.

A beech hedge retains its coppery leaves, which filter the low winter sun.

To be attractive in winter, a garden needs an underlying structure of hardscaping and evergreen trees, hedges, and shrubs. Since most evergreens have dark green leaves, this is the principal color of the winter garden, but alongside it there are many other beautiful hues. We find black, brown, gray, silver, and white in the bark of trees and shrubs; rust and copperish brown in the retained leaves of **beech** (*Fagus*) and **oaks** (*Quercus*); bright yellow in the flowers of some shrubs,

such as **mahonias** (see page 177); and various beiges, fawns, and dull yellows in the skeletons of uncut perennials. Brighter hues may be provided by **viburnums**, **hellebores**, **winter-flowering cherries** (*Prunus*), and **camellias** (see pages 180–81), as well as **cyclamen** (see pages 168–69), which have flowers in a variety of pinks and purples, and there are **witch hazels** (*Hamamelis,* see pages 177–79) with flowers in yellow, orange, and red. Some **willows** (*Salix*) and **dogwoods**

(*Cornus*) have vivid red and gold winter stems (see page 181), and there are some *Rubus* species with pure white stems (see page 176). Moreover, with climate change bringing about milder winters, many plants now flower in winter that, in the past, would have ceased to flower in late summer or fall, or that wouldn't have flowered until spring. In my English garden, hellebores flower from early fall to late spring, and *Brunnera macrophylla* (see page 62) seems to be forever in flower.

172

SMALL GARDENS

Green may be the preeminent color of winter, but in a small garden there may not be room to accommodate large evergreen shrubs, trees, or hedges. The solution can be to grow small evergreens in containers, or to plant compact ones. Among the most elegant plants to grow in containers are topiaries of *Buxus sempervirens* (boxwood) (Zones 6–9) or hollies, such as the variegated *Ilex aquifolium* 'Ferox Argentea' (hedgehog holly, Zones 6–9; see also page 77) or *Ilex cornuta* (Zones 7–9). A pair of junipers, such as *Juniperus scopulorum* 'Skyrocket' (Zones 3–7), grown beside a path or a flight of steps, also gives a smaller garden style. This conifer has grayish green, pointed leaves, which lie flat against its branches, and it grows into a tall, slim tree. Moreover, it grows slowly to 15 ft. (5 m) but spreads no more than 20–24 in. (50–60 cm).

The evergreen flowering currant *Ribes laurifolium* (Zones 7–9) is another shrub that deserves a place in a smaller garden. It is happy growing in partial shade, produces leathery, rich green, scalloped leaves, 3 in. (8 cm) long, and its lime green, dangling flower clusters appear in late winter and early spring. It is low-spreading, and looks enchanting surrounded by hellebores with greenish white flowers.

The **sarcococcas** (Christmas or sweet box) are also excellent for small gardens. They grow well in shade—even deep, dry shade—and are decorative in winter, when most produce the deliciously scented, tiny petalless flowers. *Sarcococca confusa* (Zones 6–8) has dark green leaves and fragrant white flowers, followed by black fruit; it makes a compact bush. Its smaller relative *Sarcococca hookeriana* var. *humilis* (Zones 6–8) spreads to cover an area of over 40 in. (1 m) but never gets taller

Ilex cornuta

Ilex aquifolium 'Ferox Argentea'

Ribes laurifolium

Sarcococca hookeriana var. *digyna* 'Purple Stem'

than 24 in. (60 cm), which makes it a good ground-cover plant. It has oblong, dark green leaves and scented, pink-tinged white flowers, followed by bluish black berries. Since it is low growing and shade tolerant, it suits enclosed urban gardens that are always in shade. *Sarcococca hookeriana* var. *digyna*

(see page 61) is taller and more upright, growing to about 5 ft. (1.5 m), with slender, dark green leaves, and cream and pink flowers, followed by bluish black fruit. *Sarcococca hookeriana* var. *digyna* 'Purple Stem' (see Good Companions, below) has reddish purple young shoots, and pink flowers.

GOOD COMPANIONS

The pink-flowered *Sarcococca hookeriana* var. *digyna* 'Purple Stem' (1) (Z. 6–8) mixes well with purplish *Helleborus* × *hybridus* (2) (Z. 5–8). Later, the sarcococca's reddish purple stems are echoed by similarly colored tulips, like *Tulipa* 'Attila' (3) (Z. 4–8).

Ilex aquifolium 'Handsworth New Silver'

VARIEGATED SHRUBS

Evergreen shrubs with variegated leaves can add greatly to a winter garden, although it is wise not to plant too many very close together. There are, of course, many **hollies** with variegated foliage, but a particularly splendid garden cultivar is *Ilex aquifolium* **'Handsworth New Silver'** (Zones 6–9). It is a female holly and has shiny medium green leaves with clearly defined cream borders. The leaves are spiny and grow on dark purple stems. This holly also produces vivid scarlet berries and grows into a large, dense bush with an upright habit.

The evergreen shrub *Osmanthus heterophyllus* **'Aureomarginatus'** (Zones 6–9) is similar to a holly, as it has spiny, dark green leaves, 2½ in. (6 cm)

Osmanthus heterophyllus 'Aureomarginatus'

SPECIMEN CONIFERS FOR LARGER GARDENS

Coniferous trees are not at the top of everyone's "favorite plants" list, but there are some beautiful ones that make admirable specimens for larger gardens.

Pinus wallichiana (Bhutan pine) (1) (Z. 7–8) is an unusual pine that grows into a broad, rounded tree with grayish green or bluish green needles. As the needles age, they droop, and so the tree looks elegant and elongated. It grows to 120 x 40 ft. (35 x 12 m) and tolerates some alkalinity.

Picea breweriana (Brewer spruce) (2) (Z. 6–8) is a striking conifer, with spreading, level branches from which smaller and more slender branches dangle. It has flattened, glossy, deep green needles, with white undersides, arranged radially around the smaller branches. It grows slowly into a columnar tree, 50 x 12 ft. (15 x 4 m).

Beautiful as these two conifers are, neither has quite the grandeur of the blue Atlas cedar, *Cedrus atlantica* Glauca Group (3) (Z. 6–9). It has silvery, fissured bark and sharply pointed, silvery young leaves, which become a distinct grayish blue as they mature. They are carried on curving branches, which give mature specimens their typical conical outline. When mature, this plant reaches 130 x 30 ft. (40 x 10 m).

Abies concolor 'Argentea' (4) (Z. 4–7) is a silver fir that would grace any large garden. Its needlelike leaves point upward and outward on the branches. As it grows, it loses its conical shape and becomes columnar, finally reaching about 80 x 15 ft. (25 x 5 m).

long, with a bright yellow border. Like holly, it looks marvelous in winter. The fragrant, tubular white flowers appear in late summer, followed by black berries in fall. It matures into a large shrub, and is happy in sun or partial shade. The great advantage of this plant is that it doesn't resent being clipped, so makes a good hedge or topiary.

A much less showy but elegant shrub for winter is the variegated *Prunus lusitanica* **'Variegata'** (Portugal laurel; Zones 7–9), whose leaves have a fine line of cream around their rims. They are a dark, glossy green, and grow on bright red stems. Unlike the species, variegated

Prunus lusitanica 'Variegata'

MORE PLANTS WITH STRIKING STEMS AND BARK *Acer capillipes* • *Cornus sericea* 'Flaviramea' •

Vinca major 'Variegata'

Portugal laurel grows slowly and so is a good choice for a small garden; it can also be clipped for topiary.

In all gardens, there are places where ground-cover plants are needed, and there are variegated shrubs that can perform this function admirably. The prostrate *Euonymus fortunei* cultivars (Zones 5–8), such as *Euonymus fortunei* 'Emerald 'n' Gold', are perfect candidates. This euonymus has bright green leaves with wide gold margins, tinged with pink in winter, and it never gets taller than about 2 ft. (60 cm), although it spreads over 3 ft. (90 cm); its variegations are more obvious when it is grown in sun. Greater periwinkle has a tendency to be invasive, but it makes good ground cover for larger spaces, as it thrives in all but the driest of soils. *Vinca major* 'Variegata' (Zones 8–9) is guaranteed to brighten the darkest of corners on a winter's day. Its lance-shaped, shiny dark green leaves are edged with cream and are carried on arching stems that trail along the ground and take root here and there.

WHITE OR SILVER BARK

Winter gives us the opportunity to enjoy the bark of deciduous trees and shrubs; and some, especially the white or silver ones, are beautiful when seen against a blue winter sky. **Birches** (*Betula*) have some of the most attractive white and silver bark (see box, below), but none is more beautiful than that of the evergreen *Eucalyptus dalrympleana* (Zones 9–11), which is silky smooth in a luminous, creamy white. *Eucalyptus pauciflora* ssp. *niphophila* (Zones 8–10) has less arresting, grayish white or pale tan bark. However, it becomes very eye-catching in late summer, when it sheds in patches and reveals areas of new bark that are bronze, yellow, or green. Both of these eucalyptus grow into tall trees, about 70 x 25 ft. (20 x 8 m) when mature, so they need a spacious garden to look their best.

Eucalyptus pauciflora ssp. *niphophila*

DECORATIVE BIRCH BARK

Birches have some of the loveliest colored barks; and because these trees are deciduous, these colors are revealed in all their glory in winter.

Betula papyrifera (paper or canoe birch) (Z. 2–7) has white outer bark, which peels in thin layers to reveal its new bark in pale tan beneath, while *Betula utilis* var. *jacquemontii* (Z. 4–7) (see pages 41, 54) is a white-barked form of the Himalayan birch. There are a number of refined selections available, including *Betula utilis* var. *jacquemontii* 'Doorenbos', *Betula utilis* var. *jacquemontii* 'Grayswood Ghost', *Betula utilis* var. *jacquemontii* 'Jermyns' (1), and *Betula utilis* var. *jacquemontii* 'Silver Shadow', all of which have luminously white bark that shines in winter.

Betula albosinensis (Chinese red birch) (Z. 5–6) has beautiful orange-brown bark; as it ages, it peels to reveal young cream bark covered with a whitish glaucous bloom. *Betula albosinensis* var. *septentrionalis* (2) is a selection of the species, with pinkish cream bark that peels to reveal mahogany-colored new bark. *Betula nigra* (river or black birch) (3) (Z. 4–9) has reddish brown young bark that peels so much that it appears to be rough and shaggy. As this birch ages, its bark becomes dark gray and fissured. *Betula ermanii* (Erman's birch) (4) (Z. 5–6) has peeling bark that is whitish cream, tinged with pink and cream.

To bring out the wonderful colors of these barks, some horticulturalists recommend scrubbing them with clean water in spring and fall. Birches look lovely as either multi-stemmed or single-stemmed specimens.

Luma apiculata • *Prunus serrula* • *Rosa sericea* f. *pteracantha* • *Salix babylonica* var. *pekinensis* 'Tortuosa' •

Rubus cockburnianus 'Goldenvale'

Viburnum farreri

Acer pennsylvanicum

Lonicera × purpusii 'Winter Beauty'

WHITE FLOWERS

There is nothing quite like finding flowers in bloom on cold, gray winter mornings for lifting the spirits. Some **viburnums** sport white flowers in winter, for example the handsome evergreen **Viburnum tinus** (Zones 8–9) and the lovely deciduous **Viburnum farreri** (Zones 6–8) . The minute flowers of *Viburnum tinus* are unscented, but their domed clusters are produced over a long period from late winter to spring, among long, dark green leaves. The tiny, tubular white or pink-tinted flowers of *Viburnum farreri* are lightly scented, and packed densely into clusters on its bare stems. Both these viburnums mature to become large shrubs.

Some winter-flowering honeysuckles have an intense, sweet scent that lingers in the air for months. **Lonicera × purpusii 'Winter Beauty'** (Zones 5–9) is a superb shrubby honeysuckle that has tiny, creamy white, highly scented flowers with gold anthers that appear for at least three months from early winter until early spring. Its semi-evergreen, ovate leaves are dark green, and it grows up to 6 x 8 ft. (2 x 2.5 m). (See Good Companions, below.)

Ornamental brambles need little space; and some—for instance, *Rubus biflorus* (Zones 4–6), *Rubus cockburnianus* 'Goldenvale' (Zones 6–7), and *Rubus thibetanus* (Zones 6–9)—bring an ethereal quality to a winter garden, with their gleaming white young stems. For the best effects, they should be pruned to the ground each spring. Some snake-bark maples, such as *Acer davidii* (Zones 5–8), *Acer pennsylvanicum* (Zones 3–8), and *Acer tegmentosum* (Zones 4–7) also have white-striped bark.

176

GOOD COMPANIONS

The honeysuckle *Lonicera × purpusii* 'Winter Beauty' (1) (Z. 5–9) looks wonderful in winter, but is rather uninteresting for the rest of the year. To disguise this, plant a clematis to grow through it—for example, the summer-flowering, blue-flowered *Clematis* 'Prince Charles' (2) (Z. 4–9). In winter it looks charming underplanted with pale blue-flowered pulmonarias, such as *Pulmonaria longifolia* (3) (Z. 3–8).

MORE FLOWERS FOR WINTER *Camellia sasanqua* 'Crimson King' • *Cornus mas* • *Eranthis pinnatifida* •

I cannot imagine owning a garden and not growing **snowdrops**. They are an endless source of pleasure at the gloomiest time of the year, and they are so easy to grow. There are numerous cultivars, but there is much to be said for growing only the common snowdrop, *Galanthus nivalis* (Zones 4–8), and allowing it to seed itself in grass or under tall trees. To prolong the season, you just need to plant some of the later-flowering kinds. Snowdrops hybridize easily, so to keep them "pure" plant them at a distance from each other.

Acacia dealbata

GOOD SNOWDROPS

Galanthus 'Atkinsii' (1) (Z. 4–8) Large, early flowers on robust plants that make good clumps. Ideal for the back of a border, where emerging spring foliage can conceal the snowdrop's long leaves as they fade.

Galanthus 'Magnet' (2) (Z. 4–8) Long slender flower stems make the flowers move with the slightest breeze. A reliable snowdrop cultivar that has been grown for over 100 years.

Galanthus nivalis 'Viridapice' (3) (Z. 4–8) Markings on the outer tepals give this snowdrop its name, which means green-tipped. It has distinctive small flowers on a tallish plant.

Galanthus 'S. Arnott' (4) (Z. 4–8) A fine, large, and vigorous cultivar well worth growing for its plump, classic snowdrop blooms and faint honeylike fragrance. Makes good tall clumps.

YELLOW FLOWERS

Although white flowers and stems in winter never pall, plants sporting yellow flowers bring a cheerful zest to a garden. Some of the brightest belong to shrubs such as **acacias**, **witch hazels** (*Hamamelis*), and **mahonias**. Acacias are often overlooked in the quest for winter color, perhaps because they are tender or only half hardy, but they have charming round, fluffy flowers, which are often scented. *Acacia dealbata* (Zones 9–11) and *Acacia baileyana* (Zones 9–10) are half-hardy, so need protection in cold areas. Their bright, sunny yellow flower heads, which resemble small basketballs, are collected together in clusters and appear among the leaves from winter to spring. *Acacia dealbata* has ferny, glaucous, hairy leaves and scented blooms, while *Acacia baileyana* has silvery gray, fernlike leaves and unscented flowers. These acacias are large shrubs, or small trees, and both require a neutral or acid, moderately fertile soil.

Witch hazels (Zones 5–8) also need acid or neutral soil, and produce flowers in winter. However, unlike acacias, their spidery flowers can withstand frost and all of them are fragrant. Those with yellow flowers (all those described being

Hamamelis × intermedia 'Pallida'

1¼ in. [3 cm] across) include *Hamamelis × intermedia* 'Arnold Promise', which has rich yellow flowers, *Hamamelis mollis* (see page 178), with golden yellow, strongly scented blooms, and *Hamamelis × intermedia* 'Pallida', in pale yellow. Witch hazels flower from midwinter to late winter, and these slow-growing, attractive shrubs make excellent specimens for lawns or centerpieces for small gardens devoted to winter-flowering plants. Mature specimens are about 10 x 6 ft. (3 x 2 m).

Mahonias are popular evergreen shrubs, celebrated for their striking, glossy, dark green, spiny-edged leaves and bright yellow flowers, borne in late fall, winter, or spring (see pages 125, 164, and 178), some of which are scented. *Mahonia × media* 'Winter Sun' (Zones 6–9) is an erect mahonia

Mahonia × media 'Winter Sun'

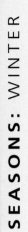
Stachyurus praecox

with bright yellow, very fragrant flowers from late fall to late winter, and dark green, hollylike leaves.

Much less widely grown than mahonias are **stachyurus**, choice deciduous and semi-evergreen shrubs, which also bear attractive yellow flowers in winter (see also page 113). *Stachyurus chinensis* (Zones 7–9) has 4- to 5-in. (10–12 cm) racemes of tiny, bell-shaped, pale yellow flowers dangling from the stems, and *Stachyurus praecox* (Zones 6–8) has slightly shorter racemes of lemon yellow or greenish flowers. The flowers appear in late winter and spring, before the medium green leaves open. These pretty shrubs reach 6 x 10 ft. (2 x 3 m). They will flourish in sun or light shade, in fertile, humus-rich, well-drained soil, but it must be neutral or acid.

Jasminum nudiflorum (winter jasmine) (Zones 6–10) is a marvelous plant to have growing in a garden in winter. Although it is deciduous, its cheery yellow flowers, on dark green, arching or climbing stems, bring a splash of color throughout the season, flowering even when trained against a north-facing wall.

Despite their small size, the bright yellow flowers of *Eranthis hyemalis* (winter aconites) (Zones 3–8) have great charm and cheer up the dullest of days. They grow from small tubers, and their buttercuplike flowers are carried above a collar or ruff of rich green leaves from midwinter to late winter. Aconites thrive best in alkaline soil that is fertile and humus-rich and does not dry out in summer. They are happy growing in either sun or dappled shade, and may be naturalized in grass or planted beneath shrubs or trees. (See also page 115 and Good Companions, left.)

WINTER REDS AND ORANGES

Bright red berries on **holly** bushes (*Ilex*) are another of winter's joys; but for those who want something different, there are other shrubs whose berries are also present throughout the season. *Cotoneaster lacteus* (Zones 6–8) bears scarlet berries that show up well against the dark leaves and persist until midwinter. It is evergreen, medium-size, and makes an excellent hedge if clipped regularly. *Cotoneaster conspicuus* 'Decorus' (Zones 6–7) is a low-spreader with stems that grow outward more than upward, making it good for a

GOOD COMPANIONS

Yellow-flowered witch hazels, such as *Hamamelis mollis* (1) (Z. 5–8) look effective underplanted with smaller daffodils (Z. 4–9), like *Narcissus pseudonarcissus* (2) or *Narcissus* 'Jack Snipe'.

The yellow-flowering *Eranthis hyemalis* (3) (winter aconites) (Z. 3–8) go well with the evergreen creeping *Asarum europaeum* (4) (Z. 5–7), which has kidney-shaped, shiny dark green leaves.

MORE GOOD BERRIES *Berberis wilsoniae* • *Cotoneaster frigidus* 'Cornubia' • *Crataegus* × *lavalleei* 'Carrierei' •

Cotoneaster conspicuus 'Decorus'

Nandina domestica 'Fire Power'

Hamamelis 'Jelena'

bank. It has dark green leaves and bears copious small, shiny red berries, which remain on the bush well into winter. Some female **skimmias** also have berries that are an attractive winter feature—for example, several *Skimmia japonica* cultivars (Zones 7–8). The male clone *Skimmia japonica* 'Rubella', although it does not fruit, has striking red flower buds.

Another source of red in winter is found in leaves. The evergreen perennial *Bergenia* 'Sunningdale' (Zones 4–8) has large round, thick leathery foliage, which turns to a rich copper color at the beginning of the season, especially on plants grown in full sun; the leaves provide a sumptuous background for the magenta flowers when they emerge in early spring.

Nandina domestica 'Fire Power' (Zones 6–9) is a dwarf evergreen with dramatic, bright red leaves all year. Reaching 18 x 24 in. (45 x 60 cm), it makes a stunning addition to the front of a red-themed border, and looks good with an evergreen shrub with red berries, or one with winter flowers—such as the strawberry tree *Arbutus* × *andrachnoides* (see Good Companions,

below). The latter has attractive peeling, reddish brown bark, glossy, lance-shaped leaves, and tiny, pitcher-shaped flowers that go on appearing from fall to spring. The flowers are creamy white, with red tinges, and hang from the stems in clusters or panicles.

Witch hazel flowers are a valuable asset in winter—for example, those of *Hamamelis* × *intermedia* 'Diane' (Zones 5–8), which are dark, rich red, and appear on the bare stems from midwinter to late winter (see Good Companions, left). The leaves of witch hazels are also a feature in fall, turning brilliant hues. One of the most brightly colored cultivars is *Hamamelis* 'Jelena' (Zones 5–8), which has copper-orange flowers in early winter and midwinter, and gorgeous autumn tints in red and orange. The flowers of both these witch hazels are about 1¼ in. (3 cm) across.

GOOD COMPANIONS

The red-tinged leaves of *Nandina domestica* 'Fire Power' (1) (Z. 6–9) make it a good planting partner for the creamy white, red-tinged flowers of *Arbutus* × *andrachnoides* (2) (Z. 8–11).

With its striking, deep red winter flowers, *Hamamelis* × *intermedia* 'Diane' (3) (Z. 5–8) looks marvelous surrounded by bushes of *Cornus alba* 'Sibirica' (4) (Z. 2–8) (see also page 172).

Ilex aquifolium 'J.C. van Tol' • *Malus* × *scheideckeri* 'Red Jade' • *Pyracantha* 'Orange Charmer' •

For striking bark, *Acer griseum* (paper bark maple) (Zones 4–7) is outstanding. It is a rich burnished orange, peels prolifically, and is revealed in all its glory in the winter months. This maple also has attractive dark green leaves and grows slowly into a spreading, medium-size tree, 30 x 30 ft. (10 x 10 m). Its leaves turn orange-red or scarlet in fall, but it is the unique orange, peeling bark that makes this maple such a wonderful treasure. (See page 47.)

Prunus × subhirtella 'Autumnalis Rosea'

PINK FLOWERS

For those who prefer pinks to orange-reds in winter, there are trees, shrubs, and perennials that fit the bill. The pretty winter-flowering cherry *Prunus × subhirtella* 'Autumnalis' (Zones 5–8) has great charm and value, as its flowers start appearing in fall, just when many gardens need a lift. They go on appearing intermittently throughout winter but are susceptible to frost; however, new flowers appear every time the temperature rises. They are semidouble, whitish pink, and bowl-shaped, and ¾-in. (2 cm) across. The flowers of the lovely cultivar *Prunus × subhirtella* 'Autumnalis Rosea' are similar but in a rosy pink. These cherries grow into spreading trees, 25 x 25 ft. (8 x 8 m) when mature, and have dark green leaves, which are bronze when young and turn yellow in autumn.

Most **camellias** start to flower from early winter onward. The varieties of

Camellia 'Nicky Crisp'

Viburnum × bodnantense 'Dawn'

Camellia sasanqua (see page 166) are the first to bloom, from fall onward, followed by the hybrids of *Camellia japonica* (see page 78) and *Camellia × williamsii* (Zones 6–10). *Camellia* 'Nicky Crisp' (Zones 7–9) is a compact, slow-growing, rounded shrub, which has large, semidouble, lavender-pink

Helleborus × hybridus

flowers from late winter to mid-spring. Camellias are best planted in a sheltered position, avoiding the early morning sun, which can damage frosted blooms. If *Camellia* 'Nicky Crisp' proves hard to find, *Camellia* 'Inspiration' makes a good alternative (see page 78).

The bright pink, heavily scented flowers of *Viburnum × bodnantense* 'Dawn' (Zones 6–8) are hard to miss. They are tiny, carried in densely packed clusters, either along the bare branches or at the branch tips, in midwinter. The flowers are a rosy pink when young, but they fade to white, flushed with pink. A mature specimen is 10 x 6 ft. (3 x 2 m).

It is not surprising that hellebores have become the "must have" winter-flowering perennials for many people, as their cup- or saucer-shaped flowers, in cream, pink, purple, green, or white, are exceptionally beautiful. The 15 hellebore species vary enormously. For example, *Helleborus cyclophyllus* (Zones 6–9) has yellowish green, saucer-shaped flowers on 12-in. (30 cm) stems; *Helleborus foetidus* (stinking hellebore, see page 94) has bell-shaped green flowers on stems 20 in. (50 cm) high; *Helleborus niger* (Christmas rose) (Zones 6–9) has saucer-shaped, white or whitish pink flowers; and *Helleborus purpurascens* has cup-shaped flowers in a range of colors from purple to slate

DECORATIVE SEED HEADS FOR WINTER *Calamagrostis × acutiflora 'Karl Foerster' • Dipsacus fullonum •*

Winter-flowering daphnes

Daphnes are among the aristocrats of the shrub world, as they have delightfully scented flowers, handsome leaves, and attractive prostrate, rounded, or upright forms of growth. Some have the added bonus of producing pink, purple, or white flowers in winter, at a time of year when little else is in flower. Daphne flowers are tubular with four lobes, and they are found singly or in short racemes or clusters. The leaves of the species described here are about 3–5 in. (8–12 cm) long.

Daphnes can be grown in any good soil as long as it is well drained and well nourished, but they thrive best in soils that are slightly alkaline to slightly acid. They are happy to be grown in sun or partial shade, but always benefit from having their roots mulched, as this keeps them cool.

Daphne odora (Z. 7–8) is an evergreen species that originates in China and Japan. It grows into a rounded shape, with glossy, leathery leaves and clusters of fragrant, deep purple, pink and white flowers. It eventually grows to 5 x 5 ft. (1.5 x 1.5 m).

Daphne bholua (Z. 8–9) has an upright habit and deciduous or evergreen, leathery, dark green leaves. The flowers are white flushed with purplish pink. Carried in clusters, they appear in late winter. This daphne reaches 6–12 x 5 ft. (2–4 x 1.5 m).

Daphne bholua 'Jacqueline Postill' (Z. 8–9) is an evergreen cultivar with especially fragrant flowers that are purplish pink on their outer surfaces and white inside.

Daphne mezereum (Z. 5–8) is an upright shrub, growing to 4 x 3 ft. (1.2 x 1 m) when mature. It is deciduous, with pale grayish green leaves and fragrant flowers in a deep purplish pink, blooming in late winter and early spring on bare stems. Its berries are poisonous. This daphne is somewhat disease-prone.

Daphne mezereum f. *alba* (Z. 5–8) differs from *Daphne mezereum* in having creamy white flowers.

Daphne odora 'Aureomarginata' (Z. 7–8) has leaves that are similarly sized and shaped to those of the species, but here they are embellished with a narrow band of pale yellow around the margins. Also, its flowers are purple with reddish tinges, and they have paler pink or creamy white insides.

gray, with tinges of pink and purple, and light green insides. Because hellebores reproduce wantonly, there are innumerable hybrids available listed as *Helleborus × hybridus* (Zones 5–8) in a range of wonderfully subtle colors, which will enhance any garden. (See also pages 38, 42, 114, 173). Furthermore, there are various spotted kinds, and breeders have bred some with double flowers. If you are happy to allow your hellebores to breed randomly, and plant hybrids in a mixture of colors in close proximity, you will be rewarded with a color selection all your own.

ORNAMENTAL STEMS

Some of the brightest winter stems are found on cultivars of the white willow, *Salix alba* (Z. 2–9). They are bright yellow in *Salix alba* ssp. *vitellina* (1) and orange-red in *Salix alba* ssp. *vitellina* 'Britzensis' (see page 48). Young stems display the best color, so cut back these willows in early spring, once every two or three years, to two or three buds from the base, to encourage new growth. Grow them in deep, moist, well-drained soil in full sun.

Some cornuses also have attractively colored winter stems. Especially eye-catching are those of *Cornus alba* 'Sibirica' (Z. 2–8) (see pages 172, 179), which are bright coral red; *Cornus alba* 'Kesselringii' (see page 38), which are dark purple; *Cornus sericea* 'Flaviramea' (Z. 2–8), with yellow, green-tinged stems; and *Cornus sanguinea* 'Winter Beauty' (2) (Z. 5–8), with shoots that are a blaze of red and bright orange-yellow in winter.

Miscanthus sinensis 'Silberfeder' • *Papaver somniferum* • *Phlomis russeliana* • *Sedum* 'Herbstfreude' •

Author's choice
Favorite color planting groups

Throughout the book there are plants with flowers and foliage in a wide range of colors. I have tried to select those that have been tried and tested and proved their worth. Here, I have grouped some of these into harmonious schemes, covering all the seasons; some are suitable for sunny sites, others for shade. All are easy to grow and should give you a basis on which to build your own, more elaborate schemes.

GREEN AND WHITE FOR SPRING (SUN)

 Tulipa 'White Triumphator' (Z. 4–8) (page 54) Bulb; elongated white flowers on tall stems, in late spring.

 Anemone nemorosa (Z. 4–8) (page 96) Perennial; creeping, low-growing ground cover, with white flowers and pretty, fernlike leaves.

 Buxus sempervirens 'Suffruticosa' (Z. 6–9) (page 77) Compact, slow-growing shrub; small, glossy dark green leaves.

 Pulmonaria 'Sissinghurst White' (Z. 4–8) (page 114) Evergreen perennial; leaves spotted white; white flowers in early spring; good ground cover.

 Osmanthus delavayi (Z. 7–10) (page 123) Rounded evergreen shrub; dark green leaves, scented white flowers in mid- to late spring.

BLUE AND YELLOW FOR SPRING (SHADE)

 Pulmonaria 'Blue Ensign' (Z. 5–8) (page 115) Perennial; unspotted dark green leaves, rich blue flowers in early to mid-spring.

 Erythronium 'Pagoda' (Z. 4–8) (page 45) Low-growing perennial; leaves deep green with bronze spots, sulfur yellow Turk's-cap flowers in mid-spring.

 Omphalodes cappadocica 'Starry Eyes' (page 127) Perennial; tiny white-edged, azure-blue flowers; bright green leaves; ground cover.

Brunnera macrophylla (Z. 4–8) (page 62) Perennial; long-lasting bright blue, forget-me-not flowers and large leaves; useful for ground cover.

Fatsia japonica 'Variegata' (Z. 8–9) (page 78) Medium to large evergreen shrub; big, dark green, cream-edged leaves; creamy white flowers in fall.

182

BLUE, LIME, AND WHITE FOR EARLY SUMMER (SUN)

 Anchusa azurea 'Loddon Royalist' (Z. 4–8) (page 134) Perennial; bright blue flowers on tall, sturdy stems, hairy medium to dark green leaves.

 Alchemilla mollis (Z. 4–7) (page 154) Low-growing perennial; froth of tiny, lime green flowers, pretty leaves that hold dew and raindrops.

 Veronica spicata ssp. *incana* (Z. 5–8) (page 135) Perennial; dark blue flower spikes, silver leaves; for front of border.

 Exochorda macrantha 'The Bride' (Z. 5–7) (page 123) Deciduous shrub; cup-shaped white flowers; will not tolerate shallow, alkaline soil.

 Philadelphus 'Virginal' (Z. 5–7) (page 138) Deciduous shrub; very fragrant double white flowers.

PINK, VIOLET, BLUE, AND SILVER FOR MIDSUMMER (SUN)

 Paeonia lactiflora 'Sarah Bernhardt' (Z. 4–8) (page 142) Herbaceous peony; large double, rose pink, scented flowers margined silver.

 Artemisia 'Powis Castle' (Z. 6–10) (page 56) Perennial; forms a dense clump of finely cut, feathery silver-gray leaves.

 Baptisia australis (page 140) (Z. 4–8) Perennial; dark blue flowers on erect stems, dark green leaves.

 Geranium pratense 'Plenum Violaceum' (Z. 4–7) (page 141) Perennial; dark violet-blue double flowers, attractive leaves.

Rosa 'Roseraie de l'Haÿ (Z. 2–7) (page 145) Dense, vigorous Rugosa rose with flat, double rich red flowers from early summer to fall.

RED, YELLOW, AND ORANGE FOR SUMMER (PARTIAL SHADE)

 Penstemon 'Andenken an Friedrich Hahn' (Z. 7–10) (page 146) Perennial; spires of wine red, bell-shaped flowers.

 Lilium henryi (Z. 5–8) (page 151) Bulb; deep orange Turk's-cap flowers in clusters of up to ten blooms.

 Rodgersia aesculifolia (Z. 4–8) (page 143) Perennial; large horse-chestnut-like, crinkled leaves, clusters of star-shaped pink or white flowers.

 Ligularia dentata 'Britt-Marie Crawford' (Z. 3–8) (page 66) Perennial; dark orange flowers on tall stems and red-brown leaves.

 Rheum palmatum 'Atrosanguineum' (Z. 5–7) (page 65) Perennial; red-veined leaves on thick stems, with tall spires of deep pink flowers.

 Acer palmatum 'Bloodgood' (Z. 6–8) (page 161) Decorative tree; red-purple, finely cut leaves that turn rich red in fall.

BRONZE, PURPLE, AND BLUE FOR LATE SUMMER (SUN)

 Agapanthus 'Blue Giant' (Z. 7–9) (page 155) Perennial; spherical clusters of rich blue, bell-shaped flowers on tall stems, straplike leaves.

 Eryngium bourgatii Graham Stuart Thomas's selection (Z. 3–8) (page 155) Perennial; spiny silver-veined leaves; blue flowers with spiky bracts.

 Miscanthus sinensis 'Morning Light' (Z. 5–9) (page 170) Grass; narrow, arching leaves with white edges and maroon or purple flower spikelets.

 Heuchera 'Plum Pudding' (Z. 4–8) (page 67) Low-growing evergreen perennial; large, ruffled deep purple leaves mottled silver, delicate white flowers.

 Penstemon 'Port Wine' (Z. 6–9) (page 49) Perennial; dark wine red flowers with white throats, semi-evergreen leaves.

 Cotinus 'Grace' (Z. 5–8) (page 162) Large deciduous shrub; wine-colored leaves turn red in fall. Smoke-like clusters of flowers.

ORANGE, GOLD, AND BEIGE FOR SUMMER/FALL (SUN)

 Achillea filipendulina 'Gold Plate' (Z. 2–9) (page 154) Perennial; golden, flat flower heads, fernlike leaves.

 Stipa tenuissima (Z. 7–9) (page 171) Grass; bright green narrow rolled leaves, buff-colored flower spikes.

 Kniphofia rooperi (Z. 6–9) (page 152) Evergreen perennial; bulbous candles of orange-red flowers on tall stems, broad, arching, straplike, leaves.

 Stipa gigantea (Z. 6–9) (page 67) Evergreen or semi-evergreen grass; tall, delicate flower spikelets turn golden when ripe.

 Heliopsis helianthoides var. *scabra* 'Sommersonne' (Z. 4–8) (page 153) Perennial; golden single or semidouble daisylike flowers.

 Acer cappadocicum (Z. 6–8) (page 164) Deciduous tree; bright green, lobed leaves turn dark yellow or gold in fall.

CREAM, PINK, SILVER, AND GREEN (WINTER)

 Ilex aquifolium 'Handsworth New Silver' (Z. 6–9) (page 174) Large holly; green, prickly leaves with cream margins. Purple stems, red berries.

 Rubus cockburnianus 'Goldenvale' (Z. 6–7) (page 176) Medium-size deciduous shrub; yellow leaves; prickly, arching stems with white bloom in winter.

 Helleborus × *hybridus* (Z. 5–8) (page 173) Perennial; saucer-shaped flowers, leathery, dark green, lobed leaves. Flower colors vary.

 Sarcococca hookeriana var. *digyna* 'Purple Stem' (Z. 6–8) (page 173) Evergreen shrub; dark green leaves, very fragrant white flowers in winter.

 Daphne odora (Z. 7–8) (page 181) Evergreen shrub; dark green leathery leaves; very fragrant, purplish pink flowers.

Betula utilis var. *jacquemontii* (Z. 4–7) (page 54) Elegant deciduous tree; brilliant white bark, dark green leaves. Numerous selections are available.

Index

Page numbers with suffix 'b' indicate plants listed across bottom of page. Suffix 'i' refers to illustrations. The letter z. refers to USDA zones.

AUTHOR'S ACKNOWLEDGEMENTS
I would like to thank Andy McIndoe, Sue Gordon, Polly Boyd and Robin Whitecross for their great patience and skill in helping me to write and complete this book. It has been a pleasure to work with them all.

PICTURE CREDITS
The publishers would like to acknowledge with thanks all those whose gardens are pictured in this book.

All photographs were taken by Andrew McIndoe, Kevin Hobbs, John Hillier or Tim Mason with the exception of:

Bridgeman Art Library: 10/Private Collection, Accademia Italiana, London, 14–15/Private Collection, The Stapleton Collection
Patricia Elkington: 89a
Garden Picture Library:
   Front cover: top/Chris Burrows, bottom left/Richard Bloom, centre/Steven Knights, right/Mark Bolton; 52b/Howard Rice, 92–93/Sunniva Harte, 93(3)/David Murray, 128a/Neil Holmes, 128b/John Glover
Simple Pleasures Nursery 114c, 115d, 121c, 131(1), 131(3)
Jane Sterndale-Bennett 21a, 32, 33a, 34, 35, 39d, 87a, 88, 127 Good Companions (1)
Terry Underhill 122c, 122 Good Companions (2), 124b